Sports Talk

*The Personality
Behind The Personalities*

Brody, Rogan, & Rhoades

Copyright 2011 David Brody, Bill Rogan, Dustin Rhoades
All Rights Reserved
Non-fiction
First Edition

This book is the pure work of the authors and does not reflect the opinion of the publisher. The stories, shared by the individuals (also known as "personalities"), categorize the stories to be accurate, to the best of their abilities, and are not intended to cause harm or unjust biased. All events are known to be true, unless otherwise stated by the authors, or personalities, and are solely the opinion of the authors and the personalities. All photographs are under the ownership of the personalities unless otherwise stated. No part of this book may be reproduced in any manner whatsoever without written permission, except in the case of brief quotations embodied in critical articles and reviews.

MaxQ Enterprises, L.L.C.
ISBN 978-0-9796238-7-5
Cover design by Linda Lee
Cover photo by Thomas Repetny
Edited by: Elizabeth J. Brody & Donna Ryan
www.sportstalkpersonalities.com
www.maxqenterprises.com

From the Authors

When we went into this project our goal was straightforward. The aim was to truly discover the personality behind the personalities we hear coming through our radios, from coast to coast, each day.

We wanted to know who these guys really are. How did they get where they are today? What were they like growing up? What moves them? What are they like off the air?

We wanted to hear their personal stories and experiences, both in and out of broadcasting.

Every individual in this book has been successful in his craft, but each had a unique arrival and gained popularity with a singular approach.

We weren't looking to make this an exposé or to dig for salacious material. Any skeletons from the closets of our subjects were willingly provided.

Fortunately, the broadcasters you will read about were very forthcoming and provided us with great content.

You will learn of the talk show host who put a gun to his head and was given a second chance. Another host in this book talks bluntly about his steroid use as a college football player. Yet another has been fired from a myriad of jobs because of his outspoken nature and railing against the industry. These stories and many others are what this book is all about.

We can argue with their stance on a subject. We can certainly debate their philosophies. But we can't dispute their testimony. These are their stories and we hope we've been able to chronicle them in an engaging, entertaining, and informative manner.

The Authors
December 2011

Acknowledgements

Embarking on an undertaking such as "Sports Talk—The Personality Behind the Personalities," can be daunting. There are logistical issues and concerns that need to be constantly addressed. To put a book together such as this takes an incredible amount of time, effort and cooperation from a myriad of people.

The authors would like to thank the following people for their generous and gracious assistance for without them this book would not have come to fruition.

In alphabetical order: Keith Allen, Don Apodaca, Robin Austin, Joe Benigno, Tim Brando, Elizabeth Brody, Laura Brody, James Brown, Tony Bruno, Chris Collins, Andy Cornell, Louise Cornetta, Colin Cowherd, Howard Eskin, Scott Ferrall, Amanda Gifford, Bruce Gilbert, Derek Jackson, Steve Kelley, KNUS Radio, Mitch Levy, Don Martin, Scott Masteller, Mark Mathieu, Kelly Michaels, Mitch Moss, Mike Mulligan, Jim Nantz, Ray Necci, Petros Papadakis, Gwyn Gantter Rogan, Mitch Rosen, Sid Rosenberg, Donna Ryan, Josh Sabrowsky, Daniel Schwartzman, Scott Shapiro, Dan Sileo, Jason Smith, Matt Smith, Arnie Spanier, Eric Spitz, Doug Stewart, Ryan Stewart, Scott Van Pelt, Mike Vaccaro, David Vassegh, Murphy Wells, Kevin Wheeler, Armen Williams and Greg Williams.

Foreword

Radio professionals David Brody, Bill Rogan, and Dustin Rhoades pull back the curtain on America's most successful and most interesting sports talk personalities, giving you a glimpse of what makes these unique personalities tick.

This first of its kind book gives you the backstories and anecdotes that have shaped the talented talk show hosts you listen to every day. You will discover that these broadcasters have taken many diverse paths to success, but all seem to be here because they have a deep passion for sports and people, not to mention an appreciation for being able to play at work every day.

Full-time, 24/7, sports talk radio was born in New York City on July 1, 1987, on 660 AM WFAN. Other stations slowly adopted the all-sports programming, and success stories began to materialize. Radio operators discovered that many of their biggest advertising customers were anxious to support a type of radio they personally enjoyed, easily understood, and vicariously participated in. WFAN's pioneering decision turned into a North American phenomenon that has fueled live public sports debates up and down the radio dial.

Now in its 25th year, sports radio is thriving and driving record revenues for broadcasters. In 2011 there are over 650 all-sports radio stations in the United States, and the once AM-only format is quickly migrating to the clearer, crisper FM radio band.

The foundation of sports, sports debate, and sports personalities makes this the most readily adaptable entertainment medium for all mobile and on-line platforms, setting it up for great success over the next 25 years. The provincial nature of sports, its inherent polarity, and the natural debate—not to mention fantasy sports and gambling—that surround the teams and the games has created legendary radio stations full of colorful characters we know as personalities.

Why the success of sports radio? What makes it so popular? Is it just a by-product of a country obsessed with celebrity in the form of freakishly talented athletes that earn billions of dollars? Could it be that outside of the weather, the games our athletes play are America's most common conversational touchpoint? Or perhaps, is sports radio popular because, as long-time sports radio programmer Mike Thompson simply says, "It's a Tupperware party for guys?"

In 1992 Arkansas Governor William Jefferson Clinton rallied to earn the Democratic nomination for the Presidency of the United States and then proceeded to win an election against President George H.W. Bush by wrapping his policies around one simple mantra: "It's the economy, stupid." When it comes to sports talk radio in America, there is a similar phrase that best describes the success of the format: "It's the personalities, stupid."

The games and business of sports generate interest and discussion among friends and neighbors. They share the pain of their team's failures and the euphoria of their team's success. That interest has been feverishly fueled by the unique personalities of sports talk radio. This book explores those personalities. What makes them so polarizing? How do they form their unique opinions? How have life experiences affected their views of the world and their perceptions of sports and sports heroes? What drives their eccentricities, insecurities, and neurosis?

Some are loudmouth fans, some are cerebral, some are witty, and many played our games at a high level. Some argue, some debate, some try to reason, others break it down like a scientist splitting the atom. All of them attract audiences that passionately play along every day. They take their listeners on a ride filled with stories, debates, and observations. They do it so well that listeners feel they are best friends with the hosts they listen to. It's a unique and powerful bond that is overwhelmingly successful, yet difficult to easily and clearly define.

As sports radio turns 25, *Sport Talk* summarizes much of what makes sports talk radio so popular, successful, and fun. This book illustrates how sports radio is a haven for boys and girls that don't ever want to grow up—and isn't that exactly the point?

Bruce Gilbert
Vice President News/Talk/Sports, CBS Radio Dallas
Former General Manager, ESPN Radio Network

Table of Contents

Sid Rosenberg	9
Tony Bruno	24
Scott Ferrall	43
Colin Cowherd	60
Arnie Spanier	75
2 Live Stews	90
Greg "Greggo" Williams	116
Petros Papadakis	133
Matt "Money" Smith	151
Photos	166
Scott Van Pelt	194
Dan Sileo	208
Joe Benigno	223
Mitch Levy	235
Tim Brando	256
Howard Eskin	278
Kevin Wheeler	291
Jason Smith	305
The Authors	327

Sid Rosenberg
"The Comeback Sid"

Controversy is no stranger to Sid Rosenberg. It doesn't matter where he has worked, Sid seems to end up in hot water for one reason or another. At times he's been his own worst enemy for a myriad of reasons. Despite all his trials and tribulations, the controversial native Brooklynite somehow always lands on his feet.

Currently, the rapid-speaking Sid mans the afternoon drive slot on WQAM in Miami, where he delivers his no-holds barred program. Make that, his highly rated no-holds barred program. A program that isn't just about sports. He'll interview actors or politicians as well.

He still has a voice in New York, doing sports reports for WINS Radio and occasionally filling in at his former radio home on WFAN.

THE ENTERTAINER

Today Sid receives attention for his job as a sports talk show host; however, he's not new to being in the spotlight. It all started at a young age.

"I was a guy who played the piano early on, sang early on, did a lot of recitals. I did one recital in front of 300 people at the age of eight-years-old that I put together myself. I was told quite a bit, great personality for a little kid, very funny, very talented. My parents of course wanted me to go to medical school like every Jewish kid. But there were certainly people along the way that thought that I had the type of personality that would lend to something in the entertainment field."

He acknowledges that he liked to be the center of attention, but to a degree.

"It wasn't like Billy Crystal and David Paymer in

Mr. Saturday Night. I wasn't standing there doing a comedy act on a Saturday night at 11 o'clock in front of my family, but did I have to be the center of attention? Was I the center of attention? Most of the time, yes."

FANDOM

As a youngster, Sid wasn't that big a basketball or hockey fan. Which is strange since over the past couple of decades he admits to being a rabid Knicks and Rangers fan.

"As a kid it was the Mets and the Jets. When I was about eight, nine years old, I went into A&S Department store in New York City with my father. And there was a box on the perfume counter, and it said fill out your name and address and we're gonna pick one lucky name out of this box and you will serve as the mascot to go see the Jets take on the Rams and sit on the bench during a Jet game. I'm a die-hard Jets fan. I'm a little kid. My heroes are Joe Namath and Emerson Boozer and all those guys."

So Sid entered the contest and quickly forgot about it until he was informed he won.

"Amazingly, they picked my name out of the box and I was going to be a mascot and sit on the bench with Namath, which I couldn't believe and went around school telling everybody. I was excited."

Sounds too good to be true, right? Correct.

"Charley Winner was the coach. The Jets were having a miserable season. I believe at the time they were 0-5 or 1-5 and Charley Winner decided that an eight-year-old kid would be a distraction. So instead the Jets actually called my house and told my father, 'We're sorry but the coach is not thrilled about having Sid sit on the bench. We're gonna send you a football signed by the whole team, jersey signed by the whole team,' all that sports memorabilia stuff. And I was like, 'Are you fucking kidding me? I was gonna meet Joe Namath. I don't want a fucking football.' That day, THAT day, I literally burned my New York Jets letter jacket and became a Giants fan and have been a rabid Giants fan for 35 years since."

That's a good story.

"No, that's a great story. Even (Scott) Ferrall loves that story!"

THE ATHLETE

Sandy Koufax may have been the best Jewish athlete ever. You can throw Hank Greenberg in there as well. How does Sid Rosenberg rate?

"To this day I still play basketball all the time. For a white Jewish kid at the JCC (Jewish Community Center) on a Saturday morning, I can still hold my own. I still play pretty good ball. I've always played ball my whole life. Baseball, football, basketball. Never great, but good enough to play in high school. Good enough to play intramural tennis and basketball in college. To this day I still run quite a bit, five, six miles three or four times a week. Still play tennis. So athletics are still important to me to this day. Never great, but always pretty good."

Sid's father, Harvey, was a good athlete and encouraged his son to play sports.

"He loved sports, and I've got two older sisters and they couldn't wait to have a little boy. He coached me during baseball, he coached me during football, so he loved sports. Because of him I ended up loving sports and together, to this day, God bless him, we still enjoy sports together."

WAYWARD

Sid's career choice didn't come to him early or often. It didn't come to him for a long time. He attended four different colleges before graduating. He was on the seven-year plan, and in his early 30s he still had no idea what he wanted to do in life.

"I was so caught up in drugs and alcohol and the

party scene I didn't know in my fifth year of college what I was going to do. As a kid I thought I was going to be a doctor because that's what my parents said. But I went to Baruch in Manhattan for accounting and financing because I was OK at that and I knew I could graduate college. But I had no idea, no idea, at the age of 32 what I was going to do, let alone the age of 10."

POINTSPREADS AND MONEY LINES

Gambling is a part of society and sports is a popular vehicle for people to get some action. Most gamblers though don't start quite as early as Sid.

"As a kid I was never in trouble, bad trouble, but I started gambling at the age of 11. Peer pressure hit me hard. Always wanted to be popular. So through elementary school and junior high school I was more worried about that stuff. About the girls and how popular I was. I gambled a little, drank a little, and drugged a little even in high school. So I never really worried about my future. Never."

Growing up in Brooklyn, Sid was a big sports fan and knew everything there was to know about the teams. There was a guy who lived next door that Sid looked up to who was into gambling at an early age and showed him the ropes.

"I was 11, he was 13, and we'd sit around watching games and the next thing you know I got to meet some people and I was involved in gambling."

He bet on football and basketball and had no difficulties doing so even as a kid.

"I had buddies whose fathers were bookmakers, whose uncles were bookmakers, and even at the age of 11 or 12 to put in a bet for $50 in Brooklyn, New York was not a problem."

While his parents didn't know of his gambling exploits at first, eventually they found out.

"Maybe four or five years after that I got into some

trouble with some pretty dangerous people, and yes, my parents did find out."

It wasn't a pleasant, sit down conversation with his parents either. It was an unplanned and unwelcome visit that tipped them off.

"It's kind of fucked up when you're having dinner with your parents and your baby sister, and the front doorbell rings and it's an associate of one of the top crime families in New York who said to my father, 'Your son over there owes us some money, so are you gonna pay it?' My father worked it out with that guy, but that didn't stop me. It scared the shit out of me and I vowed to never do it again. I meant it when I said it, but that didn't stop me. That's been the one thing my whole life, even more than drugs or drinking, that has been a constant, was the gambling."

COCAINE

It wasn't long after Sid began gambling that he delved into the world of illicit drugs.

"I was about 14 or 15 the first time I did a line of cocaine. I was a junior in high school. A little bit of drinking. By the time I was a senior in high school I was going out every weekend, Saturday night in New York City, and getting crazy."

After his graduation from high school, Sid went to the University of Miami. His first collegiate stop didn't last long.

"I went to Miami as a freshman in college and only lasted three months. I had to come home because all I did for three months, literally, was eat Captain Crunch and do cocaine. Had to come home."

Insecurities and wanting to be popular had a hand in his cocaine use, but he said the main reason he used was because it made him feel good, "like a million bucks."

His compulsive personality, simple access to the

drug, and the fact that his parents were 1,300 miles away made it easy for him.

"I went nuts."

Sid adds that he no longer uses and doesn't have the urges he once had.

"Actually, now I go out to dinner and have a couple of glasses of wine. I'll have two glasses of wine, and I don't run to my car and try to beep a coke dealer. It's not a struggle for me anymore, but there was a time during my life when I needed at least one of those three things to happen (gambling, drugs, alcohol) quite a bit."

How long has he been clean?

"It's been a while. Long time."

GENUINE

You can say a lot of things about Sid Rosenberg, good, bad, or indifferent. One thing you can't say is he's a phony. The guy who you listen to on the radio is the same guy you would get if you were sitting in the living room with him watching a ballgame.

"I don't put an act on, on the air. A lot of guys in the business are completely different off the air then they are on the air. And I'm not. The guy that you get off the air is pretty much the guy you get on the air. The passion, the opinions, the visceral responses, all that stuff that you hear from me on the air is pretty much me off the air."

IMUS

Don Imus is a radio legend. Imus, like Sid, has been a polarizing figure on the airwaves. Imus also had his substance abuse issues and was supportive of Sid when he went into rehab.

Sid worked at WFAN in New York for Imus and his role was to stir the pot. Which he did. He stirred it with an oar when a spoon would have sufficed.

"I had a role to play on Imus. And sometimes I

played that role a little too well. He wanted me to be that guy to say things that were going to shock people. Sometimes I said things that Imus wanted to say, but he's at the point of his career where he can't say those things anymore. Maybe Don would have said it 25 years ago but he ain't gonna say it now. So my job was to go in there and ruffle everybody's feathers and make people go, 'Holy shit!' Five hours later, you're at work at 3 or 4 o'clock in the afternoon, and they wanted people to say, 'Did you hear what Sid said on Imus today?' And that's what I did and sometimes I went too far. Way too far. I admit that. I said things I wish I could take back. I said some things that have been offensive, things that have been awful, and if I could take some of the stuff back I really would."

Some of the things that Sid said on the Imus program included saying that Venus and Serena Williams were "more suited to *National Geographic* magazine than *Playboy*." He said that "faggots play tennis." He also said, after the death of Palestinian leader Yasser Arafat, that Palestinians were "stinking animals. They ought to drop the bomb right there, kill 'em all right now." About the U.S. Women's Soccer team, he remarked that they were "a bunch of juiced up dykes."

While Imus would act upset on the air, he wanted more objectionable comments from Sid.

But the only comment that made Sid cringe and the one he most regrets was the crack about singer Kylie Minogue, who was diagnosed with breast cancer. He said, "She won't look so pretty when she's bald with one tit."

Sid reflects on that moment, which actually got him canned by Imus.

"As a guy that raises money for charities, I got my own charity, I raise money for Sid for SIDS, the battle against Sudden Infant Death Syndrome, a guy that helped Imus and WFAN for many years raise money for kids with cancer doing those telethons, people know how charitable and how caring I am. The Minogue thing did bother me. I did realize, literally seconds after, 'Wow, that was a bit much.' The rest of the stuff, no, I had no idea I had said anything that was going to be a big deal."

The role he played on Imus actually stopped when the program concluded each morning. Then he went on to a more traditional sports talk role.

"But the point is, that was my job. Sometimes I did it too well and that was my Imus job. But what people forget is right after I was done with Imus at 10 o'clock in the morning, for four years I hosted the midday show at WFAN, right before Mike and The Mad Dog, with Jody McDonald for two years and with Joe Benigno for two years, and I never once during that four-year period said anything that got anybody in an uproar because that was a three-hour talk show. My role there was to be the creditable sports guy. Certainly a sense of humor and to have some fun, but the Imus character was different."

That is why the Imus show kept getting Sid into jams while the midday show didn't.

"Even Miami the last five years I've never had an issue. It really all goes back to the Imus stuff."

As for the relationship with Imus now, there isn't one.

"I don't know how many friends Don Imus has. I think he was fond of me. I think if you shot him up with truth serum right now I think he's still fond of me. I think he knows I tried to please him, sometimes way too much. And I think he thinks for the most part I'm a funny, entertaining guy, but to say I'm his friend is definitely a stretch. That's an exaggeration."

BOXING CAREER

Sid got into a few fights growing up, especially when he was drinking. He was once thrown down a flight of stairs and it wasn't uncommon for him to arrive at home with facial abrasions and lacerations. But his official boxing career lasted just one fight. It was against long-time Imus producer and show cut up Bernard McGuirk.

On the show they would trade barbs that got pretty personal, even though off the air they were good friends and liked each other. Again, role playing on the Imus show. At no point was any of the sniping real.

"He was the pain in the ass Mick and I was the pain in the ass Jew. We did that type of stuff on the air."

Eventually the trash-talking led to a boxing challenge, Rosenberg versus McGuirk.

The boxing talk on the show generated a lot of interest and the bout actually raised $250,000 for kids with cancer. Sid even trained for the bout. The match was held at Chelsea Piers in New York as 500 people, including many dignitaries, spent $500 to watch the Imus adversaries duke it out.

"He beat the shit out of me. I wasn't sure at 5 o'clock that morning exactly how this thing was going to go down. We started the fight at 8 a.m. because we were doing a morning show for Imus, and it's kind of tough to get into a boxing mood at 8 o'clock in the morning. The fight started and literally 20 seconds in he punched me across the face and I said to myself, 'Holy shit, this guy's not fucking around.' And from there it was either, I'm gonna start to cry and ask for my mother or fall down and die. I was just happy I lasted. I never fell down. Now they called the fight in the third round because Lee Davis, the boss at the time of WFAN, was literally throwing his hands in the air. He was scared shit I could get killed in there or possibly sue somebody. So they stopped the fight in the third round."

So did Sid land any punches against the Fighting Irishman?

"I think I landed two to his 1,300 (laughs)."

Sid even wanted a rematch.

"That right there is the epitome of crazy."

THE FINAL STRAW

In 2005 Sid was going to host the Giants' pregame show before the season opener against the Cardinals at the Meadowlands. One problem. Sid didn't show up.

He was in Atlantic City the night before for a fantasy football promotion with the now defunct *FHM* magazine.

"I ended up hosting a party with the very beautiful Leeann Tweeden that Saturday night in Atlantic City and went out and partied and never made it back. And that was it."

WFAN Operations Manager Mark Chernoff, who had warned Sid before when he missed assignments, fired him.

"It wasn't the first time obviously that I had gotten messed up and missed a show. I had done that on occasion, not as often as people think. I still think to this day that it is wildly exaggerated the amount of partying and the amount of shows I missed over the years. But I was warned a couple of times and that was the last straw. I never made it back that Sunday morning."

Sid felt the firing was justified.

"I think they gave me enough rope to hang myself. It's very easy when you get fired to say, 'Ah fuck them and they fucked me,' but in this case it was warranted."

The firing wasn't personal. Sid is back on the air at WFAN on a part-time basis from Florida.

Sid said that despite his substance abuse issues he never showed up high and drunk.

"That's another misconception. My problem was I wouldn't show up when I was high and drunk. That was my issue."

NOBODY'S PERFECT

Since the infamous Atlantic City sleep over, Sid has worked hard to repair the damage to his reputation and image. The five years in Florida, first at WAXY and now WQAM, have been relatively uneventful off the air.

"I think people have seen that I'm not perfect. Not by any stretch. And I'm always one step away from another major issue. That's just the way I am. That's my personality. But I think I've done a real good job rehabilitating my image over the last five years. I think most people, most open-minded people have come to the realization that Sid Rosenberg was never really a bad guy. That he's a really talented guy and that it's time to move on. There are some that will never (accept him). Some that are so horrified by some of the things that I've said and I think that's a little silly. I think it's silly when you label somebody by something they say on the air for two seconds. I owned nine hours a day of real estate at WFAN. Nine hours. And you know what, every once in a while you may say something that's stupid or offensive or hurtful, but I think when people start to label people by that, to me that's equally as dangerous."

YESSSSS AND IT COUNTS

There are untold numbers of men in the New York metropolitan area who grew up with Marv Albert as their favorite announcer. Many who went on to broadcasting careers cite Marv, who announced the Knicks and Rangers, as their influence.

One of those guys is Sid Rosenberg.

"Marv Albert has always been my favorite. I love Marv. Marv and I are good friends today. If I call Marv he comes on my program pretty much whenever I want. To me I have to pinch myself, and I've interviewed everybody from Shaq to Tiger to Sampras, you name it I've had them all, even presidents. I sat down with George Bush (senior) in Don Imus' office for 45 minutes. But Marv Albert was always the guy for me. No doubt. There are guys today that I think are great. I think Mike Breen is phenomenal. But when I was a kid growing up I always loved Marv and of course Howard Cosell."

JIM NANTZ'S SOCKS AND PRESIDENTIAL CUFFLINKS

Sid started his career in the mid-1990s doing a sports talk program on Sportsline, an internet company in South Florida. In 1997 he landed on terrestrial radio when the company signed a deal with CBS Sports. CBS made their talent available to Sid's program.

"In 1998 we go to San Antonio for the Final Four. Me and my partner at the time, Scott Kaplan, who now does mornings out in San Diego. Jim Nantz is out there with Billy Packer getting ready to do the Final Four and I'm like, 'Holy shit, Jim Nantz.' So Jim Nantz comes on our show. Again, we had just hit terrestrial radio, we never had more than 10 listeners on the internet, nobody knew who the hell we were, and here we are sitting with Jim Nantz in San Antonio at the Final Four. We ended up in Jim Nantz's hotel room and, true story, he lent me a pair of socks because I brought a suit with me at the time and I forgot my dress socks at home. I sat on his bed in his hotel room for 30 minutes talking about sports. That's how I got to know Jim Nantz."

Nantz has been a supporter of Sid and used to tell him, "The President loves you." When Nantz would go on the Imus program he would ask Imus to, "Tell Sid that President Bush asked about him today."

In 2004 the Republican National Convention was held in New York.

"Imus at the time was out at his ranch in New Mexico," begins Sid. "It was me, Bernie, Charles, and Lou back in the studios at WFAN, and the dad came in. George

Bush Senior came in to do the Imus show. Mark Chernoff called me from the back on the intercom. So I went to the back to Imus' office and sitting there was George Bush. And Chernoff goes, 'Come in. He wants to talk to you.' And he went on to regurgitate four or five things that I had said over the prior week or two. So I knew he was listening. And he said, 'Barbara thinks you're the funniest guy on radio.' And him and I sat down and talked about Texas sports, everything from the Astros to Rice football to David Carr for 30 minutes. He walked out and he said, 'I love ya, Barbara loves ya,' and he gave me a pair of Presidential cufflinks which are absolutely beautiful."

Sid recalled asking the President what is was like when George W. Bush was taking a beating in the press.

"The President said it's kind of rough every once in a while. And I said, how do you think my parents feel? And he started cracking up because I was always in the papers in New York for doing something bad or saying something bad or getting into trouble. So we had a moment there where his son was the President and getting killed in the media and my parents were kind of experiencing the same thing."

MATRIMONY

Sid and his wife, Danielle, an attorney, have been married for 19 years. They met at Kingsborough Community College in Brooklyn.

"She's quiet and here I am disheveled, I was high half the time showing up in economics class, but I was smart. Always had the answers. The teachers seemed to like me and she developed an affinity for me. We started dating a little then we actually stopped seeing each for about two years. Then in 1992 we hooked up again. She's always been supportive. It's been hard for her obviously to see her husband's name and picture in the paper and have things like drugs and firings and suspensions and gambling and all these things attached to it. It's been hard, no doubt."

Sid not only appreciates her support, but he also likes the fact that she's easy on the eyes.

"She's gorgeous. I know a lot of guys say that about their wives but they're not. I got news for you guys, your wives aren't all gorgeous. My wife is actually gorgeous."

As for his parents, Harvey and Naomi Rosenberg, they've been supportive of Sid's career choice even though he didn't become a doctor. His dad, despite having been put through plenty of turmoil, remains Sid's biggest fan.

TIME MAGAZINE

Sid was once recognized by *Time* magazine. But it wasn't the way he had hoped.

"*Time* magazine used to have the 'Worst Person of the Month.' Remember that? One month it was like Milosevic, he killed about a billion people. One month it was Osama bin Laden and he killed about a billion people. And one month it was me based upon my Venus Williams remarks on the Imus show. I would say that's embarrassing."

FAVORITE SPORTS MOMENT

He's been to Super Bowls and the World Series. He's witnessed plenty of incredible sporting events and moments, but the one that is indelible in Sid's heart wasn't even a game. Plenty of people never thought this moment would even happen.

"The greatest event for me, this is very personal, was standing on the corner of Fulton and Broadway at 5 a.m. on a June morning waiting for Mark Messier, Jeff Beukeboom, Brian Leetch, Mike Richter, and Mike Keenan and all the guys to come down the Canyon of Heroes. Being at the ticker tape parade when the Rangers won the Cup in 1994 is my favorite sports moment in my life. That ticker tape parade that day was just fucking great."

ALI

One of the people that Sid wishes he could have interviewed is Muhammad Ali.

"I'd love to interview Muhammad Ali but he's not capable. All kidding aside, you give me Muhammad Ali 30 years ago, that would be the guy."

What would Sid ask Ali?

"I would ask him if he really thought he was as good as he portrayed himself to be. He talked a great game. To this day he's still the greatest boxer of all time, no one even close. I tend to do that stuff as well and sometimes I do that just to mask my own insecurities. I would love to know if Ali, with all the talking, if he really, really thought he was that good or if that was mostly a show."

A CRAZY JOB

For Sid, radio is an 18 hour a day job. He's in constant show prep mode just so he can go on the air for 4 hours a day.

"For me at least, cause I'm such a fucking crazy person, I am, I'm neurotic, I'm obsessive, I'm compulsive, I've been diagnosed with bi-polar, I'm completely fucked up, for me at least it becomes all enveloping. Now if somebody can do the job and just show up and do a good show and maybe spend two hours a day preparing, and it's a six or seven hour a day job and they can enjoy it, that's one thing. That's not me. Truth be told, it's a crazy job."

Tony Bruno
"Pure Philadelphia"

Versatile, worldly, adaptable, cultured, experienced, scholarly, candid, traveled, and entertaining are just some of the words that would describe Tony Bruno. The Philadelphia native has spread his wings and made a wildly successful career in sports talk radio; initially in his hometown, then nationally with ESPN Radio, Fox Sports Radio, and Sporting News Radio.

He's been like the coach of an expansion team, leading the pioneering efforts at ESPN and Fox when they were launching their radio networks.

A guy with a multitude of interests and talents, Bruno recently hosted 'Into The Night with Tony Bruno,' a Content Factory production on Fox each weeknight. But like a boomerang, Bruno has ditched Los Angeles and returned to his homeland, Philadelphia, where he is dealing, as usual, on 97.7 The Fanatic, the city's first FM all-sports station. He holds down the midday slot with Harry Mayes.

Looking much younger than his 59 years, Bruno is back where the winters are a little bit harsher than the ones he dealt with in Southern California.

Presenting the long and compelling journey of Tony Bruno.

THE FRIENDLY RADIO

At an early age, Tony discovered that he enjoyed the companionship of the radio because his father, Orlando, passed away when Tony was young and he grew up in a house with three women. He became fascinated with radio and realized it was what he wanted to do someday.

"Just listening to the radio at night was something that I loved to do. I'd listen to ballgames, I'd listen to talk shows, I'd listen to DJs. I don't know what it was. It was nothing ever in my background, my family or anyone that I ever knew that was involved in broadcasting. But my dad died when I was 10 and I was just a lost kid, trying to go to school, trying to live with a mother who was an Italian immigrant and two sisters, and trying to grow up and stay out of trouble." He adds, "Just listening at night, listening to the static, listening to the stations from around the country, I wasn't just listening to the local shows. Back in the day when AM radio was king, you could scan the dial and hear people in Cincinnati, pretty much all over the country, just different radio shows. Something just hit me at that point and I said, 'this is what I want to do.' Most kids at age 13 aren't even thinking about what they are going to do for a career, so that's what I chose to do and I stuck with it."

He was proactive at an early age. Tony was not content to just listen, so he got busy.

"I called DJs and guys at the old WFIL who I used to listen to late at night, and they were all gracious. Guys like Long John Wade and Dave Parks, the overnight guy. I would call in on the request line and just talk to the guys and tell them this is what I wanted to do and they were very, very gracious to me and just told me to stick with it and go to school. Then eventually, as I grew older, Long John Wade opened a broadcasting school in Philly, on Chestnut Street, and I was one of his first students. He saw my motivation, he saw my drive, and I became his biggest success story because a year after, I got my first job in radio."

Broadcast Pioneers of Philadelphia Hall of Fame member Long John Wade was a good guy to learn from.

HARDSHIPS

As you might imagine, the time following his dad's death from leukemia was difficult. He became the man of the house at 10 and was determined to do his part. His mom, Angelina, spoke very little English and money was extremely tight. Angelina sewed military uniforms for the government and Tony and his older sister, Marie, and younger sister, Gina, helped out any way they could.

"Getting over the loss of my dad was tough but my mom's the strongest person I've ever known in my life, and she worked and I tried to help her and I was also trying to pursue a career once I got into my teenage years. And I think the fact that I was focused on doing something like radio really kept me out of the trouble I could have gotten into. As the only male in the family with two sisters and a mom, with all kinds of crazy stuff going on back then with drugs and all the craziness. I mean we have that today, too, but back then that was the Vietnam War era. I had a lot of friends who went off to Vietnam. I wasn't drafted because of the death of my dad. So I saw a lot of my friends going through the ordeal of going to Vietnam or being drafted to go into the war, and I didn't have to do that. So I focused primarily on, 'what am I going to do to get myself out of this?' And I saw radio as the way to become somebody who was of substance, someone who could do something and help his family."

His mom was initially opposed to his radio aspirations. She wanted Tony to work in the construction business as he had at times with his uncle.

Tony was hired at WFIL at the age of 18, his first job in radio. He was the youngest person working at a major market radio station. WFIL was the No. 1 station in Philadelphia and one of the most successful in the country.

Angelina warmed up to Tony's career when he won an Associated Press reporting award at the age of 21 for covering a fire at a nursing home. He took his mom to the dinner and publicly thanked her at the banquet. She realized he might actually be doing the right thing with radio.

PLAYING DAYS

Tony didn't have a lot of free time to play organized sports as a kid. After his dad died, he would work after school, either delivering papers or in the pizza parlor to help his family out, but he did play pickup games of halfball or football.

"I'd go play halfball in the streets or go into the school yard and play football on concrete and asphalt parking lots. No organized real fields or equipment or any of that stuff. I never really played organized sports. I mean I did some little league, but that was few and far between so I was never really a great athlete. So that didn't drive me to be a sports guy."

Football on asphalt? No one ever said Philly kids weren't tough.

THE FOUNDATION

Tony worked overnights when he started at WIFI in Philadelphia. At the time, WIFI was an automated station playing syndicated Hit Parade music.

Tony's duties were to make sure the automation ran without problems and to fill in the gaps.

"I would sit in between the automation and do news updates. I just wanted to be on the air. I did news updates and weather updates whenever there was a local avail in there. So that was my start in radio."

He was paid $75 per week.

It was at this time that Tony was studying political science and journalism at Temple University in North Philadelphia.

He was hired at WFIL to do news.

"It was the station I grew up listening to. They started me overnights and I had no real big background other than a desire to work hard. I worked from midnight to 8 a.m. I was on the air till 6."

He wrote and re-wrote stories and learned the

business hands on.

"My start was really in the news part of it more than anything else."

THE EAGLES AND PHILLIES

Tony's first memory of sports was the Packers-Eagles NFL championship game at Franklin Field in Philadelphia.

"The Eagles 1960 NFL Championship was my first recollection as a kid. I was eight years old. I remember the Eagles winning the championship but that was during the day on a Sunday. But my first recollection of the radio and sports really affecting me was the 1964 Phillies. When we all as kids were listening to the radio every night getting caught up in 'the Phillies are going to win the pennant' and that whole thing, and not watching but listening and hearing the collapse of that team. That was probably my first real experience with listening to sports and broadcasters. And it wasn't that I wanted to be a sports broadcaster, I was just fascinated, being caught up in the emotion of listening to great broadcasters like By Saam and Bill Campbell and those guys back then who were doing the Phillies games on radio. It was just an amazing thing to listen to. I just wanted to be on the radio like those guys, but it wasn't really sports that drove me until I was in the business for a few years and the news portion of the world we live in started becoming more and more wiped out. Radio stations started eliminating news departments. I was doing news and sports and that's what eventually led me into going into sports full-time in the 1980s."

A WISE CHOICE

In the 1980s, Tony went full bore into sports broadcasting. He saw that sports radio was just beginning to take off.

"Watching sports and seeing that there was a void

and that if I could be really good at one thing, I saw the availability in the early 1980s that sports was one of those formats that was in its infancy, and that if I was good at it I could become maybe better in my field then most people and become a marketable commodity. So that's why I focused on sports. I got a job in New York working with the RKO Radio Network back then with Charley Steiner and guys like John Madden and Don Criqui, and that was my first entrée into sports. I was covering sports in Philly in the '70s when I went to WFIL. I would do the news and then I would go out at night and go to Phillies games. When Steve Carlton won his 27 games that was probably my first full season of covering sports in 1972 when I was about twenty years old. I remember going to the Vet every night for the second year of that building's existence, just sitting around and watching Steve Carlton have one of the greatest single seasons in history. And that really got me caught up in sports. I really became a sports junkie then."

NOT JUST A SPORTS GUY

Some sports talk show hosts focus on what they know best, or what they only know—sports. With Tony Bruno, you can talk to him about a myriad of topics; sports, pop culture, history, travel, wine—it doesn't matter. One important component to being a radio host is inquisitiveness and that is certainly one of Tony's traits.

"It came from being willing to explore new things. A lot of my friends who grew up in Philly, my family, they don't get to travel. The average person in most cities, they never really even leave their area. They don't even leave their state. Taking a plane ride to Florida is a big deal to a lot of people. So when I was a kid and I had the opportunity to travel to go to Indiana or to New Orleans or places outside of the city of Philadelphia, I would take it. I always had this thirst to learn. I don't know where it came from. I always wanted to be around people that were a lot better than I was so I could absorb knowledge and information. I grew up with wine at the dinner table, so when I got the opportunity to go to the Napa Valley and San Francisco and all the other great places, Italy or France, in my travels, I always tried to experiment and learn about different cultures and different things. That's what I attribute my success to. Being willing to just always absorb information. Even to this day. I don't think I know everything, I'm always willing to learn more stuff and I think if you're willing to do that and just open your mind up and learn new things and experience new things it's only going to make you a better person."

ARRIVAL

Though Tony's career began at an early age and he had success, he never felt that he had arrived. Despite the AP award, he was just going about his business in Philadelphia.

During the mid-70s through the early '80s, the Philly teams were very good—with the Phillies winning a World Series in 1980, the Sixers capturing the NBA title in 1983, and the Flyers winning a couple of Stanley Cups. This success helped Tony get noticed.

"Back then, when I was covering all those teams, the New York media, the UPIs (United Press International) of the world, Keith Olbermann a guy that I met actually when he was a young man. He was working for UPI audio in 1980, and I was working at all these games and Jim Kelly who also worked at CBS radio in New York, those guys were always looking for reporters to give them updates on major events so there was always a demand to get somebody in Philly to do a report from the game. I was the guy they would go to, 'Let's go to Veteran's Stadium now, Tony Bruno is there,' and I'd be on CBS radio networks at night and I'd be on UPI audio with Keith Olbermann. That was really my entrée into the so-called 'big time' because now all of a sudden people are hearing me all over the country, and I think it was that exposure to radio stations all over America and all over the world, that people started paying attention and noticing, 'who is this kid, he sounds pretty good,' and that's when Charley Steiner in 1982 called me and offered me a job to do weekend sports updates on the RKO radio network in New York. I go from a local kid and then 12 years later I'm on a network in New York being heard on 500 radio stations. That's when I realized, 'Wow, you know what, I could be good at this,' but again, it wasn't long form sports talk."

From there, he started covering some of the biggest sporting events. He covered the 1984 Winter Olympics, the summer Olympics, the Super Bowl, and World Series. For a guy who enjoyed traveling, it was perfect.

"I realized this sports thing is good and The Fan in New York had just started cranking it up, and so we started doing some long form talk shows at RKO, and then WIP called and that was really my first major morning sports talk show in 1990."

The RKO outfit folded so he came back to Philly.

Sports talk wasn't a stretch from his experience doing a general talk show at WCAU in Philly.

"As much as I love sports, I think the show that I did that was probably the most satisfying and gratifying as a professional was at WCAU because I got to use all of my strengths. Pop culture, news, sports, traffic, all of the things I was able to do in my career, that morning show, if WCAU hadn't pulled the plug on the thing, I think it would have eventually become a nationally syndicated full-service morning show. But CAU had all the unions they wanted to get rid of despite good ratings. In one year, my morning show was doubling WWDB's audience, and then they pulled the plug on it. That's when I was out of work for a couple of months and that's when WIP hired me to join up with Angelo Cataldi and Al Morganti to start the WIP morning show."

ESPN RADIO

Charley Steiner, who hired Tony at RKO, became an ESPN anchor in Bristol, Connecticut. In 1992 ESPN was going to launch their radio network, and when they asked Charley who they could get to be a host and start this weekend venture, he told them about WIP's Tony Bruno.

Tony's WIP show with Angelo and Al had flourished two years in. He also had a wife and two young sons. He turned ESPN down, not wanting to become a "radio vagabond."

ESPN persisted and simply asked Tony to come to Bristol to check things out, so he went to Connecticut to talk.

They made him a good offer. At the time, ESPN Radio was only on weekends and they told him he could still do his WIP work. Bruno accepted.

"ESPN really put me on the map as far as national recognition."

RAKING UP THE MILEAGE

Bristol, Connecticut, is about 200 miles from Philadelphia. Consider it a four-hour drive without traffic. If you've ever been on the New Jersey Turnpike or the Garden State Parkway, you know that there is always traffic. It's not exactly the easiest, most scenic, or relaxing drive.

With Tony working at WIP in the mornings Monday through Friday and at ESPN Radio on the weekends, commuting wasn't a breeze.

"As soon as I was done on Friday at noon, I would jump in my car and drive to Bristol, Connecticut, get there Friday afternoon, have dinner with Keith, then have a pre-show meeting, and then check into the hotel. Then Saturday we would go in at noon and we'd do six hours of prep, go on the air at 6 p.m. to 1 a.m., and do seven hours of radio on Saturday, seven hours of radio on Sunday, with no phone calls. Remember, back then we never took calls, and then at 1 a.m. when I was done I'd jump back in my car and drive five hours back to Philly and go right back on the air with Angelo at 5:30 in the morning. So I did that grind for a couple of years. I don't know how I ever survived it. I would drive back on the Jersey Turnpike and the Garden State Parkway and many nights I would have to drink like three jolt colas just to stay awake. So I would do a 24-hour cycle from Sunday at noon, I wouldn't get home until Monday at noon and then go to sleep and sleep the entire day just to catch up on the weekend of staying awake 24 hours. So I did that for a few years, and then finally it was getting to me and I had to make a decision, and that's when my contract expired at WIP."

Things were going very well at WIP and he had to figure out which job he wanted.

He knew he had to make a choice for himself, for his family, and for his health.

"Tom Bigby (WIP Program Director) said, 'go take the ESPN job because I'm not going to offer you a new deal. If you want to work there, I'm not going to pay you.' He thought I was bluffing. I guess he thought it was some sort of a contract ploy, which it wasn't cause I was serious. So I go to ESPN, they offer me a full-time contract, and I bring it back to Tom and say, 'Hey listen, I'm going to take this deal, I'm not bullshitting you, this is the deal, here's the contract.' He said, 'Go ahead and take it because I'm not paying you that.' I said, OK, I'm gonna tell them I'm taking the deal. I just want you to know that I'm being straightforward with you, here's the deal and I'm going to take it. And when my contract expires at WIP, I'm going to honor the contract, and then I'm going to go to ESPN.'"

Bruno told Bigby he took the deal at ESPN and when his last day at WIP would be. Tony claims Bigby said

'OK.'

Tony told Cataldi and Morganti he was exiting the morning show and they didn't believe him.

THE LAWSUIT

It finally dawned on Bigby that Bruno wasn't bluffing.

The week after he left, Tony got a letter from lawyers for Infinity, the owners of WIP, informing him that they were suing him to keep him for another year due to a right-to-match clause in his contract.

"I guess Bigby realized that I wasn't joking and that I did take another job, and that I'm sure his bosses and the Infinity people said 'What the hell did you do?' so they matched my contract from ESPN and had to keep me for another year. Legally I had to do it, so I did it for another year working seven days a week, but once that year ended I did the same thing. See ya guys. It wasn't fair to ESPN to put them through that."

FLAMING OUT

Tony worked full-time at ESPN radio for a few more years and hosted the morning show with former Notre Dame and Eagles defensive lineman Mike Golic for a year. Then he left. It wasn't for a better job. He had no other options.

"I just decided that I was burned out. The morning show was fun but they weren't really expanding it. We were only on in two cities and I just thought that Disney was dragging its feet on putting this morning show out to as many stations as possible, 'cause I thought we were really in a good spot to set up a morning show that could be a nationally dominant morning show that a lot of stations would carry. The plan at Disney was very, very slow, I was getting frustrated and then finally I was just like, 'You know what, I can't deal with this anymore,' so I resigned at

ESPN. At that time, I had the second highest contract behind Chris Berman at ESPN. I was the second highest paid guy in 1999."

When Tony started at ESPN, they paid him $35,000 per year. When he left, he was earning $500,000 per year. That's a lot to walk away from but he was truly frustrated.

"It wasn't one of those scam deals where I had a better offer and was just trying to get out of a contract."

He was out of work for seven months before getting a call from the West Coast.

FOX

Fox Sports implemented their own radio network. They contacted Tony.

He went back to the suits at ESPN to prove to them that he wasn't "some guy just trying to jump across the street," although that would be a pretty wide street to leap.

"I said, 'listen, I've been out of work for seven months. My intention was not to screw over ESPN. But I've got another opportunity.'"

The lawyers talked and gave him the go ahead to leave so long as he didn't go on the air at Fox until they launched their sports radio division in August of 2000.

THE CITY OF ANGELS

It was a great opportunity for Tony to start up another sports radio network. Everything was up to par legally and he was excited to move to Los Angeles and get back to work. Unfortunately, his family didn't share his enthusiasm.

"My wife was not a big Los Angeles fan and to me this was a great opportunity because, again, it was morning drive, it was Los Angeles, the opportunities were much greater to do other things, television and those other things as I got older. I said, 'You know what, this is just a great opportunity,' and so I moved to LA and took the job."

Tony never moved his family away from Philadelphia during his ESPN days. His three kids, the last of whom was born in 1982, grew up in a stable household, not being uprooted on a whim. That was important to Tony, but his kids were older. He felt the time was right to move to California.

"By the time the ESPN stuff was going on, my kids at least were teenagers and they were starting to get up there. They were not little kids that I picked up and moved from city to city. I never wanted to have my kids become radio vagabonds and then resent me. I had opportunities to leave Philly many, many times. The New York thing and even the Connecticut thing, those were short commutes so I could be home more with my family and not pick them up and displace them. They never had to move to New York. They never had to move to Connecticut. So I would commute, and while it was a tough commute sometimes I never really neglected my family when my kids were growing up and going to school and playing sports and doing little league and all those other things."

With the Los Angeles job, the Brunos had a long distance commute. Tony would go to Philadelphia; his wife would go to LA. He would go back every two weeks. Fox even built a studio in his Philly home so he could do a show on Monday before flying back to Los Angeles. It made things a little easier, but it was still a difficult situation.

In Los Angeles, he was doing TV for *The Best Damn Sports Show Period*, and EA Sports was using him for the Madden video games. Things were going well for Tony professionally and he realized he had made the right decision to go to California.

Family-wise though, the move took its toll and led to divorce.

"My wife wouldn't move to California and understand that part of my life, but that's what happens unfortunately. But luckily my kids are all grown now and they all have their own lives. It was a disappointment to me because of all the time that I spent with my wife, for 30 years of marriage, I never really tried to displace my family, but that opportunity to move to Los Angeles was something I couldn't pass up."

Tony was stunned when she wouldn't move, but he thought he could talk her into it.

"She just never bought into it."

DIVORCE LAWYERS

The divorce didn't affect Tony's show, although he did take some shots at lawyers.

"I was upset at the way the process was handled because divorce lawyers to me are the lowest form of life and I used to say that on the air all the time, and I say it to this day. Because their job is not to reach an amicable settlement, their job is to create hate and division and malice so the clock continues to run. I say on the air, 'Divorce lawyers are like cab drivers with an education. They just want the meter to keep running.' They don't care who's happy, who's not happy, they just want acrimony. I offered her everything in the beginning and she thought she could get more and then five years later, after a long, drawn out process, she realized that her lawyer really did her no good and that what she got in the end was less than I offered her in the beginning."

FOUR YEARS OF FOX

Tony's four-year contract at FSR was coming to an end. Clear Channel, which owns Fox Sports Radio, decided they wanted to cut costs.

"My contract expired and they wanted me to take a massive pay cut and they were under the edict to go cheaper. I was a victim of that. You know, 'Hey Tony, you've done a great job, we've got a lot of affiliates, we're really competing with ESPN, but we can't afford to pay you what we agreed to pay you, will you take a big pay cut?' I said, 'No, I'm not going to take a massive pay cut,' and it was really a principled thing."

That was that with Fox Sports Radio.

TRAVELING MAN

Without a job, Tony decided to hit the road. It was time to travel the world and recharge the batteries.

"I didn't let the fact that thing ended after four years destroy my life. I had opportunities to move and go other places and I said, 'No, I'm going to stay in LA and see what else is available to me.' There was really nothing going on in New York or even back in Philly."

In the seven months that he was out of work, he went to France and Italy as well as Philadelphia to spend time with his family.

"I have my family in Sicily where I took my mom back just a few years ago, so I have relatives in other parts of the world. In France I had some friends. I did pretty much travel alone but I wasn't one of these guys that just threw on a backpack and just started going on trains and going from city to city. I had a plan. I wanted to go to Italy. I wanted to go to France. So I did those things. I wanted to do things I hadn't done before and I had an opportunity for a couple of months to just do it, so I did it."

The time spent away from the radio business helped Tony learn more about himself.

"Absolutely. I learned that I'm a self-sufficient guy, that I love my wife and my family, and they were great and we were good together. She's great at cooking and cleaning. I learned that I could take care of myself. I learned that I wasn't dependent on anyone. When I knew my marriage was coming to an end I wanted to prove to myself and show myself that I can rely on myself. If I had to be on my own I could survive without being an emotional wreck and that I was strong enough. And I proved that as a 10-year-old kid, I knew I was strong enough to survive, and now a guy in his 50s, I knew that I was a survivor and that I love having friends and I love having someone that cares about me, but, if I had to be on my own and I had to travel to foreign countries and learn different languages and explore things, that's what I did. I learned that I was strong enough to be on my own and fight forward 'cause I had to keep working because that's what I love to do."

9-11

The proudest moment of Tony's career came when he was doing a morning show in Los Angeles in 2001. He was on the air with Andrew Siciliano and was discussing the NBA and Michael Jordan's ego of all things when the first plane hit the World Trade Center. Then reports started coming in on the attacks.

"We switched from sports talk, having fun mode, into 'uh oh, we have something serious going on here.' Andrew had a news background, I had a news background, and from that moment on, while other sports hosts ran away from their jobs that day, I said, 'my job as a reporter and as a responsible journalist, my background in news says you don't run away from this.' This is the biggest story in the history of our lifetime. So Andrew and I stayed on the air and we went into full news mode."

Tony and Andrew stayed on the air for eight hours collecting and disseminating information. Each year when the anniversary of September 11th rolls around, Tony gets contacted by people who remember his coverage of the tragic events.

"Many people ran away because they didn't want to deal with it. That's my finest moment and the thing I'm most proud of in 40 years of radio."

EXPERIENCE

Minnie Minoso, the former Indian and White Sox outfielder, played for five decades starting in 1949. As a publicity stunt with the White Sox, he got 8 at bats in 1976 and 2 ABs in 1980 at the age of 54, making him a five-decade player.

Tony Bruno, on the other hand, is a six-decade broadcaster. He began in 1969—he's broadcast professionally in the '60s '70s, '80s, '90s, 2000s, and the 2010s.

"The fact that I started in 1969 makes it sound like a long time but it has been 42 years in this business, which is a pretty amazing run."

What is the secret to his enthusiasm and longevity?

"I love what I do. I still have 13-year-old kids call my show. I hear a 13-year-old kid call and he's a really sharp kid and a good listener and a good talker, and I think of myself. I got that chance as a kid. I called radio stations when I was young. A lot of radio stations have this 'you can't be under 18 and call,' these rules and regulations which is all BS. To me, if a 13-year-old kid is sharp enough to call a show and can add something, what difference does it make how old he is? So 13-year-old kids call me, 80-year-old women call me. I mean, that's the joy I get out of it. I feel like I'm a performer who has to go out every night and do a good show."

JOHN LENNON

While working for WFIL in 1975, Tony became acquainted with John Lennon. The former Beatle was living in the United States and didn't want to go back to England. The USA was trying to deport him, and Lennon wanted to prove to the U.S. Government that he was worthy of staying in the country, through charity work.

Tony recalls the time Lennon went to Philadelphia. "He was doing anything it took to try and stay. He was setting up all these charity events with radio stations. He would go in and help them raise money. The Famous 56 was the frequency, but Lennon agreed to come to WFIL and spend a weekend, 56 straight hours staying awake on the air and doing stuff on the air with all the DJs."

As the evening news guy, Tony got to hang out with Lennon.

"He was just a blast. He was fun. He did not want to go back to England. I was never a big autograph or picture guy so I don't have any pictures. We didn't carry around cameras then like they do now. He really liked me and I obviously respected him, so at the end of the weekend he takes out a loose-leaf pad and just signs an autograph to me. It says, 'To Tony, Love John Lennon, nice weather' and then he draws a little rain cloud with a couple of drops in it and makes his little John Lennon face with the glasses and writes, '75' on the bottom of it."

Tony's son, Chris found it one day in a basement and put it in a frame. It's the one autograph Tony has hanging on his wall.

YOU CAN GO HOME AGAIN

After living and working in Southern California, Tony Bruno returned home to Philadelphia in October of 2011, despite what Thomas Wolfe wrote.

Philly's love affair with Tony continues to this day and with good reason. He's the ultimate local boy makes good.

"I think it's because people grew up with me. There are still people who remember me from the WFIL days. These will be people in their 50s and 60s, in my age group now, and then their kids listen to me now and their kids' kids. And there's a whole generation of people who grew up with me and they know I'm a Philly guy. I'm a Philadelphia guy."

Even when he was doing a Philadelphia show from

Los Angeles he was a Philly guy. "I said to them, 'Rush Limbaugh's not in the Beltway and he's talking about politics every day and Howard Stern's in New York doing his show but he can relate to the rest of the country.' I know. I watch Philly sports, I know what all the teams are doing. All the athletes in town know who I am, so a lot of people in Philly respect what I do."

He credits the Phillies' 1980 World Series as his favorite sporting event that he has covered. He has had to walk the fine line between fan and reporter. Yes, he's a Philly guy. Finally, he's back home.

PASSION

Passion can be an overused word, but not in Tony's case. If he ever loses it then he'll say goodbye.

"Once I lose that, then I know it's time to go."

SUCCESS STORY

"I would like to be remembered as a guy who worked hard and came from nowhere. I think I'm the original American success story. I didn't have anyone give me anything except a chance. I'm proud of what I've done. I've never hurt anybody. I try to be a good person. I just try to be the best person I can be. I try to enjoy my life every day. I'm respected and I respect others. I've achieved all my goals. I set goals as a young kid. I said I wanted to be in radio, I got there. Every goal I've ever set for myself, fortunately, I worked hard and achieved. My goal is just to be happy every day now. As long as I'm happy, that's all that matters to me."

Scott Ferrall
"On The Bench"

When Scott Ferrall was just a kid, he knew what he wanted to do. His father, Tom, was a news anchor at KMOX but Scott didn't want to do news. He wanted to be a sportscaster and sports writer.

He also knew that he wanted to be different.

While there are many different types of sportscasters, none are like Ferrall. He's different with a capital D. There is no one like Scott Ferrell, who currently plies his trade on Sirius XM Radio where he works on Howard Stern's channel.

HOWARD COSELL

In addition to his father, Scott was influenced by one of the most, if not the most, polarizing figures in sports broadcasting history.

"I wanted to be Howard Cosell when I was six years old. My goal was to be him. I thought he was smarter than everybody. By the time I was 10 and 12 I was already deeply rooted in sports, and I thought he was the greatest sportscaster that ever lived. Everybody laughed at me when I would imitate him and I can imitate him perfectly."

All the parents and grown-ups were amused by little Scott's Howard Cosell impressions. Fast forward years later to September 5, 1995. The *Wall Street Journal* called Ferrall "Generation X's Howard Cosell," complete with a picture of him chomping on a cigar in front of a microphone, screaming with his mouth wide open.

"At that point I basically just masturbated. I've made it in the *Wall Street Journal.*"

THE VOICE

To describe Ferrall's voice is like trying to describe to someone how a telephone works or why the sky is blue. He possesses a raspy, rapid-fire delivery. Silky smooth is not a way one would portray Ferrall's pipes.

"I thought I had the most distinctive voice in the business. No one else sounds like me. The only other guy who sounds like me is Johnny Most (former Celtics' announcer). I've done a lot with my voice albeit it was very painful and irritating to some."

SMART PEOPLE

Scott, not surprisingly, has had more than his share of battles over the years with radio management.

"I never listen to anybody, let alone program directors yelling at me about my style or GMs yelling at me because of my behavior. What I was trying to do on the air entertained people, got huge ratings, and made money for the radio station. There are very few people in my career I've listened to. I try to be clever when I say this but I listen to smart people. I don't listen to assholes and idiots."

He's been in the business for a long time and doesn't take to kindly to those who try to change him.

"Can you imagine? I've been doing this 28 years. Suddenly now someone's gonna fucking teach me how to do radio? I mean, honestly, I've been syndicated six times, now all of a sudden someone's gonna teach me something? Blow me. Fuck off, I don't listen to people, I'm too old. I'm 45. Fuck off, we're not friends. I go to these cheesy Christmas parties and all I do is sit there and look at people and think how much I can't stand them."

THE RADIO INDUSTRY

At times throughout his career, the battles with management took its toll. Ferrall questioned if he wanted to continue. He claims he never lost his love of being on the air and his drive to entertain people, but he was sick and tired of the business aspect.

"The reason I wanted to walk away is how cutthroat and vicious and backstabbing and lying and stealing and thievery of the people that run these radio companies are. I've never worked with so many corrupt liars and pieces of shit in my life. I've never met so many assholes in my life. Fake people. They've sucked the life out of me over the years. I just don't trust anyone. I don't look up to them. I don't admire them. I think they're scum. I think the business is scum and there have been times when I've wondered why I keep doing this, this is not working. The reason I'd want to walk away is the business side of it. I can't stand it. I hate everything about it, agents, all the rest. They'll chop your head off. They don't care if you have a wife, children. They don't care if you have lymphoma. They'll fucking fire you on the day you find out you got cancer. It is the most ruthless business in the world and I'm not wrong. The problem is nobody has the balls to say it to them, and I do, and I don't give a fuck what they think of me."

RESPECT

There are some people in the business that Ferrall actually likes and respects.

"Believe it or not, I respect everyone who does radio. I respect all hosts, all shows, no matter if they're soft, if they're gay shows, if they're straight shows, if they're sports shows, if they're talk shows, morning shows, afternoon shows, if they're Top 40, if they're rock shows, heavy metal shows or any kind of show, if you're doing it I respect people that do it. I seem to get along great with the talent and I respect them and support them."

Ferrall also singles out a couple of sports talk radio veterans.

"I love Sid Rosenberg. I love Joe Benigno. Because

they're real people, they're totally cool, there's substance there. They're laughing, they're joking, they actually care. I'm a huge fan of Sid and Joe. I used to hand off to Joe Benigno every night for five years on WFAN. I worked with Sid so many times most people think that Sid and I should be either dead together or in jail together. I think Sid's a genuinely huge talent with tremendous skill and smarts and history and just a pizzazz about him and everything even that's happened bad in his life, it's so funny to me how quick people judge him and yet they've got all the skeletons in the closet that they don't want to talk about."

INDIANA

Ferrall went to Indiana University in Bloomington in 1983 where he simply wanted to get his degree and get on with his sportscasting career.

At IU, he did sports updates for a local station, not the college station. He also did Indiana soccer play-by-play and covered Indiana basketball when Bob Knight was the coach.

He not only got his foot in the door, he kicked the door open.

"I was working so much in radio that I barely went to class. I got very good grades in journalism but I didn't care about anything else. I was on the air so much and became so popular that I became well known on campus as being the sports guy."

Out of college, he quickly got hired by CBS radio in Pittsburgh as a news writer where his confidence became evident.

A SHOT

At KQV radio in the Steel City, sportscaster Paul Steigerwald created a vacancy when he left to announce Pittsburgh Penguins games. Ferrall decided to pay a visit to the program director.

"I walked into the boss because I was pretty cocky and confident and I said, 'he's leaving, I'm the sports guy, I'm better than him, put me on the air for two weeks and that will be the end of it, and I'll be your sportscaster and there won't be anyone else that you audition.' He laughed at me and thought I was crazy. I just said give me two weeks and I'll do the rest and you'll never hear anything like it."

One of Ferrall's trademarks was saying, "THIS IS ...Scott Ferrall." He picked it up while broadcasting in Indiana. He kept it up when he was in Pittsburgh while trying to be unique.

When he broke out 'THIS IS ...' in Pittsburgh the program director wanted to know why he was doing that.

"I did everything to be different."

That job eventually led to a stint in Chicago, which led to Las Vegas in 1993, where he got a national radio show with Sports Entertainment Network when Arnie Spanier got a job in Phoenix, a position Ferrall thought he was going to land.

SEN eventually morphed into Sporting News Radio.

PASSING THE AUDITION
The people at Sports Entertainment Network wanted to hear Ferrall do his thing. They gave him a 6-hour tryout on a college football Saturday where Scott let it fly.

"The GM of the network came in on a Saturday, which he never did, cause I made so much noise and I was so crazy and just so over the top and insane I was going to get this gig. There wasn't going to be any not getting the gig. I went on there and I just went balls to the wall."

The GM took in Ferrall's show by staring at him through the window for an hour. Ferrall didn't even know who he was. But five minutes after his show he got the show permanently. He would be on over 300 markets as 'Ferrall on the Bench.'

He dropped the "THIS IS ..." as well.

"I had hats that said 'THIS IS' and I'd wear it around and people knew it was me and la-de-da when I was a young punk and an idiot. And then I started in Vegas and I immediately went on the air as 'Ferrall on the Bench.'

NEW YORK

Ferrall eventually landed in New York on WNEW, hosting a morning sports show. But he was let go when he wouldn't publicly support the station in the aftermath of the infamous Opie and Anthony sex scandal. The pair was the popular hosts of the 'Opie and Anthony Show' and they were axed after encouraging people to have sex on-air in public places in New York City. One couple decided to win the contest by getting intimate in St. Patrick's Cathedral. As you might expect, a lot of people were unhappy with the stunt and it cost Opie and Anthony their jobs.

Management told Ferrall not to cross the company line, but he knew he was getting fired anyway when he saw the bosses packing boxes in their offices.

"I went on the air that day and said it's okay for priests to fuck little boys in the ass but it's not alright for two afternoon hosts to say, 'go into a church and have sex' and then the stupid people listen to him and did it? Who do you blame—the stupid people that did it or the radio hosts who were smart enough to con him into doing it?"

Good bye, New York.

HELLO, MIAMI

After New York, Ferrall went to Miami and WQAM on morning drive. WQAM was the radio home of Neil Rogers.

It didn't take long for Ferrall to make an impact in the Sunshine State.

"I took over Miami. The first thing I said when I was on the air was 'I slept with Dan Marino's sister.' The whole world wanted me. His father worked I guess with the station in some sales capacity. He wanted to kill me. The Marinos said they were going to sue me and all the rest. I was just trying to entertain people and I sure got their attention in a hurry. And then I think I did about a half hour talking about driving down 95 admiring all the giant breasts in the area and chicks driving around in bikinis and I immediately took over the market."

The suits though were having problems with Ferrall's topics and opinions. It created some wild after-show scenes.

"Every day when I got off the air these people would scream and yell at me and I would scream and yell back at them, how stupid they were and why did you hire me if you didn't want ratings. If you want to be number one, you want to make a lot of money, you want to make millions, I'm your guy. If you want to be a pussy then let's fucking end it today. They would argue and scream at me and say no, we want you, you need to do it our way, calm down, blah blah. I hate calm down, I hate relax, I hate take it easy."

NEIL ROGERS

Ferrall was always fighting management. The late, legendary talk show host Neil Rogers gave Ferrall some of the best advice he's ever been given.

"Rogers said, 'you've got to stop fighting these people. You're never going to win. You have to just do your show and then go home and fuck your pretty girlfriend.' At the time I was with this woman who was smoking hot and then I married her and had children with her and I'm with her to this day."

Rogers told him to do the show, let his work speak for itself, not cross the line, and get out of there when the show was over.

HOWARD STERN

Ferrall has found a home on Howard Stern's Sirius XM Radio, Howard 101. For the past five-and-a-half years Ferrall has had no problems or issues with Stern and he says it's in part to the advice he received from Rogers.

"I have nothing to do with anyone at Sirius including Howard Stern himself. I would not go near him if you paid me. I'm not interested in him. I'm not interested in his social life and being his friend. I'm interested in him as a brilliant morning guy, one of the greatest morning radio hosts in the history of radio. The greatest, clearly."

Stern handpicked Ferrall to do his thing, which Ferrall found flattering and moving.

"I decided from day one I would never call him, never bother him, never e-mail him, I don't even want to talk to him. I just want my performance to speak for itself."

Ferrall has had his best success when he steered clear of people in the business. When he hasn't, it's been one headache after another for both sides.

"It's all about the show," says Ferrall.

THEATER OF THE MIND

Ferrall wanted his show to be like a bunch of guys going to get a few suds and watching a bunch of games.

He wanted to bring that excitement and bedlam to his show.

"I just felt like my show was a sports bar. A real unique look into what it's really like to go to a huge sports bar and watch a big game with all your buddies, and I felt that to do radio the right way I want it to seem like everyone's everyday life. I pictured my show at the sports bar, a rowdy, loud, raucous sports bar that had 15-20 games going, it's got a music box blaring rock and roll, it's got 300 people in a bar all smoking and drinking and talking and drinking shots and beers and laughing and throwing insults at each other and screaming and yelling and noise and chaos, but for some reason, in the midst of all that chaos everyone still understands each other and everyone still is able to hold a conversation and make their point back and forth with all that insanity going on."

He drove programmers crazy by having music playing underneath the show and playing sound effects of pouring beers.

"People are so stupid they think I'm actually serving up prostitutes and cocaine to people. And it's the funniest thing to me in the world because we're sitting in there doing a show completely sober and it's all sound tracked on a computer and it's no different than Fred playing drops on Howard's show or anyone else doing drops."

THE WORLD'S MOST PAINFUL KID

Would it surprise you if you learned Scott Ferrall was a quiet, easygoing kid? It would be absolutely surprising because it couldn't be further than the truth. Plenty of teachers would have liked to have grabbed young Scott by the neck.

"I was crazy, I was running around, I was very hyper, I was just loud and obnoxious and crazy and funny and kind of the show-off, life of the party kind of kid. I just always wanted to stand out and entertain even if it meant being painful. In school I was a troublemaker, an arguer, a confrontational child that argued with teachers. I felt that at the time when I was 10 and 15 and 17, that my best training for the real world of wanting to be a sports talk guy and a sportscaster and a play-by-play guy. I wanted to be Mike Lange, the voice of the Penguins. All of these things I did. I didn't care about school, I thought that school was boring and a waste of time, so I took advantage of school to hone my skill abusing others. I would argue with teachers, I would argue with principals, I would get suspended from school, I would call them names, I would insult them, I would make the whole class cheer and pound their tables. I would throw spitwads at teachers when they weren't looking and I would cause tremendous aggravation for people and I thought at the time, well obviously immaturity and stupidness, I was doing it, but it really was a master plan to hone my skills at entertaining and arguing and being confrontational and being an intense sportscaster. I wanted to be a sports talk guy that was so different and so argumentative and so in your face that no one would ever forget me."

Ferrall admits he was the most "painful kid in the world" and that at the age of 10 he thought he was smarter than everyone else, including his parents and teachers.

THE FAMILY

Ferrall feels his dad, who listens to his show, lives somewhat vicariously through him on the radio.

Tom Ferrall, after his stint as an anchorman at KMOX in St. Louis, worked for U.S. Steel for 42 years. While he doesn't mind that, Scott believes his dad's one regret was not having continued his broadcasting career.

Working for U.S. Steel is what brought the family from St. Louis to Indiana to Pittsburgh.

Sports was the thread that bonded father and son. He took Scott to games at Wrigley Field, Comiskey Park, Soldier Field, and Chicago Stadium.

"My dad was just a huge sports influence. It was our connection. It was the only thing I got along with my dad about. It was the only thing we ever talked about. It was the only thing I ever read about, it was the only thing I ever watched."

One reason Ferrall became a Notre Dame football fan is because his dad, at one time, was roommates with Irish coach Dan Devine.

"When he was the head coach at South Bend he would give us tickets and we would go to every game. I saw Joe Montana play every single game of his career in South Bend. I saw many more than that. I saw Vegas Ferguson, I saw them all. I went to the '79 Cotton Bowl in the freezing cold in Dallas. From the seventh grade on I rooted for the Pittsburgh Steelers, Penguins, and Pirates and my love affair with Pittsburgh has never ended. It's my favorite city in the world. Those are my favorite teams and they will be until the day I die."

Ferrall's sister and father went to University of Michigan and they, along with his mother, Elsie, tried to raise him as a Wolverine fan and get him to go to Ann Arbor. So Scott naturally went to Indiana.

As for Scott's youthful behavior, his dad wasn't a fan as you could imagine.

"He thought that I was insane and that I was out of control and immature and that I'd never make it. I just disagreed with him. I didn't want to be an anchorman. I didn't want to wear a suit and tie. I wanted to be in sports and I wanted to be crazy. He thought I was hopeless, but I guess I got the last laugh because he comes on my radio show to this day. He's a huge sports fan, he knows his sports and I think he gets a great thrill watching me over the years be so successful."

Scott's mom, who passed away in 1997, was a concert pianist and taught at Carnegie Mellon University and privately to gifted kids.

With his parents working a lot that gave Scott plenty of free time.

"I was a kid that grew up without a lot of supervision. My dad was always gone, my mother was always gone, and I would sit at home and beat up my sister."

MATRIMONY

Ferrall has been married twice. His first marriage lasted 10 years but then she gave him an ultimatum, "me or the show."

Ferrall told her, "nice knowing ya. I gave her a ton of money and got her off of my hands. And then I met 34C, which is Stephanie, my wife now, and I like her better than anyone I've ever known, and love her more than anyone I've ever known."

They have two children.

"I've always been a one-girl guy, but I have had my fair share of broads when I wasn't married. I love hot women and I'll hit on anything. I have no fear of any kind of woman. I will hit on anything with a pulse. But I always went for the hot ones. I was never interested in banging ugly chicks. I never fucked any fat chicks my whole life if that's what you wanted to know. I like hot, smokin' bodies. That's what I go for and I ended up with one so I'm pretty happy about that. My first one was hot and the second one was hotter and I'd like to do a three-way with them."

THE ATHLETE

Ferrall played high school basketball growing up in Valparaiso, Indiana. He was just 5'9" and learned to play guard and shoot the basketball. Eventually he sprouted up to 6'3". By his account he was a good shooter who could pass the ball.

But when he moved to Pittsburgh for his senior year they weren't impressed with his inside and outside game.

"They didn't want to hear about the hotshot from Indiana that could shoot the jumper. They had their own favorite sons and they sat me on the bench. The coach was a math teacher, his name was Black. I had him as a math teacher and I didn't do well in his class either. I used to tell him that he had no idea what he was fucking doing and your players suck and I'm better than them and I can school every one of them one-on-one. I can shoot better than all of 'em, I shoot 98 percent from the free throw fucking line and you're sitting me on the bench? Fuck you and I quit. I said, 'you suck, dude. Not only am I better than your top point guard, I'm going to fuck his sister.' To this day it's one of the great coups of my life that I did bang his sister."

He also played golf and while at college he played tennis for a couple of years.

"But then I decided that I liked drinking beer and having sex with sorority girls more than going to tennis practice."

As for golf, he still plays and at his best was a 6 handicap. However, without the time to play he now says he's a 15 handicap. He also cops to violent tendencies on the golf course with deplorable language.

"I'm pretty bad. I swear more than anyone I know on the golf course. Most people that go golfing with me have the time of their lives for four hours."

THE PAPERBOY

At one time Ferrall, during sixth and seventh grades, was employed as a newspaper delivery boy for the *Chicago Tribune*. His route included not only a nice subdivision where he lived but a vast apartment complex about a half a mile away. He had to drop off 250 papers, seven days a week.

His girlfriend at the time, "she was hot or so I thought. I had stuck my tongue in her mouth and made out with her and felt her breasts so I figured she was my girlfriend."

His "girlfriend" lived in a mansion, the biggest, nicest house in the neighborhood. This gave Scott got an idea.

"We decided to break into the house while they were on vacation. I delivered the paper that day and I was collecting and I had to get the money. So while I was collecting and doing the money transaction, my buddy Jeff Armstrong went around the back and unlocked the washing room door. And they were getting ready to get in their car and go on their summer vacation, so as they drove off we're waving to them down the street and they went away for two weeks."

Ferrall and his pal spent the entire two weeks making themselves at home.

"We ate their food, we played pool, strip poker, we did it all. We ate everything they had in the house so when they came home there was nothing. We were drinking their beer and I'm in like seventh grade. We were doing everything bad you can imagine."

When the family came home the father was sharp enough to remember the young hoodlums waving from the driveway and put two and two together.

The father interrogated the boys separately.

"I was smart enough to deny it for hours, I held my own. I was like, 'I don't know what you're talking about, man. I may be fingering your daughter but I didn't break into your house.' And then they finally got Jeff to break and we got busted, and I remember my dad beat the shit out of me with a fraternity paddle and grounded me for the entire summer. It was the worst summer of my life. My ass had open sores like I was set on fire on both of my ass cheeks. And if he were to do that today my dad would have served five years for child abuse. But back then it was healthy to beat the shit out of your kids and I'll never forget the lesson it taught me."

Many years later, the girlfriend in question called Scott's show and they relived the home invasion episode on the air. She and her sisters are even Facebook friends with Ferrall.

"That girl ended up really hot, too. I should have stayed with her."

REGRETS

When asked for regrets, Ferrall for once is quieted. But just for a bit.

"I loved being on KNBR in San Francisco and simulcasting my radio show on TV in the Bay Area and being number one the whole year, I was there. But I made a bad decision going there to work for Bob Agnew and Tony Salvador. I couldn't stand either one of them. They were cheesy feta and wine drinking with all the 'I'm from San Francisco, I'm better than you, we're not gonna take your shit, mister' right after they gave me all this money. They made my life miserable for a year. I couldn't stand Gary Radnich, I couldn't stand anybody there. Meanwhile, I loved San Francisco and I loved the audience. I was number one and had it all but I was so miserable with the people I had to look at every day. I regret going to work for them."

He also has a regret regarding the Atlanta Thrashers.

THE EXPANSION THRASHERS

Trivia time. Who was the first radio play-by-play voice of the Atlanta Thrashers in 1999? Probably not a difficult question since you are reading about Scott Ferrall, you could assume it was him. And you would be right.

While he doesn't have many regrets, he does have one regarding the Thrashers.

"I regret my behavior a little bit when I was with the Thrashers because all I did the entire year was party with players, drink booze, beer, I lived like a rock star flying around with NHL players."

He wasn't supposed to socialize with the players. That meant no eating or drinking with the players or even go to their homes. As we've learned with Ferrall, rules sometimes get in the way.

"I broke all the rules. One night I was with one of

their goalies and his Corvette got broken into and stolen, and we were left standing naked at like three in the morning without a car. I had a lot of bad decisions I made probably in my maturity and respect for the league and for the job. I just thought I was Harry Caray. I was rowdy, I was crazy, I broke all the rules, I defied them. They told me not to hang out with the players, I hung out with them every night. They told me not to eat with them, I went out to dinner with them every night. When we were on the road they asked me where to go cause I had been syndicated so much I knew all the great places to eat and party in every city. The players looked up to me, they knew I was a partier. I totally partied and I don't like the way I acted when I was the Thrashers play-by-play guy. I don't regret at all the way I called a game. I thought I was very good at it, but I regret the behavior I showed them in terms of defiance and breaking all their rules."

Ferrall was fired after that first season in which the Thrashes went a dismal 14-57-7 for 39 points.

"But they paid me for four years so who's the sucker?"

Despite the firing, Ferrall remained on good terms with the Thrashers organization until they relocated to Winnipeg after the 2010-2011 season.

BACK UP PLAN

"I would have been a defense lawyer. I would want to argue with people and I would want to be confrontational and I would want to have some type of sports labor to it. I would want to be in contempt of court and be thrown out of courtrooms."

Argumentative? Confrontational? Really. Now there's a stretch.

Just for the record, Ferrall and his lawyer, George Stein, are 5-0 in their battles against the FCC.

HAPPINESS

Ferrall is actually a pretty happy, contented man, excepting his battles with management and authority figures. He says they have given him plenty of stress over the years.

"I'm totally happy. I'm only happy when I'm on the air doing the show and when I'm around my wife and two kids. Whenever I'm around radio people and executives I want to vomit."

Colin Cowherd
"The Herd"

Since 2004, Colin Cowherd has held court daily on ESPN Radio's 10 a.m. to 1 p.m. Eastern time slot, previously held down by Tony Kornheiser.

A graduate of Eastern Washington University, best known these days for their red football field, Cowherd has worked in Las Vegas; Tampa, Florida; Portland, Oregon; and currently, Bristol, Connecticut, where he frequently complains about the weather.

In addition to his radio show, 'The Herd,' Colin co-hosts 'SportsNation,' a program on ESPN2 with Michelle Beadle.

ISOLATION

As a kid, Cowherd was full of imagination. He had to be. He grew up in rural Grayland, Washington, which he credits for helping his creativity.

"I was a pretty isolated kid in a small town. My sister was five years older so she didn't want to hang around me. Fifteen-year-old girls don't want to hang around 10-year-old boys. So I lived kind of on the beach halfway up Washington State. Grew up in a kind of divorced environment where I spent a lot of time playing with a couple of kids and hanging out and having to be creative. I've always thought that formed what I do for a living."

Cowherd was the nutty kid who talked to himself and filled out lineup cards to play Wiffle ball. He would turn down the sound on the TV set and do play-by-play of games, which led his mother to believe he would work in his current occupation.

"Where I grew up, you had to be creative because

you didn't live in a suburb or cul-de-sac with 15 kids. It was rural and often wet and windy and sports was a way out."

THE SPORTS FAN

One of the strange things about Cowherd's development in becoming a sports broadcaster was that nobody in his family liked sports or weather. Colin was into both.

"I remember as a kid watching television and watching the Redskins play the Dolphins, and I liked weather. I liked the local news. I used to watch the local news with my dad and I can remember wanting to do that and liking the local weather guy and liking the sports on the news."

PLAYING DAYS

Despite growing up in a small town, as a self-proclaimed "quirky, goofy kid," Cowherd found plenty of things to do to keep occupied. He played little league baseball and basketball (his dad had put up a hoop). He also had a cool mode of transportation.

"I had a little motorcycle, a Honda 150, and I'd drive around when I was a young kid. My mom didn't allow me to go down to the beach by myself because of dangerous riptides, so I'd play some sports. Kick the ball around, shoot baskets. Loved basketball. Basketball was big in the Pacific Northwest. The Sonics were very good and the Blazers were good. Basketball was my first love and I think after that [it] was baseball 'cause baseball was on TV and then I think I've segued into a football fan more."

He also played sports at Ocosta High School.

"For a small town, I was the quarterback and the best basketball player so I was pretty good. Double-digit basketball player my senior year, starting quarterback, but not great. In a very average small town league I was OK."

Cowherd never had professional aspirations and knew from a young age he wasn't big or tall enough. But he always wanted to be behind the microphone.

"I wanted to be a broadcaster. I wanted to go to the games. But I never once, when I was a kid going to a Seattle Sonics game, thought I would play. Everyone was so much bigger than me. I never had those visions."

MOM REMEMBERS

While Cowherd doesn't remember all the details, he does know that very early on, he wanted to be a broadcaster.

"My mom tells me, 'You were 8-years-old going on 40. You knew exactly what you wanted to do. You had it all laid out, you were totally organized. Nobody was going to stop you.' I don't remember that, but that's what my mom recalls."

THE STUDENT

While Cowherd knew what his career path would be, that didn't mean he slacked off in the classroom.

"I had a lot of interests. I was always a good B-plus student. I loved literature class, English, and psychology. I never liked foreign language much. Wasn't much of a math student. I was interested in geography and writing and reading. I was always a pretty good student."

Even with his varied interests, he related everything to sports or broadcasting in some manner.

"I liked writing and reading because it helped me become a better broadcaster. And I liked geography because I liked all the teams and the leagues and could follow them in the papers. I wanted to know where Cincinnati was 'cause I liked the Cincinnati Reds, so I wanted to look up that state and what's it like. So I've always been into that. I've always been into geography and demographics and particular regions of the country. As long as it tied itself to sports I liked it."

THE OPPOSITE SEX

In many cases, the quarterback of the high school football team has little trouble finding a girlfriend. Cowherd was no exception.

"In high school I had a really cute girlfriend, Lisa Maples. She was the homecoming queen. I was always personable so I've never been a guy that stays home on a Friday night. I always thought my personality got me dates that were better looking than I was. I've always thought I've dated better looking, more attractive people than myself. Plus, I was kind of jocky and had a good sense of humor. I mean, let's face it, in high school, if you're a jock, and I was the editor of the newspaper, and if you're kind of quick on your feet you can usually get a date."

EWU

After high school, Cowherd went to Eastern Washington University. While some students are on the 7-year plan, Colin wasn't.

"I was really focused in. I wanted to get out of college as soon as I got in. I was taping games, just micro-focused on it. Completely into it. I would stay at home at night for the first two or three years of college and just turn on the radio and listen to AM stations all across the country."

Cowherd's broadcasting goal was to do play-by-play. He had no interest in becoming a DJ or a public address announcer. It was all about PBP. He hounded the program director at the school station, Dave Ackerley, and another guy, Ron Breitstein, to call the games.

"I was all over them. Any game, any inning, any minute I could do it. To me it was all about play-by-play. There was no talk radio. There was play-by-play and I wanted to do play-by-play."

After college, while still enjoying play-by-play, Cowherd got into television and then sports talk radio in the late '80s early '90s when it began to get popular.

NEVER IN A HURRY

Cowherd enjoyed his journey to ESPN. He wasn't the guy who had to jump from one market to another higher up on the food chain.

"I was never in a hurry to get anywhere. That's the weird thing. I've always been really happy where I was. When I was in Vegas I stayed there for six years. I was single, I was dating beautiful women, I was having fun, making good scratch, I didn't care, I loved it. Then I went to Tampa. I really didn't love the city but when I went to Portland, I loved living in Portland. I would go to a market and try to win the market. I would try to be the number one guy in that market and I wasn't looking at the network. I wasn't eyeing the network at 18. I wanted to get a good job and be really good in that market."

FUN TIMES IN DENVER

During Colin's stint on TV in Las Vegas, he was covering the 1990 Final Four at McNichols Sports Arena in Denver. UNLV won the title that year under Jerry Tarkanian, 103-73 over Duke. His career could have taken a major hit that night, but disaster was averted.

"I did interviews and lost the tape. And as I was running to the truck I couldn't find the tape with all my interviews, and I had like eight minutes to get on the air. And 30 seconds before I hit the air some young guy ran across the parking lot saying, 'Hey dude, here's your tape.' And for about 20 minutes, I was literally, as UNLV won the National Championship, they were going to throw to me and I had nothing. To this day it gives me goosebumps to think about it. It went from the worst nightmare to the greatest relief in a matter of seconds."

ESPN

Cowherd was working in Portland when ESPN called, but they didn't reveal their identity to him for several months. Eventually, in 2003, Colin was hired to replace Tony Kornheiser.

The jump from local to national radio could have been daunting and intimidating, but Colin knew he was ready.

"There was no doubt in my mind. First of all, I had lived in all four corners of the country, so I knew my depth of information and understanding of each region would help a lot. I also knew that West of the Rockies, Kornheiser wasn't going to spend a lot of time on, didn't like to fly, had spent little time there, I knew I would beat him in all the West Coast affiliates. I knew I'd beat him in LA, Portland, Vegas, Phoenix, that kind of stuff. So I knew immediately. And I also knew that in the South, I talk college football, and I knew that I would get an audience in the South and sure enough about a year in I was starting to get a following in the West and in the South."

Bruce Gilbert interviewed Colin for the position. The story goes that Cowherd started talking and Gilbert understood that he was doing his show for his potential future boss.

"Everybody always says that. Everybody always says 'you basically walk around the office, sound like you're on the air, you're kind of auditioning segments.' I think that's just the way I am. Even my wife or kids will say that from time to time. They'll be like, 'Dad, you're not on the air. You're barking at us.' I'm doing everything shy of giving out the phone number. So I think I'm pretty authentic on the air."

He knew he had a chance of getting the job but he wasn't overconfident. There was never a point in the interviewing process when he knew he would take over for Kornheiser.

"I knew they wouldn't fly me out unless I was one of the five or six guys and I thought the interviews went well. I think I've always interviewed well. I've interviewed seven or eight times and I've gotten every job I've interviewed for. I think I'm a pretty good salesman. I can sell my rants on the air, I can sell myself. When you're a host on radio you're basically selling you, not just your platforms or ideas. I knew I was close and then they called and offered some money and I thought, 'Well, they're not offering this to a lot of guys' so I knew I was getting there."

LOCAL VERSUS NATIONAL

Adjustments had to be made when Cowherd made the move to ESPN. Discussing the Blazers' game-winning shot to beat the Warriors wasn't going to cut it on a national level.

"Local radio is very different from syndicated radio. In local radio you can break down one play in a game and talk about it for two hours. That's death for me. I have to get Buffalo and Los Angeles to simultaneously care about a sport or a subject. So in the syndicated level, you have got to think macro. Big stories, strong opinions, big stars, Yankees, Duke basketball, Ohio State football, Los Angeles Lakers, Dallas Cowboys, lots of NFL. Locally, in Buffalo you can talk hockey for four hours and every region's different. But what we've seen over the last several years is an emergence of one dominating sport and that's the National Football League. So I spend 70 percent of my time on that."

THE HERD

How would we describe Colin's radio show? How about we let him characterize his program.

"I've always believed that I do sports for a guy

who likes sports but has a life. That's probably the best way to describe my show. I don't do my show for nerds. I don't do it for guys who have no social life. I do it for a guy who has a great job, a sexy girlfriend or wife, kids, who really likes sports but would rather laugh. I've acknowledged this. This is a badge of honor. Other than five or six events a year, I would choose a date over sports every time."

For the record, the sporting events that Cowherd would choose over dates are the Rose Bowl, the Super Bowl, Game 6 or 7 of the NBA Finals, and Game 7 of the World Series. He would choose the date over a Predators-Maple Leafs game in January or an early December hoop match-up between Western Michigan and Bradley.

"If you gave me a night out with my wife that was sexy or romantic, or a game, I would choose the woman every time. And that's how I brand my show. I'm not for die-hard, 13 fantasy leagues, still memorizing the back of baseball cards guy. That's not who I attract, it's not who I'm attracted to. I don't have a single friend like that."

His show deals with his life and the lives of others. He calls his interviews "conversations." He explains that if two guys are having a compelling conversation in a bar, you'll stop and listen. If one guy is interviewing the other, you'll walk right by.

"I just want to be conversational. I'm going to bring my life into sports, my sports into my life, it's just all one. My life, my kids, my sports, my politics, it's all one. I don't have this compartment where, OK, I'm radio guy. Alright, I'm goofy dad. This is me, I turn on the radio, me comes out, this is what I am. Both of my wives, my ex-wife and my wife now, they understand the game."

Cowherd says he knows where to draw the line, although he doesn't know where that line is.

INFLUENCE

Howard Cosell was willing to not be liked and wasn't shy about asking tough questions. As he would say, he was "just telling it like it is."

Is it any wonder who had the greatest influence on Cowherd's career?

"Howard Cosell," Cowherd says without hesitation. "Not afraid to have a political standpoint or opinion. Took stands. Brutally opinionated. Polarizing. He started all of it. Howard Stern opened the door for a lot of DJs. Howard Cosell opened it up for a lot of talk show hosts. As a kid, one of the reasons I liked boxing was Ali and the other was Cosell. I thought he stood alone intellectually from a standpoint of courage. There was some self-loathing there as well and some bitterness at the end, but I thought he had real courage at the height of his career."

THE TOUGHEST MOMENTS

"Brutal."

That's how Cowherd describes doing his radio program while going through his divorce.

"Easily the toughest thing I've ever gone through. I'd get off the air and cry, you know, that's just awful. That was one of those things where I wouldn't wish on my worst enemy. I lost like 10 pounds in a month. I was very dark, very guilty, and that doesn't lend itself to quality broadcasting. I think you bring your mood to the show and if you're sad and dark you'll do a sad and dark radio show. I think I'm doing my best radio show when I have good energy and a good night sleep and I'm in a good mood."

It was for about eight weeks that Cowherd admits it was probably a hard listen for people.

"They were hard shows to do. I can remember doing two shows where I had not slept the previous night. I came on the air and I had been up for like 36 hours. Just awful and what are you going to do? Thinking about it now makes me sad."

Cowherd hasn't failed at too many things. Whether it's been getting in better shape or doing better financially, he's been able to do it. He's put his mind toward goals and achieved them. The divorce humbled him. It also made him feel guilty since children were involved.

"You start to second guess yourself and there are times when driving to the radio show was the biggest downer and there were other times it was therapeutic."

THE SITCOM

CBS television was developing a sitcom based on Cowherd's life and relationships. His role was inspirational.

"I'm not allowed to write it. I'm not a writer. They have taken parts of my life and they think there is an interesting story there with the wife, the ex-wife, the funny co-host. I'm a radio guy and a TV guy and I'll write a book. It's not something I'm depending on. If it can add nourishment to my career I'm all for it. But I'm certainly not relying on it to pay my kids' tuition or to pay my mortgage. It's an ancillary project that could be beneficial to my career, but if it never takes place it won't be a negative. There are really no negatives with it, only positives."

Cowherd wouldn't have appeared on the show if it had gotten off the ground.

"I'm not an actor. I think I've got a lot of faults but I think I'm authentic. I know what I'm not. I'm not a chef and I'm not an actor and I'm not an engineer, I'm not a scientist. I think a guy has to know his limitations and I'm not a guy who's going to appear on the screen anytime soon."

DISFUNCTIONALITY

Cowherd was the featured speaker at a sports broadcasting seminar in 2005, in Hartford, Connecticut, hosted by Broadcaster Marketing Services. At the event, he said that to be a great talk show host, you have to be dysfunctional.

"This is not a job for accountants. You talk to yourself. A lot of people would be embarrassed. A lot of people would be incapable of that. A lot of people would think it's silly. There's an art to it. It's a craft. It's like play-by-play or writing a great column. I think there's a little artistry in it. I don't think there's a lot of artistry in being a beat reporter. I think being a columnist, where you have to craft ideas, or a talk show host, you've got to believe that your opinion really matters. If you don't believe that you'll never create a popular show. You've really got to believe your stuff is important and maybe it's delusional, but you have to believe that. You have to turn a mike on and think 'My opinion really matters and I'm going to say it forcefully and with great conviction and I'm going to argue it if anybody disagrees with me.' That's not typical. Most people don't even like to speak in public. Yet I can stand up in front of people and forcefully argue things or talk to myself for hours, and I just think you have to come from a background of some isolation generally speaking. To be the black sheep in the family, to have a chip on your shoulder, there's something either missing or there's something you're trying to prove."

For Cowherd, some of that comes from a family history of divorce (eight between his biological mother and father), his quirkiness, and being a guy who enjoys ribbing people and being contrarian. He doesn't feel he was gifted but had ambition and drive.

"I can remember being like 12- or 13-years-old thinking about my career a lot. I think that's fairly atypical."

ADVICE

Sports casting hopefuls grow up with a desire to be like Howard Cosell, Marv Albert, Al Michaels, Keith Jackson, and so on.

These days, there are legions of future broadcasters who would like to be in the shoes of Colin Cowherd.

Cowherd's advice is simple: "Radio is an unglamorous business. I consider myself mostly a mason. I lay one brick on top of another brick. Nothing at all replaces work. Be coachable and work your ass off. Those are the two things I would say."

Cowherd says that he could still be coached and his bosses would agree.

"I think what happens is you make a little money, you get up there in high six or seven figures territory, and everybody thinks they know it all. And I think there's a little bit of insecurity before the mic goes on every day and I use that to my advantage as I try to get better every year. I tweak my show. Once or twice a year we'll tweak the show and it's paid off."

He also says to read everything you can get your hands on and get reps.

"Just because you're in New York or syndicated doesn't mean you've figured it out. I don't want to be one of those guys at 55 where people go, 'Ya know, he used to be really good.' I want people every day to tune in and say, 'Every time I turn him on he's a little better and a little more interesting.' And I take a lot of pride in that. I think someday I'll wake up and won't feel that way. That will be the day I say, 'It's over.' Young guy, take the show."

THE BEST PART

The most fun Cowherd has on his show is when he stirs emotions and connects with his listeners. He likes sports topics that have social connections.

"One of the things I've noticed, and this is without

debate. What I'm about to say is not even an opinion, it's fact. The further you get away from breaking down the game and talking Xs and Os, the smarter your callers get and the smarter your e-mailers get. That's why I've never catered to hardcore fans because where are they going to go? I work for ESPN, where are they going to go? That guy's going to listen. My job is to get the guy who might listen to FM, who might listen to the local FM show, how do I get him, how do I get his wife? Cause I know the diehard sports guy is listening to the station all day long. I've always thought sports radio is at its best when you can talk about a sports topic, whether it's racial, polarizing topics that can deal with sports in our economy or sports and race or sports and entertainment. You broaden it out and the callers get significantly smarter and the e-mailers similarly get brighter."

The worst part?

"Summer. July, All-Star break can be really slow. That's why we all take our vacations in July and August."

THE FUTURE?

Colin Cowherd loves his career, but don't be surprised if he disappears from sports talk radio.

"I'm not sure I'll do sports radio forever. I say that with great admiration and respect for the industry and the people who do this and do it well. I have always been a person that after about seven years gets bored with stuff. I don't know where this career is going to take me. I'm in my mid-40s and I'm in pretty good shape and have a decent appearance for my age. I don't know what I'm going to do. If somebody told me in 10 years I was producing a movie, doing specials for HBO, I mean even though I love this business, Rush Limbaugh to me will die on the air. If Jimmy Kimmel left tomorrow and somebody offered me that job I'd be wildly interested. I was wildly interested in Larry King's job. I like challenges. When I feel I'm repeating myself I tend to move. I talk to my wife and agent about this. I really don't know what the future holds. I would not be shocked whatsoever if I ended up on cable TV doing something else or working on other projects. That's not to be critical of this industry. I love what I do for a living. I've just never done anything for 10 years, 15 years, 20 years, and I don't know if that's my personality, so I think it's going to be a really interesting journey for me."

A SIMPLE GUY

It might have been different for Cowherd during his time in Las Vegas, but these days, he describes himself as a homebody. He likes spending time with his family. When he's away from the job, he's hardly a big radio star.

"I work out, travel, hang out with my kids. I'm pretty much a career, kids, wife guy. Not a social animal. I really like spending time with my wife. I've got one or two close friends, maybe two or three. Lot of time with my kids. I'm a pretty simple guy. I don't need two-week European vacations or Central American hikes. I like the beach. I like being athletic. Going for a jog. Going to a local reservoir or state park for a run. I like beautiful views, glass of wine, cocktail with my wife, laugh with my kids, go to the beach, go to an amusement park, I'm pretty simple."

PARTING SHOT

"I've always thought it's about being thought provoking. And the people that I like make me think. Jon Stewart, Bill O'Reilly, Bill Maher, on whatever political side they're on. I always like the discussion. I like storytellers. I never really cared if I was right or wrong. When I create a show in the morning, I don't go right or wrong, I look for interesting or not interesting. What's thought provoking? What's compelling? If I'm retired someday and kids said 'Colin had a unique style and he elevated your typical talk radio narrative to broaden it out and make people think.'

"I always like [how] guys come up to me or women and they say 'Ya know, you make me think.' That's a great compliment, 'You make me think.' I don't listen to anybody regularly who doesn't make me think. I like to listen to people that I think are smarter than me."

Arnie Spanier
"The Stinkin' Genius"

When you listen to Arnie Spanier on the radio (now on KRLD in Dallas), you hear a calm, even-keeled, measured, smooth-talking sophisticate. Wait …no, you don't. He's somewhat loud. Okay, he's very loud. Arnie's the guy with a voice that you would hear from the upper deck at a hockey game or in the bleachers at a baseball game. If you want a guy who is quick with a one-liner and who is simply flat-out funny, then Arnie is your guy. He doesn't know the meaning of that word 'serious'. He doesn't know the meaning of 'syndicate' either. We'll get to that later. He's entertaining with a capital E.

What would you expect from a guy who named his kid after a stadium? That's right, he named his son after a ballpark and if it was a girl he was going to name her after the world's most famous arena. Keep reading. It will all make sense later. Maybe.

HOOKED

Sports broadcasters, including some in this book, will tell you that they harbored dreams of being behind the microphone at a young age, calling games and talking sports. This is not true for Arnie.

"This is not something I thought about doing or wanted to do. I was working after college at an advertising agency and I just kind of fell into the job."

Fell into the job?

"I went to go watch my brother play basketball when he was in high school. When I went there they were filming it for the local cable company and the play-by-play announcer didn't show. So I went over to the guy and said, 'Hey, I know my brother's team pretty well, I can do this for ya.' And then I did the game for him and I guess I did a pretty good job, and I kind of got the fever right after that, and I'm like, 'Yeah, I think I can do this for a little bit.' One game and I was hooked but again, sports talk wasn't my thing. I was just thinking play-by-play. Sports talk didn't come till later on in the future."

When Arnie looks back on that first play assignment, he is honest in his assessment.

"I was bad. I was horrible. I'm not a play-by-play guy, which is why they didn't give me a play-by-play job after that. You have to have a special forte for that, a special voice, just a keen quick sense. That does help in sports talk but I don't quite have the voice or pipes for the play-by-play aspect of the whole thing."

In fairness, nobody is good at play-by-play after one game. He did end up improving after doing more basketball games. He also called Loyola Marymount basketball during the Bo Kimble and Hank Gathers era when they were lighting up the scoreboard.

"Unbelievable. If you were ever going to do LMU basketball it was during those two years. And to do it on TV, I had a heck of a lot of fun."

A SHORT STINT IN THE KEYS

While working at the advertising agency and getting a taste of broadcasting, Arnie decided to pursue his new passion in earnest. Despite barely making any money calling basketball games, "It was kind of like a voluntary basis," Arnie packed up his car in Los Angeles and headed to work at a radio station in Florida. Key West to be exact. He was in his late 20s.

"That lasted like four days. I didn't like that aspect, doing the weather and pressing buttons and reading the news. I drove up to New York and back to LA and I couldn't find a job to save my life. I was just looking for work."

VIVA LAS VEGAS

In 1991 Arnie caught wind of a new sports talk operation in Las Vegas. Originally called Sports Entertainment Network, it eventually morphed into One on One Sports and then Sporting News Radio.

Arnie decided to give it a shot.

"I'm like, 'I'd love to do a show there.' I used to listen to them on the radio out of a station in Las Vegas. It would be sports talk and the guy wouldn't get too many calls so I would call into the show. And I'm like, this guy's stinkin' horrible. I could do a better job than him. I guess that's how it happens with a lot of us."

Arnie kept hounding them for a job. The guy in charge told him to "keep in touch." So he did. Relentlessly.

"He's like, 'Where have you worked?' I'm like, 'I've never had a show. I've never worked in radio.' He's like, 'I'm not gonna give you a show. Go to Arkansas and work your way up and call me. I tell ya what, I like ya, you're nice, I think you're funny, so keep in touch.' So I kept in touch for seven, eight, nine months."

Nothing happened until one day, completely out of left field, the guy called Arnie at his parent's house. It wasn't a prime offer but it was a chance.

"He was looking for someone for Christmas Eve and Christmas, New Year's Eve and New Year's, midnight to six. He wanted to know if I was still interested and I'm like, 'Hell yeah.' So I drove to Las Vegas and did the four shows and now I had a tape to try and get a job."

It is almost unheard of for a person to start out doing a national show, but then there was Arnie—his first show ever—on a network with 200 affiliates.

"That was my first job. You want to talk about getting a break and falling into your lap. You can't get any luckier than that."

How were those first shows, by the way?

"I never met the boss during those four days. He

never came in to tell me what to do. I didn't have headphones. I didn't know how to punch up callers. I didn't know you had to create topics and have stuff to talk about. I really didn't know what I was doing. I was just having fun. I didn't know if I was any good at it or not."

After a year working in Las Vegas, Arnie was excited to move to Phoenix to do radio. He went to school in Arizona and felt comfortable there.

YOUNG ARNOLD

Arnie was born in the Bronx in 1963 and, as you might imagine, stood out as a kid.

"I wasn't really the full class clown but I certainly knew how to get into trouble. Especially as a kid growing up in New York in the Bronx. It just wasn't easy with me with the teachers; let's just say that. Teachers were not a fan of mine growing up."

How could a teacher not love Arnie?

"This one time, I was in the fifth grade, and I was just a terrible, terrible student. We were having an exam on different parts of the eyes and the ears and all that. And my dad said, 'Here. I want you to read this half a page over and over and over again until you know it frontwards and backwards.' It was probably the last time and only time I studied in my life. I read the thing over and over and over again."

Arnie took the test and really didn't have a feel for how he did.

"I had no idea. The teacher comes back and she goes, 'I'm really disappointed, everybody did bad. There was only one A and he got 100 percent, and that person was Arnold,' which was my name. And I fell out of my chair backwards and hit my head. I thought she was bullshitting. And she thought I cheated. She wanted to give me the exam again. I just read that half a page over and over. I never had the guts to cheat. I wasn't that type of person."

HIGH SCHOOL

His family moved to Los Angeles when Arnie was 13. High school went by quickly. He wasn't sure if he had enough credits to graduate from Pacific Palisades High, the school that graduated Steve Kerr, Jay Schroeder, and Kiki Vandeweghe. Arnie was classmates with Penelope Ann Miller.

"I think they just pushed me out of high school and said, 'Get the hell outta here,' ya know."

HOOP IT UP

Arnie was a pretty good basketball player as a kid. He played JV basketball in high school.

"Basketball was my sport. I was a good shooter but I hurt my knee and had injuries and I wasn't good enough to get the big-time scholarships."

But he did get a small amount to play ball at a small school in Pueblo, Colorado.

"I got 100 bucks to go play off my $12,000 tuition. I thought I was a big shot."

PARTY ON

Arnie went to the University of Southern Colorado to play basketball. He lasted a year before transferring to the University of Arizona.

"This ain't for me, man. I had to get out of this yahoo place," he said regarding Pueblo.

Arizona was the next stop, a school that has a reputation for being a party school, which Arnie doesn't deny.

"Absolutely! If you can't party there you can't party anywhere. I did my share plus everybody else's share, I would think."

When asked if he needed a map to get to class he

said, "I didn't go to class so why would I need a map?"

His first semester grades at Arizona?

0.3.

"I got four Fs and a D."

Maybe that map would have come in handy.

NOW WHAT?

Following college, Arnie still didn't know what he wanted to do with his life.

"I had no idea. I didn't know what was going to become of me. My parents were always worried. My brother became a big real estate agent. Had I not got into radio I might have gotten into real estate or law but I really wasn't the student. I don't know what the hell would have happened. I'd probably be working at 7-Eleven right now to be honest with you."

DYSFUNCTION

There is some discussion in this book about dysfunction. Colin Cowherd says that a great talk show host has to be dysfunctional. Kevin Wheeler, who worked for Arnie at one time, says, "absolutely not." It's obviously a subjective question. So, is Arnie Spanier dysfunctional?

"To a tee. If you're not dysfunctional you're probably not a good talk show host. Oh yeah. I'm dysfunctional in so many different ways I'm trying to figure out how am I normal. You gotta have a colorful life and not be afraid to tell anything. I agree with Colin on that, that's for sure."

He claims his entire family and extended family are dysfunctional.

"Cousins, aunts, uncles, all very dysfunctional."

Arnie has two cousins he hasn't spoken to in 10 years because he didn't go to their weddings,

"I was working."

Meanwhile, he's been out of the loop with his

brother-in-law, Howard Saffan, for 15 years after he tossed Arnie out of his home.

"He was having a briss and it was at noon and I had two tickets to the Knicks-Bulls game at Madison Square Garden. He lived in New York. That game was at 6 o'clock, it was Jordan's last game in New York. And he's like 'You're not gonna go, are ya?' Why the hell wouldn't I go? The briss is at noon, the game's at 6! And then of course we had it out and he said 'Get the fuck out of my house.' I said fine and we haven't spoke since."

It should be noted that Arnie's favorite team at the time was the New York Islanders.

"He's super rich and he ended up buying the Islanders with Charles Wang just to hate me. After he threw me out of the house I became a Sabres fan. But he does send good Chanukah presents to my kid so I gotta give him credit for that."

THE WINNER

Arnie used to go on the radio to find dates. It worked.

"I used to do a segment on the radio show in Phoenix called The Blind Date of the Week. I used to have girls call up and say they would pay for the entertainment, I would pay for the meal at a local restaurant, and Beth [Arnie's wife] was one of my blind dates."

Beth's sister set it up saying the she had tickets to the Suns game. That sealed the date. It was an evening that apparently went well—they've been married for 15 years.

Ironically, it wasn't the first time they met.

In college, Arnie went out with Beth once. Once.

"And when she wouldn't put out I never called her again. So we only had one date."

Did you really think she would put out on the first date Arnie?

"Well, it wasn't really a date. I just picked her up at

a local bar, you know what I mean. And I expected her to put out, yeah. That's college for you. I mean you go to a bar and get drunk and 'hey, baby, what's going on?'"

WEIGHTY ISSUES

Arnie's wife has always been on him to lose weight and get in shape. There were rumors that he would sneak in food while he was doing his radio show. Beth put a plan in place to prevent that.

"She took away my wallet so I wouldn't have any money to order anything. I'm sleeping and she went by and took my wallet! 'Hey, you got no money for food, what are you going to do now? Here's your driver's license, you can have that.'"

Of course Arnie worked a deal with the vending machine guy so he didn't go hungry.

All those years she was after Arnie to lose weight and it didn't happen. He was up to 270 pounds. Now? He's 180 pounds of Tungsten Steel and sex appeal.

"I didn't want to go on a diet. Slim For Life offered me money to go on a diet and read their commercials. I still didn't want to do it but my wife's like, 'YES, we need the money!' So I said, 'Ah, what the hell.' I know she's happier with me now than she used to be, that's for sure."

APPROACH

One thing that you can't say about Arnie is that he takes himself too seriously.

His self-deprecating humor is one of the reasons for his popularity. The day he becomes sanctimonious and preachy is the day he'll probably hang up the headset.

"If you take yourself seriously you're in the wrong business. If you can't take criticism you can't be in this business or you can't be an actor. You better get used to rejection and criticism when you're in radio and television, that's for damn sure."

OFFSPRING

Being a Mets fan, Arnie named his son Shea after Shea Stadium. Good thing he wasn't a Red Sox fan. Fenway Spanier doesn't quite have the same ring to it. He also had a name picked out if he had a daughter.

"If it was a girl it was going to be Madison for Madison Square Garden."

While Shea Stadium is now gone, replaced by a parking lot, the human Shea is a hockey goaltender and a pretty good one. Could there be a Spanier playing in the NHL?

"I'd say it's such a longshot," says Arnie. "It's always the slim and none chance. But then I hear stories about Ovechkin, how they thought he wasn't even good enough to play over here in the states and not even make the NHL, I mean who am I to tell my kid 'you're not good enough' for something?"

It would be a nice story if Arnie's kid did make it to the NHL—with the Islanders!

Arnie says that his son uses hockey to work hard on his grades.

"And hockey will get him into an Ivy League school I believe or a great college."

Finally, Arnie's serious about grades.

What if Shea wanted to follow in dad's footsteps and become a broadcaster?

"I think it would be great. I really would. I would say, 'you better hope your grandmother dies and leaves you a lot of money so you have money to live on.' If that's what he wants to do and he's good at it and he wants to have fun, I'd support him 100 percent. I'd encourage him whatever he wants to do. I wouldn't tell him to stay away from any occupation."

TANK MCNAMARA

A caller to Arnie's show way-back-when asked him if he had read that morning's Tank McNamara cartoon in the paper.

"I'm like, 'no, why?' I read it once in a while, I don't read it every day. He's like, 'Ya gotta go read it.' So I pick up the copy and it has Tank in the hospital with his wife and they just had a baby and Tank says to his wife, 'I just read about a sportscaster that named his son Shea for Shea Stadium. Shea's a nice name.' And the wife goes, 'I will not name my daughter 3com. There won't be a digit in my daughter's name.' So I called him up, had him on the air, they sent me the original cell. They framed it for me and they signed it for me, and I have it hanging in my kid's room right now."

THE STINKIN' GENIUS

Ask any sports talk radio junkie who The Stinkin' Genius is and there can only be one answer. Arnie Spanier. He thinks he may have given himself the moniker but he's not sure. Still, it is a well-earned nickname.

"When Nebraska beat Arizona State one year in Lincoln, they scored a late touchdown to run up the score like 70 or 77 to like 21 (The actual score was 77-28 in 1995). It was embarrassing. The next day, and I don't like Arizona State because I went to Arizona, I said, 'You watch, Arizona State will not only kick the crap out of Nebraska when they come back down here, they're gonna shut them out like 21-0. It's gonna be 21-0 and Nebraska is gonna look stupid.' Nebraska's never been shut out in like 10 years. Son of a bitch, next year Nebraska lost to them 19-0. I was two points away from a final score that I predicted a year ahead of time on a shutout. I'm like, 'I'm not even a genius, I'm a stinkin' genius!' That's incredible. And it took off after that."

MEMORABLE GAME

The most memorable sporting event Arnie ever attended was with his dad, Sy, at the Los Angeles Coliseum; December 26, 1977. It was the Vikings-Rams divisional playoff game, better known as the Mud Bowl. The Vikings won the game. It was also Joe Namath's last game. He sat the bench as Pat Haden quarterbacked LA.

Arnie remembers the day well.

"I was young. I was with my dad and we were at a McDonald's and it was raining like crazy. The guy next to me had like six or eight tickets. Me being the smartass kid that I was, I turned to him and I go, 'Hey! Which two tickets are for me and my dad?' And son of a bitch if the guy didn't take two tickets out and just hand them to me! And I turned to my dad and said, 'Can we go?' And he said, 'Yep, let's go.' And we had to sit there in the pouring rain, no umbrella, because you weren't allow to lift your umbrella because people couldn't see. We just sat there getting soaked. And the Rams actually lost that game 14-7 so it wasn't even a great game. But it was just fun going with him. Me and my dad had a great time."

Arnie's dad was a big sports fan and passed it along to the Spanier boys.

"He was my biggest advocate. He used to listen to the radio and go to sleep with the radio to his ear and listen to the sports guys. He'd ask about all the guys. As a matter of fact, a lot of the sports guys knew and liked my dad. He liked calling in. He did like having fun and having people with personality. That's probably why he would listen to Rome. He always liked Tony Bruno too. 'Ah, that Bruno's full of shit.' He was important for me. He was always there to help me and encourage me to continue."

Arnie says his father was the only guy who believed in his radio career. His mother felt it was too much like acting and he couldn't do it.

When Sy passed away, Arnie heard from a lot of

guys in the sports radio industry, which he found to be touching.

THE GENERAL

Arnie's most memorable interview was with Bob Knight. The legendary basketball coach, not always a fan of the media, grabbed a chair and sat directly across from Arnie. They were alone in the room, knees almost touching, for half an hour.

"Quite an intimidating figure. He got right in my grill. It went pretty well. I enjoyed talking to him."

Arnie also enjoys talking to celebrities.

"When Chick Hearn (Lakers beloved broadcaster) passed away, I called four people. We called Dyan Cannon. She called back in about 30 minutes in tears. That night we get off the air, the phone happens to be ringing, I pick it up and, who is it, 'Hey, it's Jack.' Well you don't have to go any further than that. I go, 'Jack, it's Arnie. I appreciate you calling back. We're off the air.' He goes, 'No, no, you're on till 7.' I said, 'Yeah, we're on till 7 Jack but today we got off at 5:30 because we have a pre-game show.' He goes, 'I want to come on to talk about Chick.' I said, 'If you want to call tomorrow, at 3 o'clock, you can be the first on.' He called at 2:55 and stayed on hold for five minutes. Great having Jack Nicholson on the show. And then Denzel Washington couldn't apologize more about not calling back immediately and he came on. It was only the fourth person that gave us an attitude because he was on vacation and that was Chevy Chase."

CHUCKLES

Arnie's favorite encounter with an athlete didn't come in the locker room where so many of these moments occur. It actually came courtside at a Nuggets-Suns exhibition game where Arnie was taking in the game with his friend, Steve Levy of ESPN, and involved the inimitable Charles Barkley.

"We're sitting courtside and it was kind of quiet, early in the game. Pre-season game, it's not a full house, and Barkley's on the court and I yell to Barkley, 'Jeez, why don't you just play defense for ONCE in your LIFE?' And he turned to me and goes, 'Why don't you go FUCK yourself.' So that was pretty memorable to be honest with you. You're gonna print that now, huh?"

Sure. Why not?

ARNIE IN THE JUNGLE?

When things were kicking into high gear in Phoenix, Arnie got a call from a boss about syndicating his show.

"I didn't even know what syndication was. I go, 'I don't even know what that is. I'm kicking ass in Phoenix. I don't want to go anywhere. I went to U of A, I love giving ASU fans crap. Syndicate? What the hell you talking about? Why do I gotta do this? Can I live in Phoenix? They're like, 'No, you gotta move to LA.' I'm like, 'I ain't moving to LA. Goodbye.' Of course that was the job they gave to Jim Rome. What's so funny is the guy that hired Jim Rome to do that show is Brian Purdy, who is my boss right now. So it's interesting how things kind of come around. I guess maybe that's my one regret that I wasn't smarter in business decisions and kind of looked into everything when I first got in the business."

Another regret Arnie has is that a couple of people who helped him out in Chicago passed away before he could thank them and tell them what they meant to him.

One of them was Bob Collins, the WGN radio morning host who used to listen to Arnie's show and told WGN-TV to put him on the air, which they did. Arnie never had a chance to call Collins, who passed away a week later in 2000 in a plane crash in Waukegan, Illinois.

Arnie became friends with Randy Salerno, the guy

that Bob hooked him up with at WGN-TV. In 2008 Salerno died in a snowmobile accident in Wisconsin.

"It kind of hit me hard that these people who were nice enough to help me out, and I never found the time to thank them and show them how much I appreciated them passing my name back and forth to each other. I think that's a regret that I have to this day."

BELIEF

There were a lot of people who were negative towards Arnie's radio career aspirations. They probably meant well but it certainly didn't help.

"I was getting it from friends, fraternity brothers, girlfriends, my mom, everybody but my dad."

One friend even called Arnie's radio goals a "pipe dream."

So what would Arnie say to a young broadcasting hopeful?

"You have to believe in yourself and you have to be innovative and you have to think of a way, if you're not getting hired, how to get yourself on the radio. It's tough to get your name out there but if you work at it and if you really think of it and you really work hard you can figure a way to get yourself on. And if you're good enough you can find your way into a good local market and make yourself a living and enjoy yourself and have a lot of fun. Don't listen to the naysayers. Abraham Lincoln lost every election before he became President. What would have happened if he quit? What if Thomas Edison quit, we'd be living in the dark. Never quit, believe in yourself. It took me a long time to get that first job, and once I got the first job I've never been without a job."

ONE OF A KIND

Arnie doesn't think of himself as a "radio guy." Quick with a laugh or quip, Arnie simply considers himself a guy who has fun on the radio.

When the day comes and he steps aside, will we turn on the radio and hear another Arnie Spanier?

"Oh jeez, I hope not my friend. I don't know if there's gonna be anybody quite like me. Hopefully there won't be, I gotta tell you that."

2 Live Stews
"Get in the Dog House!"

The 2 Live Stews are a most unique sports talk show pairing. While tandem hosts are not uncommon at all, hosts who are siblings are. The Stews, Ryan and Doug Stewart, have been working and honing their act unintentionally since they were kids, Doug being the oldest by three years.

The Stewarts are headquartered in Atlanta, Georgia, and are the ratings winners on WQXI, 790 The Zone.

They've been syndicated by Sporting News Radio and Syndication One.

In a business where cookie cutter shows are common, there is not a more unique listening experience than tuning into the 2 Live Stews. You will be unquestionably entertained and likely bust a gut listening to these two engaging characters.

THE BEAVE

Growing up in Moncks Corner, South Carolina, Ryan Stewart was a happy-go-lucky kid who loved to play sports and hang out with his friends and older brother, Doug.

"My brother called me Beaver Cleaver because I was kind of mischievous; at the same time our parents were very demanding when it came to respecting other folks.

"Not just my childhood, and it's a blessing to be able to say it, it's really been about having a good time and that's something that I'm very thankful for."

It was just Ryan and Doug. There were no other brothers or sisters, so you can imagine the Stewart boys were close.

"Pretty close," says Ryan. "Pretty close in an 'I'm

gonna get you' kind of way. We've always tried to one-up each other from a very young age. Being the younger brother, whatever my older brother was doing I wanted to do it, and whatever he was doing I wanted to do it better."

THE TAG ALONG

While they always played sports and hung out together, there were times when older brother Doug wanted to ditch Ryan.

"I think the three-and-a-half year difference was kind of an issue growing up through middle school and teen years," says Doug. "I wanted to hang out with my other friends my age. He always wanted to hang out with me and tag along with me and I didn't want him to do that. But when we were at home we always did everything together. If he had a problem as school and somebody was bothering him, he knew he could come get me and I'd defend him."

ATHLETIC TALENTS

Looking back at his days playing sports, Ryan realizes he was a little bigger, a little faster, and a little stronger than the other kids.

"When you're a kid it's no big deal. As early as five or six years old, when we started playing sandlot basketball, football, and baseball in the yard and we had to pick teams, I didn't realize I was always being picked first but I was. As a kid that stuff doesn't matter to you. You just want to get out there and play."

One would assume that since Ryan played in the NFL for five seasons that he was a superior athlete than Doug.

"Of course," Ryan says without hesitation. "I was a better athlete than my brother but I've always, from day one, given the credit for my athletic ability to my brother."

Doug played football at Newberry College and South Carolina State. He didn't make it to the NFL as his younger brother did, but that doesn't stop him from answering the following question quickly and emphatically. Who is the better athlete?

"Me," says Doug in a clear and strong voice. "It's not even close. He made it to the NFL but if you ask people from our home town, I'm the more fluid, more athletic person out of the two. He has the resume and making it to the NFL so people who don't know would believe it. That's fine, but whenever the question is posed, I'll be honest with people and let them know."

Doug also cites a few examples of his athletic superiority over Ryan.

"He can't beat me in basketball. He can't hit a baseball better than me. I got better agility than him in football. I catch better than him. He can't beat me in a footrace, in a 40. He can't beat me at anything."

Except maybe NFL paychecks. Ouch!

SPORTS

Like most kids growing up in the '70s and '80s, the Stewarts were activity oriented. There were no computer screens to stare into or vapid reality shows to occupy their minds and time.

"We played football in the front yard and the back yard pretty much every Sunday after church," Doug remembers. "We played all day long then went in and watched football on TV. We were the house in the neighborhood that had the basketball goal, so kids from all over our area came to our house to play on our basketball goal. We had one of the nicest goals, which our father put up. We were little kids but the big kids would come over to our house and play basketball all day Saturday and all day Sunday. Sports was always a huge part of our life."

SAGE ADVICE

Since Doug was older, he gladly passed advice along to Ryan.

"I'll never forget," Ryan says, "one day, I was in the eighth grade, and I was on the junior varsity team, he came home one day because he was on the varsity team, and he was a great athlete, but he was a little small in stature. One of the starters was one of the best athletes we'd seen in our town. His name was Mike Dingle. But from time to time, Mike wouldn't practice and Doug would get his chance, but when game day came around Mike told the coach he wanted to play and Doug would be forced to go back to the bench."

Doug was discouraged but he gave his younger brother some sage advice.

"He said, 'You need to start running every day and lifting weights three to five times a week. Don't rely on a coach to tell you. Don't rely on mom and dad to pick you up. If you have to do pushups and self-squats in the yard, do that. But every single day you need to work out because you're already bigger than me. You're gonna be faster than me, you're gonna have the opportunity to get a full scholarship.' I remember clear as day saying, 'A full scholarship? What are you talking about?' He said, 'Because of your size and speed and you're already good in sports, when you get your grades and you keep playing the way that you're playing, you'll be awarded a full scholarship to go to college wherever you want to go to college for FREE.' That resonated with me every day of my life."

Ryan applied that advice immediately. Well, an hour later he ran two miles through his neighborhood, something he did every day throughout high school and college.

"That's the effect my brother had on me. So yeah, I was the better athlete, but I think I was the better athlete because he instilled it in me at an early age to do the best that I could do to be the best athlete that I could be."

Ryan was a wide receiver who, despite being bigger than everybody else, "had trouble catching the football," according to his older brother.

One particular day, with the game on the line, the coaches sent Ryan deep on a Hail Mary pattern and he jumped over three guys and came down with the ball with no time on the clock.

Doug remembers that play and his thoughts vividly.

"It's kind of like I stepped out of my body and I looked at him, and me being a little bit older and knowing how things worked, I knew that this guy had an opportunity because of his size and his skills. At the end of that season I told him, 'Look man, you need to first of all change positions. You need to play safety because you're the right size to play safety at the college level and you're aggressive and physical. You can't catch that great so I don't think that wide receiver is going to get you to the next level.' He did that. We started working on him catching the ball a lot better, you know at the house. And the rest is history. It all worked out for him."

If this radio thing doesn't work out then Doug could certainly be a talent scout or motivational speaker.

DOUG'S NFL DREAM

Most every kid who plays football dreams of one day playing in the NFL. The odds of that happening are astronomical. Doug not only harbored those dreams but believed in them.

"I know a lot of this sounds crazy because it's after the fact," Doug begins. "But from the time that I started playing football until the day that I tore my ACL in college, I thought I was going to play in the NFL and that's the honest to God's truth. Whether or not I was imagining or my expectations were far more than what I thought they were, that was my mindset."

Doug wasn't recruited as much as he felt he should have been after a very productive senior season in high school.

"I didn't start for my high school until I was a senior because my sophomore and junior years I played behind a guy that was like Gatorade player of the year in the United States, a guy by the name of Mike Dingle. He was basically Marcus Dupree when Marcus Dupree was coming out."

Dingle, the 1986 player of the year, ended up going to his home state school, South Carolina, and played a year in the NFL with the Cincinnati Bengals.

MIXING IT UP

Like any pair of rambunctious brothers, there were some scraps between the two. Alright, many scraps.

Doug remembers it as, "an everyday occurrence."

There were some big-time altercations back in the day. Some even resulted in visits to the emergency room.

One trip to the hospital occurred when Doug was crawling along the floor with a blanket over him. It was dark and little Ryan decided to take action.

"I knew it was him but I was still scared and I grabbed the first thing I could find which was a belt and I swung the back end of the buckle and it hit him and he fell straight on the ground and I just ran out of the room."

Fifteen minutes later, his mother told him, "You've done it this time." Ryan didn't know what happened but mom filled him in. "You busted your brother's face!"

Doug spent five hours in the emergency room and probably retired from crawling around covered by a blanket.

"We had knock-down, drag-out battles all the time," Ryan remembers. "When it comes to destroying the house and putting holes in the sheetrock and throwing a shoe and missing and cracking a window, there's way too many stories to tell because it happened all the time. Looking back at it, it was the time of our life."

Ryan recalls one of those times when he was a senior in high school and Doug came home from college with a friend.

"We got into fussin' like we typically do and my dad was like, 'you guys know the deal. Not in the house. Take this outside.' He would let us go outside and wrestle and fight all day with one rule, we couldn't punch each other in the face."

As Ryan was putting on his shoes his dad said to him, "today's the day."

It's the first time his father said that to him.

"My brother used to throw me and pin me down and I couldn't get up. So when he said that, I just walked outside and I was like, 'you know what, I've been lifting and running, I've been working my ass off, yeah, today is the day!' (laughs) So that was the day we went outside and I tossed him around like a rag doll in front of his buddy. It was an embarrassing day for him but it was a very good day for me. That was pretty much the last time we've ever had a physical confrontation."

Doug's recollections of the first time his baby bro got the better of him was a little different, but close.

"He was a freshman in high school and I was a senior. One day, I think I was home, this was after a football practice, we got to the age where we got so big and so physical that our father told us to take it outside and I'd throw him around. So this particular time we went outside, it was like 10 o'clock at night, and we were in the front yard rasslin', I did say rasslin', and he picked me up and tossed me a good little ways. So that was the last time we did that."

INSPIRATION

Despite the altercations, physical and verbal, Ryan has always held his brother in the highest regard.

"He's been the inspiration for me to do good in everything that I've done. As I got into school, he was the reason why I studied hard and never missed a class and asked questions to the teachers. He pretty much taught me what to do and what not to do because of his experiences growing up. I've applied those things in my life and everything in my life has pretty much has been pretty good."

As a side note, the verbal wars must have been somewhat hysterical around the Stewart household. Maybe not to Ryan and Doug's parents, but they still must have been funny and entertaining nonetheless. Only now they get paid to do it on the radio.

EMPHASIS ON EDUCATION

Doug didn't waste time daydreaming while in the classroom. He took his studies seriously due to his parents demanding it.

"I was a good student. I was in college prep courses, honors courses. I'd say probably a B, A-minus student coming through middle school and high school and in college as well."

During his days in school he never thought of becoming a sports talk show host.

"In my mind, I was going to play in the NFL, even though I went to a small college first to play and subsequently went to South Carolina State. I was going to get a shot to play in the NFL, as crazy as that was. But my Plan B in the courses that I took initially were physical education because I wanted to be a coach."

Doug soon discovered that coaches, especially starting out, didn't make that much money. He decided to study business.

Ryan also knew the value of education and accepted a scholarship to play at Georgia Tech.

Earning a degree really entered his mind as a junior following the opening game of the 1994 season. Georgia Tech hosted highly rated Arizona. Ryan had the game of his life with a bunch of tackles and pass breakups. However, late in the game, he hurt his knee and had to miss a few weeks of action.

"It brought me back to reality. You really need to focus on school. This is why my mom and dad have talked to us about school, school, scholarship, scholarship, learn, learn, learn, and you can get your degree."

Ryan got that degree from Georgia Tech but he does have a regret.

"Now that I'm 37 years old and I've got a son of my own, I'm pissed off at myself because I could have done much more. I didn't apply myself nowhere near as much as I could have. I was a socialite. I had a good time. I liked to party and hang out. I focused on school, yes. Never missed a class, sat in the front of the class, asked questions when I needed to, but after class didn't put in the time that I probably should have."

MEET THE PARENTS

Perhaps the best compliment a parent can get is when their kids try to raise their own children the same way they were raised.

Ryan knows how he wants to rear his children—just like Ralph and Brenda Stewart did with their two boys.

"When it comes to raising my kids, I want to duplicate every single thing that my parents did. They worked hard. They stressed discipline. They stressed respect. When we did things that were good we got praised and congratulated. And when we did things that were bad they would light into us, whether it be verbally or with a belt or a hand on the back of the behind. But we definitely grew up knowing right and wrong and respecting our elders and respecting authority. I just absolutely love my parents to death."

Some parents these days see big paychecks in professional sports and direct their kids to athletics, hoping against all odds the kid makes it. That was not the case with the Stewarts.

Ryan recalls what his dad told him.

"All he really wanted us to do was go to college and graduate. I remember, 'where you going to go to college? What are you going to study? What are you going to major in?' I remember hearing that stuff at a very young age. It wasn't, 'you're going to get to the NFL.' My dad never told me that. He never, ever said that."

A man of character, Ralph wasn't interested in getting deals or cars when Ryan was being recruited. Money, according to Ryan, was offered all the time but his dad would simply say, "We really appreciate it but Ryan's not even interested in your school so thank you but no thank you."

Ralph Stewart, a businessman who also coached his kids in sports, passed away in 1997. Brenda Stewart retired more than a year ago and spends much of her time traveling around the world.

BARRY

When he was drafted out of college by the Lions, Ryan was excited for two things. He would have the chance to put on the helmet and wear the uniform of an NFL team, something most college players never get the chance to do.

Secondly, he was thrilled to be teammates with perhaps the greatest running back in the league's history.

"I was never really star struck. We didn't grow up idolizing people. But Barry freaking Sanders is my teammate! That was big to me. At practice and every single Sunday I had a front row seat to watch Barry Sanders do what he does. That was one of the highlights of my career, being able to call Barry a teammate."

The first time Ryan saw Sanders, he went up to him in the locker room and introduced himself.

"I said, 'Barry, what's up? My name is Ryan Stewart, just got drafted here and I just wanted to shake your hand and tell you that I've always liked your work and I'm looking forward to working with you.' He gave me a little smile like, 'hey man, that's pretty cool. I appreciate it.' He knew me because I introduced myself the first time I saw him. He was just a great player."

WELCOME TO TRAINING CAMP

As a wet-behind-the-ears rookie out of Georgia Tech, Ryan knew that training camp with the Lions would be tough, but he didn't realize how tough. Even though it was 110 degrees he figured, "it's not gonna be that bad." Wrong.

After his initial practice, which was pretty demanding, he was walking off the field with veteran Bennie Blades.

Ryan remembers asking him, "So what's next?'"

Blades looked at him and said, "Rookie, this doesn't stop. You're asking me what's next like you're looking for a break or something. We're gonna be here in Saginaw, Michigan, for the next month and it's all football."

"I thought to myself," Ryan said, "holy smokes, this is really gonna be tough. We went two-a-days every day. After that third day, physically I didn't know how I was going to be able to do it because my body was dinged up and I was just mentally drained from all the meetings and thinking, OK, now I'm starting to understand why we make the amount of money that we make because this is a very daunting task and I don't think the average person could do it. It was an eye-opening experience for me."

SO THIS IS THE NFL

Off the field, Ryan and his fellow defensive backs hung out. They'd go out for drinks, watch film, or go to someone's house for dinner.

One day, a veteran, who will remain nameless, decided to invite the rookies to a little get together at his house. It was to start at 8 but the rookies were instructed to show up at 9 with four bottles of Dom Perignon.

"We were like, 'That stuff is expensive.' And he said, 'are you gonna do it or not?' Of course. We'll be there."

They got the Dom Perignon and arrived at the desired time.

"We walked inside with our bottles and there were about 20 people inside and no one had clothes on. It was the women that didn't have any clothes on. It was one of the best days of my life."

VERY PROUD

When Ryan made it to the NFL, Doug was excited and took joy in his brother's success.

"I was very, very proud."

While Doug doesn't take a whole lot of credit though for his baby brother's achievements on the football field, he feels he played a small role in Ryan's success, mostly through his own experiences.

"The errors that I made coming out and the path that I took. I knew the ropes. I knew what it would take to get to the next level based on how it worked out for me and the path he was going."

Since the Stewart boys were always competing in everything, was there ever any jealousy on the part of Doug that Ryan made it to the NFL and he didn't?

"No, never," Doug says assuredly. "Never any jealousy. Not even an ounce of jealousy as for how far he's made it. I wish that I would have had somebody like me in my life at the time when I was coming through, but I didn't and it is what it is. But everything's worked out perfect for me."

THE LIONS

The Detroit Lions last won an NFL championship in 1957. They've won just one playoff game since then and even had an 0-16 season to their credit in 2008.

But when Ryan Stewart played for them, they weren't bad. During his tenure they had two playoff appearances, in 1997 and 1999.

"We had some of the best talent and some of the worst breaks of any NFL team in the history of the NFL," Ryan reflects. "We had three of the best receivers in the game at the time, Brett Perriman, Herman Moore, and Johnnie Morton. We had Barry Sanders. We had one of the best centers to ever play the game by the name of Kevin Glover. We had one of the best defensive ends in Lions history, Robert Porcher, got double-digit sacks every year. On the other side was Tracy Scroggins, another great defensive end. In the middle was big Luther Elliss. Big Hank Thomas. Stephen Boyd. The list goes on and on. My rookie year Bennie Blades was there, one of my favorite safeties growing up. When Bennie left Mark Carrier came in. We had talent. We just had bad breaks and a lot of injuries. We dealt with more injuries the five years that I was there than probably any NFL team. We were a good team but we just had some tough breaks."

THE PICK

When asked about his one career interception, Ryan says, without hesitation, "Rick Mirer versus Seattle."

It was during his rookie season, and when the Lions broke the defensive huddle, Bennie Blades, who was diligent in his film study, asked Ryan, "What's gonna happen here?"

"I said, 'I think it's gonna be a draw or something.'"

Blades wasn't buying it.

"You don't study one ounce of freaking film. You got all the athletic ability in the world but until you start using your head you're not gonna be a good player."

Ryan recalls, "I'm sitting there like, 'this dude is bustin' at me and they're about to snap the ball.' Me being the smart alec that I was sometimes, I said, 'OK, well you tell me what's gonna happen then.'"

Blades told him, "they're gonna run the bootleg to my side because I'm gonna be the linebacker on the line of scrimmage. With this defense I called you're supposed to play half field back there and I want you to do that. However, after you take two or three steps back, I want you to stand right there and as the tight end or number two receiver drags across the field, you run straight down as fast as you can in front of him and you should get an interception."

Ryan said, "what if that doesn't happen?"

"It's gonna happen," Blades barked at him.

"What happens if that doesn't happen?" Ryan shot back.

"You get in trouble and you'll probably get fined a couple of thousand dollars," was Blades response.

The Seahawks were set to snap the ball.

"I said to myself, 'I can't take this chance. I'm not gonna do that.' They snap the ball. As I get off the hash and drop two or three steps, I see the number two receiver dragging across the field and I'm like, 'Holy shit, it's the boot!' I fire up and Mirer doesn't even see me because his eyes are locked on the receiver and I get the pick. The minute the ball hits my hands I'm like, 'holy smoke, I got this damn ball.' I run about 15 yards, I get hit extremely hard and the first person to get there and pick me up was Bennie Blades."

Blades was pumped up.

"I told you! Didn't I tell you, didn't I tell you?"

Ryan has a picture of him and Blades hugging on the field after the interception. He also kept the football.

ONE DOOR CLOSES, ANOTHER OPENS

Like almost every NFL player, Ryan suffered through his share of injuries. The worst was a torn groin in his fourth season. In his haste to return he tore it again. The Lions placed him on injured reserve. The injuries took their toll and he was done during his fifth and final season. No other team wanted him. The phone wasn't ringing.

"I started realizing 6 or 7 months later that my time in the NFL was probably over. I just started trying to figure out what was next."

Doug was a big sports talk radio fan while Ryan didn't listen much to talk radio. Doug knew that his little brother certainly knew sports and encouraged him to call Georgia Tech to put in a word for him to learn the business. Since Doug suggested it, then of course Ryan followed up and was put in contact with several stations.

"I did that and started filling in for guys who were on vacation or who were sick from time to time."

It wasn't as if Ryan was ill-prepared. He had done internships for radio and TV stations in Detroit during his playing days. He was also an eager guest for teammates who had their own shows. A future in broadcasting was always in the back of his mind.

TALK RADIO

Doug graduated from South Carolina State with a management degree. His first job out of school was managing a Foot Action USA store in Pensacola, Florida. He left that position and started working in the mortgage and finance industry. He moved to Atlanta in 1994 where he also spent a brief time working for a sports agent but didn't like it. Doug was a recruiter and hated chasing down these young athletes looking for handouts coming out of college.

At his mortgage job, Doug developed his interest in radio by simply listening to the medium all day long.

"I just started listening to radio every single day. And it really wasn't just sports talk radio. It was talk radio. The Rush Limbaughs, the Sean Hannitys, those conservative guys, and I listened to talk radio and kind of fell in love with it."

From talk radio Doug began to listen to sports talk radio.

THE GENESIS

It was at Ryan's house, in the basement with a bunch of friends, that Doug and his brother got into a lengthy and passionate debate.

"I remember it like it was yesterday," Doug begins. "It was a debate on the effectiveness of an option style running quarterback in the NFL because Quincy Carter was playing for the Dallas Cowboys at the time. And I was saying they should just let Quincy just use his athletic ability because that's something that's God-given. Why, whenever these athletic quarterbacks get in the NFL, they always try to turn him into a pocket passer? So Ryan went off about how you can't do that in the NFL. These guys would get killed. We basically argued about this for 30 minutes. No lie. And there were like 10 guys in his basement and we were drinking beers, watching the game, playing Madden. And after 30 minutes of arguing one of the guys there was like, 'You guys should have your own radio show.' And when he said it we were still in the moment of screaming and arguing about this particular topic."

While driving home that day, Doug had an epiphany.

"Why shouldn't we get our own radio show? Why

shouldn't we try to do our own radio show?"

Doug called Ryan.

"Are you thinking what I'm thinking?" Doug asked Ryan.

"About the radio thing?"

"Yes."

From that short conversation they put together a business plan to put the Stewart brothers on the air in Atlanta.

Their platform was genius in its simplicity and practicality.

Doug explains.

"The whole thing was, we played sports. Ninety percent of these guys on radio didn't play sports at the levels that we did. We can carry on an interesting conversation. We can debate with the best of them. We're in Atlanta, a city with a population of 70 percent African-American and there's no African-American sports talk guys. This is our concept."

Their presentation was intriguing. They said they would do the show for free just for the opportunity to back up their promises. The program director loved it and two weeks later asked them if they could come in tomorrow night.

"Well hell yeah we can," was Doug's answer. "We went in at 9 o'clock on a Wednesday night. The signal is down, nobody can really hear us. We just started going. We kind of had a format on how we wanted the show to flow. Halfway through the first show the program director and the owner of the station called and said, 'You guys are on the payroll from now on.' And the rest is history."

The success these days of the 2 Live Stews might surprise some people, but not Doug.

"Knowing us and knowing how passionate we were about sports and knowing how driven we've always been, we've always been guys that want to win. We never like losing at anything. I knew that if we got the opportunity, knowing us, I knew that we would be successful. To this degree? Yeah, yeah. Because I knew there was an audience out there that hadn't been addressed and I knew that we could address it. So yeah, I thought we could be this successful. As a matter of fact, I think we should be more successful than what we are right now."

THE ARRIVAL OF THE 2 LIVE STEWS

During their first show, they asked the listeners to name the program, even though they didn't know if they would even be around for a second show.

A caller said, "You guys are really live. You guys remind me of the 2 Live Crew."

The producer of the show, Matt Edgar, said during a break, "2 Live Crew sounds good but that name is already taken. Because both of y'all are Stewarts why don't y'all be the 2 Live Stews?"

"We thought that was pretty cool so we rolled with it," Ryan said.

GRASS ROOTS MARKETING

The 2 Live Stews were an immediate hit in Atlanta. They were different, brash, opinionated, loud, and funny. To spread the word they hit the streets.

Doug recalls their marketing efforts.

"We passed out flyers. At the time there really wasn't e-mail. We told everybody we knew. We told them to pass the word. We had a lot of people listening to us from day one as opposed to most people, they have to build an audience. We basically tried to get the word out about us from the very beginning. We got on and kind of did this 'hit you in the mouth' type radio. It was something that the city of Atlanta was looking for and it was kind of like the perfect storm."

In six months everyone in Atlanta knew of the 2 Live Stews. A year after that, they were manning the midday shift before taking over afternoon drive shortly after. Within four years The Stews were nationally syndicated.

A SHOW!

One thing that the 2 Live Stews didn't want to be was bland. They approached the program with the idea that they would be different from every other show. That meant they wouldn't dwell on stats or typical interviews.

Or as Doug says, "we wanted to be entertaining. We wanted our show to be a SHOW!"

That is why, when you listen to the 2 Live Stews, you'll hear sports talk infused with comic bits, comedians, guy talk, and entertainment segments. In other words, you'll never know what you will get from the Stews but you know they will bring it. They never take a show off.

"When I listened to talk radio," Doug explains, "whenever I heard a boring interview come on, a boring interviewee come on, I turned the channel. What I tell people is, separate yourself from everybody else. Don't sound like everybody else because if you sound like everybody else, what's the point?"

The natural chemistry they have as brothers is also quite apparent.

"It's very energetic and it's very enthusiastic," says Ryan. "We're not like a lot of other guys that try to push statistics all day long, because this is 2011. Everybody has got a PDA or a 3G or 4G phone where they can find out who did what, how many yard or points this person had. We try to take people into the locker room, the folks that weren't blessed to play at the level I did or play college ball like both of us did. We try to help them understand what's taking place in that locker room. That's something that a lot of guys who do what we do for a living can't do because they didn't have those experiences."

The goal each day for The Stews is to make their listeners feel good and enjoy themselves.

"If you're in the car listening to us, you're leaving work where you probably got a job that you don't like or a boss you don't like," Ryan explains. "And you're driving home maybe to a wife you don't like (laughs). So while you're in the car listening to us we want you to be able to enjoy and laugh while you're listening. We want to inform you about sports. We want to take you inside sports and more importantly we want you to enjoy us. We want you to enjoy that listen. That's what we've attempted to do since day one. We want people to listen and have fun with our show."

Like their days growing up in South Carolina, the Stewart boys will go after each other. There are no secrets.

"I know Doug's total history," Ryan says. "He knows my total history. When certain things come up we take shots at each other that a listener will understand is truly a sibling rivalry on the air."

The brothers have never sat down and said what can and what can't be said. But they know where to draw the line. Still, embarrassing things do get out.

"Oh yeah, embarrassment happens weekly," Ryan says with a chuckle. "Our lives are an open book but because we are brothers and blood is thicker than water, there's certain things that just can't and won't be said because it's not supposed to."

Which is the more sensitive Stewart?

"I would say Doug but when you talk to him he's gonna say me," says Ryan. "We're two different people. I'm more of an extrovert and he's more of an introvert. I'm kind of the wild child, always have been."

THE DOG HOUSE

Doug and Ryan are both Qs, the nickname of the fraternity Omega Psi Phi. The fraternity mascot is a dog so they are known as the Q Dogs. It's only natural that the show is also known as The Dog House.

"We try to infuse a lot of that stuff with show as well," Doug explains. "The name of the Dog House came from one of my frat brothers. We bark throughout the show and a lot of people don't get that but when our fraternity brothers listen they definitely know what it is. We play hip hop music throughout the show. So we always wanted to make it bigger than just a talk show."

Just for the record, they've toned down the barking but bring it out from time to time to keep with the theme of the show.

The male listeners are known in the Dog House as simply 'dogs' and the female listeners are known as 'poodles,' because "it's kind of a cute dog," says Doug.

THE JUICE

While many people consider O.J. Simpson a pariah, the former football star was an in-studio guest of the 2 Live Stews.

"O.J. is my favorite football player of all-time," Doug says. "This was after the murder trial and everything. This was probably in 2004. He's the only person that I was actually geeked up or in awe of. I said to myself, 'I can't believe this guy is in here.' I played running back my whole life. When I was in little league I had number 32 because of O.J. Simpson. This was the only guy that I was like, 'This is pretty cool here.' Plus, surrounding everything that happened, this was a huge interview to get at that time. This was before he went back to jail for all of the stuff he's in there for now. That was probably the biggest interview that we've ever done."

Simpson was in town for a golf tournament and a

radio morning show host set up the interview. There were two things that struck Doug about Simpson.

"It was strange to see him walk. He pretty much needed a cane to get around. The other thing that was interesting was how big his head was (laughs)."

It wasn't a pressing interview and the Stews didn't delve into the murders and trial.

"I don't want to say it was a cupcake interview," Doug recalls. "But we really didn't go there. It was kind of like an agreement before he came in there that we wouldn't ask. 'O.J., since the trial how has your life changed? Since the trial, how have people perceived you in public?' We asked those type of questions, but specifics about the trail and the murder and all of that, we didn't even go there."

Another thing that Doug came away with was that O.J. wasn't angry or bitter.

"To me, it seemed like the guy was just ecstatic that he was free. It was almost like there was nothing you could say to get this guy mad. In his mind he was supposed to be in jail anyway so anything outside of not being in jail or worse is gravy at this point. He was smiling and happy. He was very likeable. He was very charming."

Simpson won't be doing any more in-studio appearances with the 2 Live Stews anytime soon. He's serving a 33-year sentence, with the possibility of parole, in Nevada, for multiple felonies.

SPARE TIME

With busy schedules, time away from the job is spent primarily with family. For Ryan it's being with his wife and baby boy.

"I spend every moment I can with him. Before he was born and before I was married, I loved to travel the world. I'm the guy that would get on the phone and book a trip to Amsterdam, Germany, Brazil, Aruba. I did a lot of traveling because I wanted to see the world and had fun doing that. I ride motorcycles. I like cars. I work out and hang out. That's what I do. The solo trips don't take place anymore. It's all with my wife and son."

And is Doug a good uncle?

"Yes, he's great. My son loves him to death."

Away from the rigors of the job, Doug enjoys going to the opera. Wait, no he doesn't. He likes to attend sporting events among other things.

"I love all sports. Love going to basketball and football games in particular. Traveling. And the big thing, the number one thing, I'm on this golf trip. I play a ton of golf. I've been playing golf seriously for the last five years. Before that I played a ton of Madden. I basically got rid of the Madden and I've been playing golf real hard. I play probably at least twice a week. Sometimes three or four times a week."

He admits he's "not great" but adds, "but I'm better than Ryan once again! We've played against each other probably 30 some times and he's beaten me once."

The competitiveness between the two never ends. Doug adds, "His lifelong goal is to just beat me. It's not been a good run for him though. That's the problem."

Back to the course, on a good day Doug shoots an 82. On a regular day add 10 strokes to that.

ON THE TUBE

Ryan Stewart, former Georgia Tech Yellow Jacket and Detroit Lion, a man's man, views sports on TV and he also watches—*The Young and the Restless*?

"Every day. I set my DVR to tape *The Young and the Restless* every single day. On days when I travel and I can't see it, when I get home I'll watch from day one that I missed. I've got four episodes that I'm catching up on now."

His mom watched *The Young and the Restless* and that's how Ryan became a fan of that soap opera and only that soap opera. He would watch it with her, the only rule being he couldn't say a word. It's perhaps the only time Ryan was quiet as a kid.

Unlike his brother, Doug doesn't watch *The Young and the Restless*.

It's pretty much sports for Doug along with a dose of old time TV shows like *Sanford and Son*, *Different Strokes*, or *Good Times*.

As for more current television, he watches the HBO series *The Wire*.

"As far as movies, I like Mafia-type movies. My favorite movie of all time is *Goodfellas*. The other 90 percent of the time my TV is on whatever game or SportsCenter."

As for his brother's habit of watching *The Young and the Restless*, Doug says, "it's kind of strange."

CHARITIES

One of the nice things about the radio show is that it gives the Stews a platform and an opportunity to do charity work.

Being benevolent isn't difficult for the Stewart brothers. It's not something they are forced to do or do with minimal effort. They want to do it and the worthy causes they've supported are numerous.

"We've just always been taught to give back," Doug says. "Our father was a guy who did a lot of charity. Our father was the type of guy that went around and saw the sick and shut-ins on Sundays after church. That was his routine. So we grew up with that as well as our fraternity and our Masonic lodge that we're a part of. We're Masons as well and it's always about giving back and about charity. God loves a cheerful giver. So we've never had a problem with giving and as a matter of fact we love giving."

Big Brothers and Big Sisters is one of the charities that are special to the radio tandem and they have helped get hundreds of mentors involved in the program.

"They mean a lot," Ryan says of their charitable endeavors. "It's because those charities assist kids and I've always been a firm believer in that. The kids are going to be our future. When it comes to the youth I'm a huge believer in giving back and helping out, and Big Brothers and Big Sisters of metro Atlanta does a great job when it comes to finding mentors for these kids that don't have a brother like I did growing up or a father to take them out and shoot some hoops."

SPIRITUALITY

How does every morning start for Ryan? It begins with God.

"Every morning I wake up, since 2000, the first thing I do is read my Bible and pray and go through scripture. Every single morning because I'm a believer in God and there's no doubt in my mind that we wouldn't be where we are today if it weren't for his grace. At the end of the day, I'm a huge believer in God and I'm very, very thankful for that. Some listeners may not know that and it's OK."

THE END?

There is no end in sight for the 2 Live Stews. They have no intention of shutting it down or looking to close shop. So how much longer do The Stews want to do the show?

"Man, I could do this forever," Doug says immediately. "The reason I say that is because we would be doing this no matter what. That argument we had in his basement 10 years ago wasn't the first time we had done that. We've done that our whole life. I can see myself continuing to do this for a long time."

LEGACY

"Trust me, they'll never forget us," Doug says. "We basically came in and changed sports talk radio forever. Not just in this city but nationally. All of the shows and hosts were pretty much the same but you got to hear from us. People are going to look back and say these guys said the things that most of my friends, and a lot of it is from the African-American perspective, wanted to say but never had the voice to say before."

Greg Williams
"A Second Chance"

Greg Williams, affectionately known to his audience as Greggo, is currently working the afternoon drive shift at KRLD, 105.3 The Fan in Dallas, Texas, with co-host Richie Whitt.

The fact that Williams is hosting a show of any kind is a miracle considering he shouldn't even be alive.

Like a rubber ball, Greg Williams has bounced back and continues to thrive on the air. As you'll come to understand, it has been anything but a smooth journey for brutally honest and extremely candid Greggo.

"I've always admitted what I've done because I think this story is going to have a happy ending for me."

WORLD TRAVELER

People frequently say, "one day, I'm going to travel the world." For many travelers that day comes in retirement. For Greg Williams and his three siblings (two sisters and a brother), traveling the globe began at an early age. He was born in Fort Worth, Texas, but thanks to his father who was in the Air Force, he didn't stay there long.

"We lived all over the world," Greg recalls. "I started school in Nebraska and then I went through Spain and Libya, then I went through Turkey."

He also lived in Florida, Virginia, and back to Texas.

Greg's high school years were spent in Boyd, Texas, his dad's hometown.

"It was a small town of about 700 people. There were 51 people in my graduating senior class. I think that later on, being able to move and being able to make new friends and new acquaintances, I think that that really helped me 20-something years later when I got into the radio business."

While some kids may not have enjoyed all the moving, it didn't bother Greg. It's what he knew.

"I had a tremendous childhood. Tremendous. I had what I needed and I was very content."

His parents divorced when he was 12.

"Looking back, maybe that had some unknown psychological effects on me, but at the time it was just part of it. You were sad but you moved on."

THE PET

Greg was the oldest of the Williams' children, and he was his mom's pet.

"I was always the pet of the family. That's a known fact. I could get away with stuff that others couldn't."

He was also able to make his mother crack up, which was important since she was the disciplinarian in the family.

"I always had a way of amusing my mother. I always had the gift of gab and I could always say something that would make her laugh. I wasn't a problem kid. I never got into any kind of trouble. I was just mouthy. I had a teacher one time that said, 'Greg Williams, with that mouth of yours, you're never going to amount to anything.' And that's what made me successful; my mouth. I was a smart aleck. I couldn't keep my mouth shut. I was a very good student [and] made excellent grades; never really challenged that much, but I was just mouthy."

MR. ZERO GRADE POINT AVERAGE

After graduating from Boyd High School in 1978, Greg went to Ranger Junior College, about 90 miles east of Fort Worth, on a baseball scholarship.

"It was there that I discovered that there was nobody to wake me up in the morning to go to class. So basically, I didn't go to class. I'd go to baseball practice. [And] I played baseball for them one year. I left after one year with a 0.00 GPA."

There were also distractions at Ranger J.C. for Greg that prevented him from achieving success in the classroom.

"There was too many girls, there was too much partying to do. I was 18 years old. I was out from under my parents for the first time. I was playing baseball and in my stupid little world and mind, 'hey, if I show up for baseball practice that's all I need to do."

The baseball coach took note of Greg's grades or lack thereof.

He asked Greg, "Do you know how hard it is to flunk out of Ranger Junior College? But you're managing to do it."

THE BAR

No, Greg didn't end up going to law school. Following his less than stellar academic career at Ranger JC, he went into the bar business.

"I was a bartender. And then I got into that lifestyle for which I had nothing but fun for about seven years. It was Caligula. It was Sodom and Gomorrah. I can't tell you how many times that I was bartending and you'd meet some girl and she started drinking and you'd say, 'I'm about to take a break, why don't you come back?' And you'd go into the liquor storage room and have a little sex. Then go back and bartend. It wasn't uncommon at all."

Greg worked at Billy Bob's, the famed honky tonk nightclub, from its inception in 1981.

"It was just a big party scene back then."

One of his goals each morning was to make money, which he was doing to the tune of $800 to $1,000 each week.

"Cash money," he says, which he spent on nice cars

and clothes. "I made a lot of money bartending but I spent it all. I was like a gypsy. From the age of 18 to 25, I had fun every single day."

Despite the fun and income, something was building up inside of him.

MORE BILLY BOB'S

Celebrities would pour into Billy Bob's. Stars such as Johnny Cash, Merle Haggard, Willie Nelson, and Waylon Jennings performed at Billy Bob's when Greg was working there.

Greg worked in the VIP room and served drinks to untold numbers of celebrities, including Ray Price, who cursed him out for the way he made him a Kahlua and cream drink.

"He told me what a stupid motherfucker I was for doing that. He was just like barking at me."

Greg just made him another drink.

He also worked as an assistant to one of the owners as Billy Bob's was getting into management of Country and Western stars. Greg would run errands and shuttle singers to and from the airport. One singer that they briefly managed was George Jones.

One day, Greg had to go pick up Jones, who was at another owner's house about 30 miles outside of Fort Worth. A routine, easy assignment, but Greg was warned by his boss, "if you don't get him back here, don't even show up."

Greg thought, "How easy can this be? Just go pick up the guy and drive him here and that's done."

Greg picked Jones up and it was soon apparent to him that the singer was very irritated.

"I got him into the car and I tried to make small talk and he wanted to hear none of it. Then he told me, 'hey, I need to get a dress shirt.' I'm like, 'well, we'll get back to the club and then they'll take care of it.'"

Jones insisted he needed a dress shirt and persuaded Greg to take him to the mall.

"I took him into this store and I turned around and he was gone. He was out of there, to which I was in horror."

In these pre-cell phone days, Greg had to use a pay phone to call the owner who told him, "You just better find him."

Greg finally tracked him down at a bar in the mall.

"He was finishing up about his fifth drink already. He had no money. The bartender was telling me to get him out of there because he was being belligerent and to pay his tab."

Greg paid the bill, finally took Jones to the club and told the owner, "Don't ever involve me with this guy again."

One morning, Greg woke up with a massive hangover. He had $1.18 in his pocket. "I knew that there was something better out there. And I always knew that I wanted to go to college and get a degree. That was kind of like a challenge to me."

The day of the hangover, at the age of 25, Greg decided to get out of bartending and to work on earning a college degree.

BACK TO SCHOOL

Greg applied to four schools: University of Texas, Texas Christian University, University of Virginia, and the College of William and Mary.

He liked Virginia when he lived there as a kid, but decided to go to TCU, although he didn't have a career destination in mind.

"I just assumed I would get in there and get a degree and it would all take care of itself. But I was always a sports nut. I played all sports in high school and always knew I wanted to do something in sports. It took about 15 minutes of my first workout at junior college in baseball to figure out, 'you know what? You ain't going to the Major Leagues.' I always knew I wanted to get into sports, I just didn't know what it was gonna be."

Of the four schools he applied to, the only one that didn't accept him was Virginia. Greg still holds a grudge against the Cavaliers.

"To this day I still root against them in everything they play. It doesn't matter if it's swimming or football or basketball. I can't stand them because they turned me down."

Can a guy really hold a grudge against a school that turned away someone who recorded a zero grade point average in junior college?

"That was before there were computer records and transcripts. So when I filled out applications, it said, 'Have you ever attended college?' and I just lied my ass off and go, 'No.' And so that 0.00 kind of ended there."

TCU

Unlike his days of sleeping in and skipping class at Ranger J.C., Greg did an about-face at Texas Christian, a private university in Fort Worth.

"I knew if you had a degree from TCU it looked pretty good. So I went back to class and I was a professional student. If they were holding class I was there. I was ready to roll. I went in the summers, I went during the holidays when they had the mini-semesters, and I really buckled down and really got a good education."

Greg set his sights on journalism in hopes of becoming a sportswriter.

It took him three years to graduate with a 3.0 grade point average.

"Which I'm very proud of."

DRUGS

In high school, Greg first was confronted with pot. He went to concerts and couldn't believe how many people were smoking pot, "which always scared the hell out of me. They're smoking pot here at this concert and there are cops everywhere. Why aren't they being busted? And I was always fearful of jail and authority."

The first time Greg tried drugs was in 1981 at the age of 21. While drugs were around he says they weren't a part of his life.

"Drugs always sort of scared me. But yeah, I had experiments with social drugs at the time. It was at a time when cocaine was flowing, Quaaludes were flowing, and pot was flowing, and if you were in a nightclub and you weren't doing one of the three, you were in the minority. But it never became a serious problem for me. Because I could have a drink and have as much fun. But they were around in abundance."

The first time Greg used cocaine was when he was working at Billy Bob's and a roadie for a band offered him some.

"I'm like, 'I've never done it.' And he goes, 'well, here, try it.' And I tried it and I'm like, 'oh my God. This can't be good for ya' because it's so great.' And then I had just small dalliances with it. I might buy some here and there and usually when I bought it, it was to get girls. To share it with girls."

Was Greg dependent on cocaine at that time?

"No. Never. Never even close."

He was never concerned that it would become an addiction.

"I only did it when I wanted to. And there would be long stretches of not doing it."

RADIO

After getting his degree from TCU, Greg hoped to parlay his writing skills into a job as a sportswriter.

"I was really good at it."

But he ended up getting a job in radio.

"Somewhere along the line I got an internship at a TV station and then I worked as a production assistant, and then I was offered a job as a radio guy. I never thought about radio. This is 1988. I never thought of it. But I got the job and we had a small sports department. It was WBAP, which is one of the largest, oldest radio stations in the country, 50,000 watts. I was like the lone reporter. I would go out and do interviews and bring quotes and actualities back for the sportscasts."

WBAP had three sportscasts per hour on morning drive and in the afternoon as well as a nightly two-hour sports talk show.

"I was way down as just a reporter but I was getting to cover the Rangers, the Mavericks, and the Dallas Cowboys. I was making like, no money, but I was getting to cover all these teams. I just pretty much worked my ass off. At one point I worked 144 days straight without a day off, but it was no big deal. It wasn't like a job to me."

SPORTS TALK

The transition from reporter to sports talk show host wasn't a major leap for Greg.

"It just evolved. You're a reporter and then you get to fill in on the weekends on the post-game show for the Rangers or the Mavericks. Got to do that. And then you get to fill in doing sportscasts during the week. I just kind of worked my way up after five years there."

Greg says that he was a complete novice when he started doing sport talk shows.

"I was real green. And there's really no way you can practice for that type of stuff. I had a gift for the gab and I had a line of bullshit that I could use, but I had zero talk show host skills. I was told I would never work in this market because of my voice. But I was able to hang in there, and when the opportunity came along for the first all-sports station in Dallas I was offered a job as a full-time talk show host. But up until then I was just a reporter slash producer slash fill-in talk show host."

RHYNER AND THE TICKET

While at WBAP, Greg met his broadcasting idol, Mike Rhyner, at a Texas Rangers game. Rhyner did sports on the number one rock-and-roll station in town and Greg thought that was the perfect job. Somebody pointed him out to Greg in the press box.

"I was, like…dumbfounded," Greggo recalls. "I'd been around Nolan Ryan and all the big baseball and basketball names, but he was a guy larger than life to me. We struck up a conversation and we really hit it off. It was the greatest thing ever. He became a genuine friend."

KTCK launched as an all-sports radio station in Dallas in January of 1994 with the moniker of The Ticket, and Greg was one of the first people to get a call.

Rhyner was one of the people responsible for starting the station and hired Greg to be his afternoon drive co-host.

"He was always a hero of mine," Greg says. "Still is. A lot of people said, 'wow, how'd you get this job on The Ticket?' I go, 'I knew Mike Rhyner.' They're like, 'no, how'd you get it.' I'm like, 'that's the truth.' That's how I got it. If I ever had to apply for that job there's no way I would have got it."

The pairing was almost immediately successful and the show took off, as Greg says, "like a rocket."

The station was finding itself. Instead of filling a two-hour block with a sports talk show like other stations would do, they had to fill 24-hours with sports programming.

"We were flying by the seat of our pants," is how Greg termed it.

The listeners flocked to the station. The reviews from the media weren't as glowing.

"The media thought we were jokes. They were like, 'Who is this guy? And who are they?' Because there were some low-level guys with low-level positions at other stations and all of a sudden they were doing talk shows."

Does Greg remember any of the criticisms?

"Oh yeah. No business being on the air. Don't know what they're talking about. Not entertaining. Don't talk enough sports. Joke. I mean it was unbelievable what they said about us."

As for the listeners?

"They loved it. When we went out on remotes and met the crowd, we noticed that all they remembered and talked about was the entertaining stuff. It's there that we kind of developed the guy talk. And The Ticket was one of the first ones in the country to do that. There were other all-sports but they were Xs and Os, hardcore sports. I mean, we were sports. We covered all the local teams and this is when the Cowboys were really getting good."

GEORGE W.

Greg got to know George W. Bush when he was managing general partner of the Texas Rangers. A well-known baseball fan, Bush attended many Rangers games, first at old Arlington Stadium and then the new ballpark.

"Interviews I'd done with him, he was always very cordial. Very nice. And it was just shocking to see him do a State of the Union Address and know he's one of 40-something presidents and not only does he know my name, I've heard him use the F-word a lot."

TALK RADIO

Some guys like to listen to sports talk radio to get an idea of what's happening, but not Greg. He rarely listens to sports talk.

"I don't want any idea that somebody else has. I don't want to subconsciously use that. I like to do all my own research from scratch every morning on the news and entertainment of the day. So I don't listen to sports radio. And subsequently, I don't listen to talk radio."

Greg does have opinions on some current sports talk show hosts.

"I used to like Jim Rome until he became so national and became an ass-kisser of all the players. And the same thing with Dan Patrick. I don't think Mike and Mike have anything. They're ridiculous. I do like Mike North in Chicago. He's got something. Tom Tolbert, former NBA player, I think he's got something. I always get amused by Mike Francesa. He's such a blowhard and so arrogant. I love arrogant people. You can't be arrogant enough for me. It amuses me. I'm a very arrogant person. It's confidence. I wear it as a badge of honor. Controlled arrogance, if there's such a thing. I don't think you can succeed in this business without being arrogant. When I say business I'm talking about the entertainment business. I don't consider myself a talk show host. I don't consider myself a journalist. I consider myself an entertainer."

I'M GREGGO

While arrogance may have helped drive Greg to heights in radio that couldn't have been predicted, there is a clear-cut example of where his arrogance contributed to his downfall. He turned back the clock and it backfired.

"After putting in 14 years at The Ticket and being number one for 10 years and just thinking, 'You know what, I think I'm going to go back to the days when I was 25, and I think I'm just going to party on this cocaine because I'm Greggo and they can't touch me.' And they found out and I got fired."

The station found out because all the obvious signs of cocaine use were there.

"I was fooling no one except myself. Arrogance."

After blaming the station for a while, Greg came to the realization that he was justly let go.

"They were 100 percent right. I was 100 percent wrong. That started my two-year trip through beyond hell. I would have loved to have gone just through hell. I went beyond and below hell."

FIRED

Greg's show with Mike Rhyner on The Ticket had a great run, but like all good things it came to an end.

Greg still doesn't know for sure what happened with his relationship with Rhyner but it deteriorated.

"For the life of me, I don't know. I think it was a matter of growing apart."

Today there is no relationship. According to Greg, "He refuses to talk to me, which pains me to no end."

In October of 2007, Greg was late for a remote broadcast on a Friday afternoon.

"I just absolutely overslept. I tried to get there as soon as I could but I was late."

During a break they told him to leave immediately and he needed to go take a drug test. Greggo refused to take the test because he knew he couldn't pass it. The drug in question was cocaine.

Management then said he had to be at the office Monday morning at 9 o'clock.

There was suspicion about Greg's cocaine use but he always denied it.

The general manager, Dan Bennett, told him he had to take a drug test and even if he passed he wouldn't believe it.

"That's when I came clean," Greg says. "It was totally my fault. It was my choice. The reason I'm not working at The Ticket is because I screwed it up. Not because anybody screwed me, not because anybody had it out for me, it's because I'm the one that screwed up and ended up getting my ass fired ...which was the right move."

Greg admits to being delusional as to how much power he wielded being part of the number one show for over a decade.

He also cops to doing a few shows under the influence of cocaine.

"A couple of times. I didn't make a habit of it, but a couple of times. Being honest, yeah, sure did. From my point of view those shows were OK. But, looking back, there was probably need for suspicion. They weren't disastrous. Weren't horrible. But it was under the influence and any time you're under the influence that's not real. I was 46 trying to act like I was 23, which you can't do. I would call it a mid-life crisis but that's a stupid term."

Greg went into rehab although he didn't think he had a huge problem. He was an in-residence patient for a week and then an out-patient for three weeks.

"This was just a vehicle to go to, to satisfy the employers and then I was going to go come back to work. They promised me that my job would be waiting for me."

Following treatment, it was time for Greg to return to work. But there was a problem.

"I had a meeting with all the other hosts and they pretty much unloaded on me for a number of things. Then I was told to go home and I thought I was coming back to work that Monday. And then they called me and said that it's best that we sever relations. They had had enough of my scene and my actions."

Greg did file a suit against The Ticket.

"I had to."

He didn't think what was offered to him was fair.

While he can't get into specifics of the agreement, he does say that a compromise was reached. The suit never went to court.

WHERE'S GREGGO?

Legally, while in rehab, the station couldn't say why Greg wasn't on the air. But when a guy who is on the air daily for nearly 14 years suddenly turns up missing from the airwaves, people notice. Fans of Greg were going to events holding up "Where's Greggo?" signs.

"I had a lot of listeners. I had a lot of people that really liked me. They wondered what was going on. The people at The Ticket, they couldn't really explain."

LUCKY TO BE ALIVE

Part of Greg's post-rehab treatment involved counseling. They also had him on the drug Xanax. He was taking 10 to 12 pills a day.

"So for like a year, that's pretty much the way I was going through life. In absolute Xanax-induced fog. There was no way I could go on the air."

At this time he was officially diagnosed with depression. Depression runs in his family. His brother committed suicide at the age of 29. Upon reflection, Greg believes the genesis of his depression started around 2005 when his relationship with Mike Rhyner started to sour.

While unemployed, Greg became suicidal.

"No question. I actually put a gun to my head and it misfired. I shouldn't be here. I just couldn't take it anymore. Thought that was the way out. As a gun collector, I still got that gun and it's never misfired once since then. But it did that day."

He can't explain why there was never another attempt to do himself in.

"I don't know. And I've never considered it after

that. That's never been a consideration."

Does Greg feel he got a reprieve from death?

"I wouldn't call it that, but I appreciate things a lot more."

He still takes medication, not Xanax, every day to deal with depression. He's also ditched therapy.

"It didn't help me at all. Zero. I'm not anti-therapy, but it doesn't work for everybody."

RADIO GOALS

Greg certainly is focused on his radio goals.

"You better believe it. To be number one. I was number one. We had one of the most successful sports talk shows in the country. You started ranking sports talk shows and we made everybody's top 10. And realistically, I don't know if that goal is achievable. But when you have the type of personality that I do, then it's always good to be chasing. You have to be driven in this business."

All the ingredients are there at The Fan in Dallas for Greg to be successful. He cites a great on-air partner in Richie Whitt, a 100,000 watt station, the backing of CBS, and a great program director in Bruce Gilbert.

What would stop Greg from reaching number one again?

"Just not being good enough. I've got a tremendous opportunity here. It's just a matter of making it work."

HOMEBOY

These days, what kind of exciting lifestyle does Greg Williams lead?

"I basically have no life. I work and go home and watch TV."

He loves cable channels such as the History Channel, Discovery, the Learning Channel, and the Military Channel.

"I've seen every single show on the Military

Channel."

Since he's an avid collector, Greg also likes the show *Pawn Stars*. In addition to a baseball memorabilia collection and gun collection, he has one of the biggest Coca-Cola memorabilia collections in the country, which includes a mint condition 1939 Coca-Cola vending machine.

Just to clarify, the show is *Pawn Stars* not *Porn Stars*. But Greg volunteers, "Ya know, we're being open book truthful here, yes, I have searched the internet for porn, which I don't think makes me unique in any way. Most of it is for my own amusement because I can't believe that people would actually do this."

In addition to his viewing habits, he gets away on the weekends by going to his lake house where he goes boating and jet skis.

MUSICAL TASTES

It's a safe bet to say that Greg doesn't have the latest Lady Gaga or Justin Bieber album.

"Today's music I don't like too much. I'm 51-years-old and I still like the old stuff. Led Zeppelin, the Beatles, the Rolling Stones, I still listen to that all the time."

GOING FORWARD

The Greg Williams story seems to be on track for a happy conclusion. Just like he was proud when he graduated from TCU, he's gratified to have bounced back from certain doom.

"I have a big sense of achievement from coming back from where I came from. It's not like I came back from some kind of terminal disease or being abused. I'm coming back from things that I did at my own hands. But sometimes that's mentally harder to come back from that than it is the other things, 'cause you know that you've been so self-destructive."

His parting thought is that he may be misunderstood by some people for what has happened in his past.

"I'm not a bad guy. A lot of people, because of the things that happened, might label me a bad guy. I use this all the time, I say, 'The lower someone is on the totem pole the better I treat them.' Management, other talk show hosts, fuck them. They've had their success. But board ops and producers and office people, those are the people I want to connect with. Those are the people I try my best to be nice to."

Petros Papadakis
"Fight On"

The Gregarious Greek would be an apt nickname for Petros Papadakis, part of the prominent radio program 'Petros and Money.' Matt 'Money' Smith is also spotlighted in a chapter of this book.

Full of opinions, enthusiasm, and self-deprecating humor, Petros is a busy man during football season. He works every day in his job as a football analyst and talk show host. Every day as in no days off.

In an age of conformity, Petros stands out like a Trojan horse in a fish bowl.

The former Southern Cal running back and team captain has taken to the airwaves and distanced himself from most others. Actually, all others. No other person on the air, radio, or television sounds quite like Petros Papadakis, although one might conclude upon first listen that perhaps Petros won an Arnie Spanier soundalike contest. But additional time spent listening to the California native would lead you to reach the undeniable conclusion that Petros is one-of-a-kind. Whether that is good or bad is up to you. We lean on the side of good.

WORKING BOY

One reason Petros Papadakis was a skinny kid is because he was always working. While most parents can't get their 18-year-olds to work, Petros had a job at the age of eight, working in his father's Greek restaurant in San Pedro, California.

"My father owned a very popular restaurant which we worked at constantly," Petros recalls. "During the summers we worked at my grandfather's liquor warehouses during the day delivering liquor. There's not a lot of eight-, nine-, ten-year-olds who know what Hiram Walker Root Beer Schnapps is, but I did. We worked hard and we played football."

SCHOOL

With a strong work ethic instilled in him as a youth, one might conclude that Petros was a pretty good student, able to discipline himself enough to get good grades. Well, perhaps we should let Petros tell us what kind of scholar he was.

"I was a horrible student. Not attentive at all. Really awkward. Didn't kiss a girl until I was, like, 18, but I had this older brother that was a football star, so I kind of did everything with him. I had issues all throughout high school. I was pretty confused."

All of his family members were straight-A students. Petros, not so much.

"I had a 1.4 GPA in high school."

SPORTS

Despite being asthmatic as a kid, he started playing football when he was nine in part because of his family history. His father, John, a linebacker, played at the University of Southern California as did his brother, Taso, also a linebacker.

"My older brother was kind of like an Adonis figure," says Petros. "Really, he was. I've never met anybody so celebrated in a local area. This is before everything was viral."

Taso Papadakis is now enjoying an acting career.

In addition to football, Petros played basketball, and in junior high he played on the boys' softball team.

"I didn't play hard ball because I was horrible at it," Petros says with a laugh. "I'm not very coordinated hand-eye wise. I was just a really violent football player and I didn't mind hitting people with my face. When you stick your face in there and drive your legs you'll probably be pretty good at football."

INKED UP

When Petros was 13, he got a tattoo. The first of many.

"I grew up in a port town," Petros reveals. "There's a lot of tattoo parlors and a lot of sailor types and swarthy sea folk. And I got my name in Greek tattooed on my back at 13. There was nowhere to go but down from there."

Were his parents accepting of his body art?

"Hell, no, they weren't OK with it. My dad saw it like a year later and cried."

Was his dad strict?

"No. I have a dad that's crazy. Strict, I don't know. He just saw the tattoo in the shower. He came in the shower to dump ice water on me as he often did and he saw it. It's a tiny little tattoo."

Later on, at 15, Petros and his brother got the same reggae-themed tattoo.

"Yeah, that was a good decision. When I got to SC, dudes had these big old tattoos. I was like, 'well, hell I could do that.'"

John Papadakis is still upset at his kid's tattoos and wonders when he will finally stop.

For the record, Petros has eight tattoos.

"And they're all stupid. I mean, some are dumber than others and there are some that are just inexcusable."

BABES

Despite being a football player and owning a gregarious personality, Petros was a flop with the girls in high school.

"I didn't do well with chicks," he shares. "There were a couple of girls that did have sex in high school but it certainly wasn't with me. I'm hosting Love Line tomorrow night, so I'm obviously a sex expert so I understand these things."

He continues.

"I'm kind of like a sea monster. I'm sort of awkward, I have a really big nose and a lisp and my tongue is too big for my mouth. I had some issues. I had real bad eczema when I was young. I carry an inhaler with me all the time. Think of Paul Pfeiffer from the Wonder Years but really fast and really violent and able to pick up the blitz. And that was me."

MISTER ALLERGIES

It might be easier to list the things that Petros is not allergic to than the things he is allergic too.

"I had a lot of problems growing up," Petros says with a hearty laugh. "I'm just like a kid who's allergic to everything. I'm allergic to dogs. I'm allergic to cats. Allergic to dust. Allergic to being outside. Allergic to salt water. Allergic to wool …"

We get the picture.

BLOSSOMING

An average player initially, Petros turned into a great football player between his junior and senior seasons at Palos Verdes Peninsula High School for Head Coach Gary Kimbrell.

The reason? Speed.

"I started to be able to run. I mean, elite track speed kind of running. I got really fast. I don't know why or how it happened. I was just able to fire my legs and I was running a 4.4 40 legitimate by the time I left high school."

To his surprise, the 6'0", 195-pound Petros ended up starting his senior season at fullback and he ran wild for the Panthers.

"I ran for 2,000 yards. And I was a smoker! I smoked about a pack a day. It was sort of like watching someone else," a still surprised Petros says. "I ran all these long runs and knocked dudes over and went deep in the playoffs. I went from going to a JC or trying to be a busboy for the rest of my life or just wait tables at my dad's restaurant to having a scholarship."

CAL TO USC

After his stellar senior season, Petros signed with the University of California.

"I signed with Cal out of high school. I don't know why, but I signed with Cal. I love Cal, that's why! I loved the place, I love the campus, I loved the idea of going to Cal."

Even though his dad and brother played at Southern California and the Trojans did recruit Petros, he went to Cal partly because USC was going to grayshirt him.

Another Pac 10 school showed interest in Petros.

"Washington State dropped me because they said I had character issues. Which I did. I didn't have good grades. I got into a fair amount of trouble. I wasn't a great kid. I was just kind of an idiot (laughs). This huge fucking idiot. But I was fast and violent. If you're an idiot and you're fast and violent, you can go pretty far in this world, as long as you show up to fucking practice."

Boston College, Penn State, and Miami were also interested in Petros.

"I ended up going to Cal and leaving in the summer. Nothing against anybody at Cal. I go up there and I love it. When I call games in Berkeley it's one of my favorite places to be. My favorite restaurants are there. I love walking in Berkeley. I love drinking in Berkeley. I love that town, love it. Especially around the campus and up in the hills. But I got into camp and was actually their second string back and I was playing really well. I was really fast and breaking some runs and having some success and getting in fights. If you're a white tailback you gotta fight people. But I left. I just left."

He was on campus for three months and in football camp for just one week.

"I just royally fucked up. I was just a stupid kid. Just beyond dumb. I was really immature, really emotionally unprepared. I'm embarrassed about it because I signed a letter of intent there. Who knows what would have happened in my life if I stayed up there."

Part of his leaving Cal was being homesick. So he just went back to Los Angeles, where his dad wasn't pleased with his son's decision to leave Berkeley.

"He put a hit out on me, like literally," Petros says. "I was staying at my Uncle Matty's house. He didn't want to be around me. It was a bad scene."

After kicking around for a while Petros made a decision.

"I agreed to go to USC so then I kind of had some direction and he was happy about that. He didn't care that I didn't go to USC in the first place. He was happy I had a scholarship."

He walked on in the spring of 1996 with the Trojans; however, because Cal wouldn't release him from his scholarship, he was told he had to sit out two years.

"So I quit," Petros says.

But when a coaching change was made at Cal they released Petros from his scholarship.

He finally got a chance to play at USC in 1997 and earned a scholarship.

THE INJURY

Petros played in 10 games for the Trojans in '97 and all 13 games in '98 as a backup to tailback Chad Morton. In his second season, he ran for a then career high 113 yards, including a 65-yard touchdown run against—Cal.

But before his senior season, Petros suffered a horrible freak injury to his right foot. He knew right away there was something wrong when he was tackled in practice.

"I was a team leader type of guy, kind of climbed my way up, and about a week and a half into camp my foot buckled. All the bones popped out at the top. I mean, it just shattered. It was a debilitating injury. One of the worst they've ever seen."

They put several pins and screws into the foot as well as a cadaver bone.

"But that wasn't the worst thing that happened," Petros recalls. "I was legally crippled after that but the worst thing that happened was I had osteomyelitis, which is a staph infection in the bone. So I was 22 and I went from being this athlete who was really fast and strong and felt like he could jump over a car, to laying in a hospital bed for months and months and months. But they put it back together. I had a PICC line to my heart with an IV every eight hours. Even at home I had to do that. But I came back and played in 2000 basically on one leg."

Petros admits that the injury brought him down to earth.

"The foot injury humbled the shit out of me."

He was named a team captain for his delayed senior season, and before every game he took a shot to the bottom of his foot. Despite the damaged foot he scored 8 touchdowns that season.

The team finished 5-7 after a promising 3-0 start.

"I was the captain of the worst team in USC history," Petros says softly. "The only one ever to be last place in the conference."

Prior to the injury, at 220 pounds, he ran a 4.3 40. The injury ended any possibilities of an NFL career.

So why go through grueling rehabilitation and play his senior year?

"I wanted to walk off on my own terms, which is what I did."

After that senior campaign, Petros was named the team's Most Inspirational Player, which had a lot of meaning to him since his dad won the same award years earlier.

To this day the pain exists and if Petros runs around his foot will turn purple. A nice shade of purple but purple nonetheless. He also needs another surgery in the future.

MARRIAGE

It might come as a surprise to some that the 34-year-old Petros is married. He got married two years ago in Greece on the island of Rhodes. His bride even converted to Greek Orthodox.

"I'm obviously an acquired taste," Petros says. "I'm not the kind of guy you find at the club on Sunset with leather cuffs on his hands dancing to the house music. There were some girls that liked me (laughs). One enough to marry me."

He met his future wife, Dayna, when she worked on the film crew at SC when Petros was a Trojan.

"We dated briefly and of course I fucked it up royally," he admits. "I begged her for years to date me again but I always had a girlfriend or something going on. Finally she agreed to go out on a date with me and I was, like, shocked."

So how did he mess things up the first time?

"I was playing college football. You play high school football you think your world is like this epic struggle, that you feel like you're Odysseus and you live in this little bubble and everybody's watching every move you make and you're really special, and in college it's that times 100. You think that every time you fart everybody's clapping."

SMOKING

Petros began smoking cigarettes when he was the ripe old age of 13. Not a lot but a cigarette every other day or so.

"I worked in a restaurant. Everybody was smoking. I quit smoking the day before I got married. I haven't had a cigarette in two years. I don't even smoke cigars."

He smoked a lot for a long time, including the years he played football.

"I could sprint but I couldn't run a mile."

BROADCASTING

Some of the people in this book harbored dreams of becoming a sports broadcaster at an early stage of their lives.

Not the case with Petros.

"I was never a practice in the mirror type of guy or a guy who even thought he could look into a camera and speak. I had no aspirations of this. I had no idea who was who. I was a bit of a sports fan but nothing like the people that I work around. I never envisioned anything like this."

In his senior season at USC, Petros was named the captain of the team in 2000 and with that came the reporters.

"I just did a lot of interviews. I became a bit of a sound bite because I'm a little different than what you normally get from a college football player. It just kind of developed that way."

Even when he was done playing for the Trojans, Petros had no thoughts or desires to pursue a livelihood in the media. His career started out of the blue.

"I got a call from a guy who worked at Fox, who was the head of the news department, a guy named Mark Houska, who asked me to come and work. I thought that they wanted me to have an internship. I was still working at the restaurant and had just finished up. I'm sure people feel weird when they graduate college. But when you graduate college the captain of the worst football team in USC history, your coach is fired (Paul Hackett), you're completely spit out. I didn't know what was going on and this guy Houska called me up. He said he was going to put me on the air. And then the sports information director at USC, Tim Tessalone, said, 'No, no, you can't put him on the air. He's crazy.' And Houska said, 'No, I'm gonna do it.' They put me on their pre-game radio broadcasts and post-game call-in show. It was one year later. I just went from being on the field to being in a booth. And it kind of moved very quickly from there."

If he didn't get an opportunity to get into broadcasting, Petros says he probably would have ended up running his father's restaurant.

"I learned to use a computer three years ago. So I'm not a very useful person. I don't handle my finances. I don't know how to do taxes. I'm a pretty useless guy. I can help you out with a lot of things that really don't matter. I'm not very practical. But I sure as hell know how to put on a suit and sit in a make-up chair and talk. So that's what happened."

Petros started out doing a lot of TV and some radio work and each year he was afforded more and more opportunities. One certain reason is because the audience was drawn to his humor. Simply put, Petros is a funny guy. To which he says, "Not everybody thinks so."

He admits to his good fortune.

"I got lucky. There was a guy that saw something in me and pulled me out. What also helped was my first year out was Pete Carroll's first year in. And I was a USC football analyst. So by 2002 I'm spending two weeks in Miami covering the Orange Bowl and there was a lot of interest in USC football."

All that led to doing national college football games for Fox.

NO HOMER

As a player, USC fans grew to love Petros, especially since he came back from his terrible foot injury.

Now though, his candid nature has turned some Southern Cal fans against him.

In his role as an analyst he calls it as he sees it and doesn't mince words or show favor towards the Trojans.

"How can I walk into Chip Kelly's office or Mike Riley's office or anybody's office and shake their hand?" Petros wonders. "Yeah, USC people may love me for being full of shit but where would my credibility be? I wouldn't have any."

While the criticism from SC fans rolls off his back there is one bit of criticism that sometimes bothers him. That's when people say that he was no good when he played and that he couldn't play today for the Trojans.

"It's like, motherfucker, I ran a 4.3. Shut up. Don't tell me I wouldn't play. I'd compete and play anywhere in college because I was a good football player. I was a good, hard-nosed football player. So I don't like that. I don't like when people go back in time and say 'Petros sucked.' But all the other stuff, I don't care if people call me fat or stupid or ugly or say that I have a lisp or I'm an idiot or a moron or gay. I mean, I hear it all. But attacks that I couldn't play used to bug the shit out of me. I need to get over it."

THAT'S ODD

Most sports talk show hosts are big sports fans. Or at least they were at one point before becoming jaded over time. Still, just about every sports talker immerses themselves in the games in order to shape their knowledge and form opinions.

Again, Petros breaks the mold.

"I'm not much of a sports fan. I'm kind of an observationalist. I'm a football analyst by trade as far as a lot of the television stuff goes."

As a kid, was he into sports?

"I was. I loved the Portland Trailblazers with Clyde Drexler. I watched sports but not with the intensity of a lot of these guys."

Is Petros a stat geek?

"No, no, no, no. I don't play fantasy baseball. I don't play fantasy football. I used to be really cynical about that kind of stuff and call those people dorks. I'm a little older now and I think people should do whatever floats their boat. I mean, fuck, I watch the *Real Housewives* of whatever city, ya know. I'm not that macho I guess."

DAD

Earlier we mentioned that Petros' father, John, was a linebacker at USC before opening up his restaurant, Papadakis Taverna, in San Pedro. If you want to check out the Greek food at the restaurant, you're too late. It closed in 2010 after a 37-year run.

"My father was a good football player, really good," Petros says. "He's bigger than any of us, personality-wise. I put him on the show once a week cause he's crazy."

That was established earlier when we learned John used to throw ice water on Petros in the shower just for kicks.

When his dad was a high school coach, Petros was the water boy. He also remembers as a youngster coming out of the tunnel at the Los Angeles Coliseum and watching the Trojans play.

"My father used to take us into the locker room at USC. I just remember being really young on that sideline staring into the yellow asses, 'cause these guys are all wearing the gold pants. I'd just be standing there with the team just staring at everybody's ass."

THE SHOW

While 'Petros and Money' is a show that is more than just sports, sports tends to be the backdrop of whatever is on the minds of Petros and Matt Smith.

Their interests are varied and Petros wouldn't mind branching out in that regard.

"I always feel like I could do, or maybe one day with Matt, a general talk show because we do so much stuff that is not sports related. There's nothing worse for me than being stuck at a dinner party or something with some guy across the table who's a Yankee fan or a Red Sox fan or some super fan of sports not radio. 'What do you think about Joba Chamberlain (in a fake, sports fan voice)?' It's like, 'dude, what do you think about Joba Chamberlain? Because you don't care what I think. You want to just say it.' That sort of stuff, I'd rather poke out my eyes. I'm lucky that Matt's with me when it comes to that stuff."

Does he listen to other sports talk shows?

"Oh God, no. I can't listen to sport talk radio. No. I don't want to hear what anybody else says 'cause I might just take it (laughs)."

Working with 'Money' wasn't easy at first for Petros. He had to learn to work with a partner and make the show work despite their differing personalities.

"Matt's got a wife and three beautiful little kids. He's a very dedicated father. I have a lot of respect for him in that way with his family and stuff. It's been a nice example for me as I've been kind of growing up and maturing, getting married and thinking about starting a family."

TYPECAST

In 2005, the TV show *CSI: NY* was looking for a Greek sports talk radio host. Somehow they found a guy named Petros Papadakis who happened to be a sport talk radio host.

Petros remembers his acting debut as Rico Savalas.

"That was a long day man. That's a long ass day. I was only in one scene and then I did some radio stuff for them. Emilio Estevez was the director. I knew him from my dad's restaurant a little bit and he was a nice guy. It was fun. It was a long day. I had to take the day off work and my bosses were pissed, I remember. I think my line was, 'Sorry the guy's dead.' Something like that. It's like cue the smoke machine to make it look dark. They had a reel-to-reel in the fake radio studio they built in Studio City. I was like, 'Really? Reel-to-reel?' It was fun. Everybody was really nice. Most of the TV I do is live. The thing that struck me about it was just how tedious it was."

While Petros didn't win any awards from his performance he does get royalty checks totaling about $100 every year.

"Every once in a while I'll get a check for like 35 cents. Seriously, why did they write the check?"

PROS VS. JOES

For the first three seasons of the *Pros vs. Joes* reality show on Spike TV, Petros was the host. He didn't even know what it was all about when he auditioned.

"When I left there I thought it was the dumbest thing I ever heard of."

The show was about mostly former professional athletes competing against non-pros, or as the show title says, the "Joes."

He also told the producers that it probably wouldn't work for him since his workdays were booked with football.

Of course they called Petros and wanted to hire him.

Petros says, "I told them, 'You shoot on Saturday's. I have a game at Stanford.' They said, 'Well, we'll get you a private jet.' I was like, 'whoa, shit. Maybe they're for real. Maybe they are really going to do this.'"

It was a nighttime shoot at first in Carson, California, and then they took the show on the road in year three.

"It was fun," says Petros. "It was a great experience and I made some money. I wish I could still do it. I'd love to do another show like that."

Among the "pros" to participate were Jerry Rice, Bill Romanowski, Bo Jackson, Clyde Drexler, Herschel Walker, Rebecca Lobo, Dave Winfield, John Rocker, Dennis Rodman, and Jim McMahon.

Petros recalls a few interesting stories from *Pros vs. Joes*.

"John Rocker mooned me like 14 times. He was very well liked by everybody."

Roy Jones, Jr, was on the show, but Petros accidentally called him, several times, Roy Williams. The boxer's angry bodyguard confronted Petros. "I said, 'are you going to beat me up? What are you coming at me for?' That was pretty awkward. There's a safety named Roy Williams. What do you want from me, I'm a football analyst."

Then there was another incident involving a boxer, the late Arturo Gatti.

"We were shooting in Washington, D.C., and at 6 in the morning after we got done shooting he was in a full suit in the lobby of our hotel, which was in Crystal City which is all Pentagon military people. There was nothing going on in Crystal City and he was like, 'where we going? Let's go out!' And I said, 'what?' You're kidding me.' The guy literally just fought 15 rounds and we're in Crystal City and he put on a full suit and he's all gelled up and he tried to get me to go out with him. It just blew me away. This guy must be absolutely insane (laughs)."

For the record Petros went to bed and Gatti presumably went wherever the 6 a.m. hotspots are in Crystal City, Virginia.

Finally, hockey player Claude Lemieux was on the show. Petros remembers Lemieux, on his last night on the program, telling Petros about his upcoming one-hour flight home from Los Angeles to Phoenix.

"These idiots here. They book me to go home tomorrow first class. Idiots," Petros says imitating Lemieux's French accent. "Let me tell you. I change. I put in coach. That's $200 in my pocket. In MY pocket!"

SO MR. PAPADAKIS, WHERE DO YOU SEE YOURSELF ...

Read any number of self-help books or go listen to a motivational speaker and you will hear about goal setting. The importance of writing down your goals has been a topic that many great leaders have broached. Having a clear and concise mental picture of what you want to accomplish is important in the minds of many. Not in the peculiar mind of Petros Papadakis.

"I'm not trying to accomplish anything. People say, 'What's your goal?' I want to get up and leave when guys would say, 'Where do you see yourself in 10 years?' It's like, 'Where do you see your fucking self in 10 years dude?' I just want to keep my job. What are you talking about where do I see myself in 10 years? I want to keep working. Do you have a job for me? I'll do it. Shut up, where do I see myself in 10 years. What the hell is that? What if I asked you that? Stupid question. People say, 'What do you want to end up doing?' I'd like to call games and do a radio show every day that somebody listens to. I don't have any long-term goals. I just want to be able to make a living and have a family and that's it. I'm not that complex."

FACTOID

Former teammate and Heisman Trophy-winning USC quarterback Carson Palmer had his first date with his future wife at Papadakis Taverna. The waiter was Petros.

MUSIC

One of Petros' passions is music. He used to go to concerts a lot when growing up.

"I collect music and always had a big interest in music. I was always a little odd I guess in that way. I listened to dance hall reggae the whole time I was in high school while everybody else was listening to grunge rock or Pearl Jam."

The love of music is one of the common threads shared by Petros and his on-air partner, Matt Smith.

VIEWING HABITS

While he may not watch every sporting event there is to watch on the tube, Petros does have his favorite shows.

"I watch a lot of trash reality TV. I watch a lot of *Hawaii Five-O* reruns. I watch A LOT, and I mean A LOT of cartoons. I've been watching cartoons forever. I watch old cartoons. I don't like the *Flintstones* or the *Jetsons*. I watch new cartoons and old cartoons. I watch the *Wacky Races*, I watch Dastardly and Muttley, I watch the *Herculoids*, I watch *Thundarr the Barbarian*. I just watch a lot of cartoons."

He also reads comic books.

Perhaps one day there will be a cartoon or comic book featuring Petros. There have been worse ideas.

SURPRISE

The success that Petros has had post-USC football could not have been anticipated by anyone, least of all Petros.

"If you had told me when I was 21, when I was still at SC, that I would end up a national type of broadcaster and be fat and married to Dayna, living in a house on a cliff in San Pedro, I would have …well I don't know. It did work out pretty good (laughs). I'm happy. It's not something I envisioned or tried."

He knows he is cut from a different sports broadcasting cloth.

Petros adds, in a voice mocking a smooth-talking, deep-voiced announcer, " 'Welcome back!' I see these type of guys, these generic guys who went to Syracuse, they've wanted to do this their whole lives and it's their dream, so when you do this for a living and there's only a handful of us that have these shows and people always are e-mailing or calling, young people, saying, 'how do I get into this?' And, 'what do I do?' and this and that. Wow. I don't know. I just kind of backed into it (laughs). It seems like the harder you try in this sort of business the more generic you are."

If you are an aspiring broadcaster and want to follow in Petros' footsteps, it's simple. Become the captain of a major college football team, overcome a gruesome injury, give the media entertaining interviews, and wait by the phone for a broadcasting executive to call and give you a shot. Also, make sure not to write down any goals and don't worry about where you'll see yourself in 10 years. Actually, never mind. No matter how much anyone tries, it will be in vain. There will never be another Petros Papadakis.

Matt 'Money' Smith
"Money the Sports Guy"

Matt Smith is a common name. There are likely thousands of Matt Smiths roaming the globe. But add the 'Money' part and people know you are certainly talking about Matt 'Money' Smith, part of the blistering hot 'Petros and Money' show based in Los Angeles on KLAC and nationally at Fox Sports Radio.

THEY CALL HIM MONEY

If you are stuck with a nickname, 'Money' isn't a bad one to have. Better than many others. Certainly beats the nickname 'Lack of Money.'

The moniker came about from Matt's first radio job at KROQ, an alternative station in Los Angeles. He worked on the morning show 'Kevin and Bean' as a phone screener when he was a junior at Pepperdine University. The sports guy there was Jimmy Kimmel. Jimmy's cousin Sal was always around, too. They gave Matt the nickname 'Money,' although time has clouded the exact origin.

"It's hard to remember exactly why they gave it to me," Matt struggles to recall. "And any time I ask them they don't quite have the answer, but we think it's because Sal and I were always looking at gambling lines and betting games and things like that. So I think that's kind of the genesis of it. But I'm not 100 percent sure."

The nickname stuck and has been with Matt ever since.

"The first time I think they introduced me on the air they introduced me as 'Money.' I became the sports guy after Jimmy left and I just became 'Money the Sports Guy.'"

GAMBLIN' MAN

Looking over sports lines wasn't just an idle way for Matt to pass the time. He was no stranger to wagering on sports.

"Oh yeah. Absolutely. And that started back in high school," Matt says. "I had a guy that I went through in high school."

In 1990, the Pittsburgh Pirates were dominating the National League while the Chicago Cubs were having another difficult year. Matt remembers what happened.

"Pittsburgh was just crushing the NL and the Cubs were terrible. After probably three weeks of the season a friend of mine and I just kind of said, 'You know, I bet if we bet the Pirates everyday and bet against the Cubs every day we could probably come out ahead big time.' So that's what kind of got it rolling for me."

His parents never knew. He never got into any debt difficulty and that's probably because his system worked.

"That year we did well. We did real well that year. We were probably each up, I don't know, 600, 700 bucks. At that time it's a lot of money."

Of course in the world of wagering sometimes the ball doesn't always bounce the way it is expected to. Or in this case the puck.

Matt got a big time jolt back in 2002 when the Stanley Cup Finals featured the heavily favored Detroit Red Wings against the Carolina Hurricanes.

"A couple of us got together and loaded up on the Red Wings. You had to bet them heavy. I think you had to put something like five Gs down to win a grand. So we multiplied that a few times."

The Red Wings lost the first game in Detroit and Carolina put up a battle in Game 2.

"For those three days it was pretty stressful because Detroit was such an overwhelming favorite. It was two and a half days of 'Oh no. This could go terribly wrong.'"

The Wings ended up winning the Cup in five games.

"That was enough for me to go, 'Alright, done with that.' I would have been able to cover it but it would have been a big hit."

Following that scare, Matt scaled back on his gambling.

"Waaaaay back. Probably for the next three or four years all I did was professional football and it was no more than 500 bucks a week."

He doesn't gamble any more. When Matt started working for the Lakers he said to himself, " 'You know, I should probably just stop.' Not that they would care. Broadcasters do it all the time. But I figured it's not something I'm that attached to. So just in case it would cause a problem I better cut it loose."

Matt doesn't believe his gambling was ever a problem and that he always had it under control.

"I've always been able to manage addictive things. Whether it's alcohol, drugs, gambling, or whatever, I've been very good about moderation."

There was a genuine benefit to gambling on sports for Matt.

"It got me to study. When it's your money, you either make it or don't. You really are paying attention cause you're financially vested. It really did help me. That's when I really started getting into sports."

OLD COMISKEY

One early sports-related job that 16-year-old Matt held down for a summer was at the original Comiskey Park in Chicago, home of the White Sox.

He was a Coke vendor and it was a fun job for Matt—watching the games, that is, not selling the soda. Lugging the soda crate around was tiring.

"Selling the soda was kind of a pain but you'd be

done by the 6th or 7th inning and they'd let you go out to left field and sit. There was never anybody out there and you'd just watch baseball."

Many people wax poetic about the long ago demolished Comiskey Park, some remembering it as 'The Old Lady of the South Side.' Others get misty-eyed when recalling the grand old yard on 35th and Shields.

Matt's thoughts?

"A dump."

JIMMY KIMMEL

As mentioned earlier, Matt took over for Jimmy Kimmel as the sports guy at KROQ radio. Kimmel is now the host of his own late night show on ABC.

One can reasonably assume that Matt holds Kimmel in high regard since he calls him "The best guy ever." The two remain friends.

"I still reach out to him for advice," Matt says. "He still sends me links to stories, I send him links to stories that we think are interesting and can help one another. He's the guy that basically put me on this path. He always took the time. Any questions I had when I was just a dumb junior in college, he would talk to me. He planted the seed that was, 'You have to be different. You can't go on the air and give scoring updates and who scored the most points and this player's great and this player sucks. You gotta be different. Always remember that. Separate yourself so that you have a recognizable style. It doesn't have to be the same style I have but figure out what you enjoy and what you like.' And I've done that my whole career. Whether I'm doing play-by-play or the show or public speaking, whatever it might be, I've always tried to be different."

Matt says that Kimmel has been the biggest influence in his career.

"Without question."

Kimmel's success comes as no surprise to Matt.

"Knew it the moment I met him. Same with Adam Corolla. Both of them worked on that show. It took me all of two minute to realize as great as Kevin and Bean were, and they are very good at what they do, that Jimmy was just on a different level. Just his wit and his ability to create comedy at the snap of a finger."

Which brings us to one of Matt's favorite Jimmy Kimmel memories, the bacon pinned to the wall story.

Jimmy was eating a breakfast sandwich and didn't want the bacon. So he did what most people would do...he took a stick pin and stuck the bacon on the wall. Alright, he did something only Jimmy would do.

"He pulls out a sharpie," Matt says, "And writes, 'In one year from today' and he wrote the date, 'Jimmy Kimmel will eat this piece of bacon.' Wrote it on the wall (laughs). And no one touched it. It never came down. It stayed there for a year. One year later we forced him to eat the bacon on the air."

Dr. Drew was doing 'Love Line,' which was only local at that time on KROQ. He went on the air telling Jimmy that it was a bad idea to eat the bacon. But, Jimmy ate it anyway.

Matt adds, "I can still hear the crunch when he took the first bite. I can still remember his face and the pain that he was in and just how disturbed he was and how upset he was for the rest of the day and concerned for his own well-being. I remember him saying, 'It tastes like nothing,' which really scared him. 'Why does it taste like nothing?'"

EXPERIENCES

Matt has experienced and experimented with many things. It was one of the reasons why he ended up on the West Coast.

"I was always one to try everything. It's just kind of my nature. I guess it's probably one of the reasons why I just decided to leave Chicago and go to California with nobody. None of my friends. They all kind of stayed in the Big 10 or went to the Ivy League. I just said, 'Screw it. I'm going to California and I'm going to go to a school that's as much California as I could find' and that was Pepperdine 'cause it was on the beach. And I think that was just kind of my nature when it came to anything else. Food? I'll eat anything, I don't care. Girls. Back then, whatever, didn't matter. Asian, black, white, Mexican. Didn't bother me. I was fine. I was open to everything. I wanted to experience everything and that was the case with alcohol and drugs, I guess, as well. I started drinking when I was real young. Smoking when I was real young. Probably 13, 14. Drugs came in right around, I don't know, probably 15? Marijuana and psychedelics really was all it was. I never touched cocaine. I guess that was just me recognizing my limitations."

Matt was a big fan of the Grateful Dead and that is how he was introduced to acid.

"The first couple of shows I went to I really enjoyed. And then someone suggested that if you really want to enjoy them take some acid or some shrooms or something. And that led to me just doing it when I went to Grateful Dead shows and that was really it. The first time I caught myself doing it outside of that realm, I said, 'OK, no more of that. That's not cool.' And then pot I never enjoyed. Just never did anything for me. So that was very limited."

These days, Matt simply has a few glasses of wine and drinks on a limited basis. The drugs are no longer part of his life.

"Yeah, that was fine but I'm over it."

THE FAMILY AND THE CUBBIES

Born in East Chicago, Indiana, and growing up in Chicago, Matt's early memories of his dad weren't pleasant. His dad was an alcoholic and wasn't fun to be around, though his father has been sober since Matt was 10.

With his mom and dad working, Matt's maternal grandmother spent a lot of time rearing him.

"That's how I got into the Cubs. She was always at home when I got home from school, and the Cubs always had that 2:20 start, so I'd just sit down with her and we'd watch Cubs games together. The Cubs were kind of my first love when I was a little kid. I remember doing that with my grandma."

Both his parents, Ralph and Antoinette, are still alive.

"We get along great. Very close family. Two brothers. My older brother is a lawyer back in the Chicago area and works for the Indiana Democratic Party. My younger brother is an IT guy based out of Chicago."

INDEPENDENCE

As a kid Matt got along just fine. He considered himself to be independent in his youth. He would get up before the rest of the family, fix himself breakfast, and head out on his bike. He'd return for lunch, then disappear again on his bike before returning home for dinner.

"I was always out. That carried all the way through until I left for college. In high school I was never home. I was always sleeping on somebody's floor or couch. I was always gone."

He did make sure his parents always knew where he was.

"I was always good about that. I credit them for that. They just said, 'Hey look, call us, let us know where you're at all the time and you can go. Enjoy yourself.' They were always overprotective of my older brother and that kind of backfired on them a little bit, so they tried the complete opposite approach with me. And it seemed to work."

It also helped that Matt was a good student.

"Probably like a high-B average. I think it's one of my bigger regrets that I didn't take it more seriously. Had I paid a little bit more attention, even just a little bit more attention, I probably could have been a straight A student. I was just more interested in other things."

He did well enough at Morgan Park Academy, a small private school in Chicago with a graduating class of around 45 kids, to allow him to go to Pepperdine University.

THE ATHLETE

It is no secret that the older some guys get the better they believe they were as athletes when they were young.

In Matt's case, no one has to look up his athletic achievements. He is quick and to the point when asked what kind of athlete he was.

"Mediocre. Average. I started at shortstop my sophomore, junior, senior year of high school. I was a starting forward on our soccer team. I was on the basketball team one year. I played all of maybe one minute of one game. My older brother was a really good athlete. I was average, maybe a little bit better than average. But by no means was I a great athlete."

PEPPERDINE

All Matt knew about Pepperdine is that it was in Malibu and on the water. Good enough for him. After a visit with his mother he made his choice.

"Pepperdine just stuck in my head. I was like, 'Wow. Yeah I'd like to go here. This would be great.' And that's really all I knew."

Attending school at Pepperdine was an enjoyable experience for Matt although he was surprised by some things.

"You'd think a school on the water, you'd wake up and go surfing every morning and then party every night. It definitely is not like that. It's a very religious school. That's a big part of the curriculum and I think a pretty big part of the student body as well."

As a college student, he spent a semester in Italy. He lived in Florence and everything made an impression.

"Unbelievable. Something I would recommend everybody do. It was probably the best experience of my life. It was just so different. Being in a foreign country on your own. Given the freedom to travel four days of every week. Just hopping on a train, having a couple of drinks, falling asleep and waking up the next morning in Germany. Or in Amsterdam. Or in France. Or in Switzerland. Or in Austria. We covered all of Western Europe and a little bit Eastern Czech. We went to Prague. Greece. It was just amazing. You realize what history is and I love history."

Another benefit of his college days at Pepperdine? It was where he met his wife, Kerie. They have three young daughters.

THE MUSIC BIZ AND KROQ

Matt initially considered following in his big brother's footsteps and become a lawyer.

But he was sidetracked by two things.

His brother told him, "Law school sucks."

The other thing was he found he enjoyed working at the Pepperdine radio station. He decided to try and get a job in music after college, and ended up getting an internship in the record business.

"I love music. I'm a big music guy. I worked in admissions at Pepperdine and a girl that I worked with, her boyfriend had a job at Polygram, the record company. He said, 'Hey, if you really like music I could probably help you out and get you a job at a record company.' That followed me putting applications in for a job at local radio stations, which went unanswered."

He started interning at Polygram. And a few months

after that an opportunity emerged. His boss at Polygram alerted him to a job at KROQ, knowing it would be a great opportunity for Matt.

"There was some luck involved. I was very fortuitous. Things worked out. I was in the right place at the right time, got the right internship that hooked me up with the right person that told me to apply for this right job, and then I had my foot in the door. One thing I've always done, is once I get my foot in the door I try to make the most of the situation. I think that's what I did in both instances."

It was a case of making and leaving a good impression.

"More than anything else, I work very hard."

PRESIDENT MONEY SMITH?

One thing you can't accuse Matt 'Money' Smith of is lacking ambition. His initial career goal was to become a politician after becoming a lawyer.

He wasn't looking to becoming a small town mayor or councilman. Nope, not Matt. He wanted to take it to the White House.

Did he really want to become the President of the United States?

"Yes. Yes, but those little drug incidents popped into my head and I realized that probably wouldn't happen," he laughs.

Not to mention his foray into the wonderful world of gambling! Not sure if that would have helped the Money Smith campaign.

PETROS

When Matt was at KROQ, the University of Southern California football program went on a run that made them the most popular team in Los Angeles. He recalls one former USC player, Petros Papadakis, as a guy who produced pieces on Fox Sports West.

"At KROQ, when the SC thing started to go, we would talk to reporters but we were different as a morning show and these guys were a little too technical," Matt recalls. "I said, 'We ought to call this guy. He played at SC, he was a captain, he's pretty funny, and I think it would be a better way for us to do the SC stuff in a segment then by talking to a play-by-play guy or a beat reporter for our purposes.'"

The decision to get Petros turned out great for the morning show and for Papadakis. The two hit it off immediately with a natural chemistry right from the start.

Did Matt think, in the beginning, that they would go on to host a hugely popular sports talk show?

"Yes and no. No because I was also the music director at KROQ at the time. When I first met him I was still in the music business. I worked for a record label for almost 10 years. So I was still doing that and that was my primary career. I did the "Kevin and Bean" stuff almost as a favor. I had already had a career when I graduated college. I was working for DreamWorks. When Jimmy left they hired someone else to replace him and he was terrible. So they fired him after like eight months and they said, 'Hey can you help us out?'"

With football season on the horizon, they needed Matt to help out on Mondays and Fridays. He agreed.

"That became an everyday thing. Before I went into work I would stop by there, do the sports, then go to my day job. Then that turned into a full-time job along with being music director at KROQ. But then, when I left KROQ to do the Lakers radio and sports talk then most definitely he was the guy that I said ultimately that would be great, it would be a great partnership to work with him."

The tandem began as 'Petros and Money' in January of 2007 and clicked almost immediately.

"It took us about maybe two, three weeks to get

comfortable and then we were rolling."

The show got great reviews and surged in popularity from the get go. They are now on over 200 affiliates across the country with no end to their success in sight. It's exactly how Matt envisioned it, right?

"Never, never imagined it. Never had any aspirations to do a national show. Cause LA is such a huge market and you can make a heck of a living just by winning in LA. That's just what our vision was—win in LA."

THE SHOW

Not much has changed with the 'Petros and Money' show since they've gone national, other than the content.

"Just what we cover," says Matt. "As opposed to doing Lakers, Dodgers, Kings, Ducks, USC, UCLA, and being very local with our non-sports-related stories, we're just a little bit more general. And the teams that are involved now are what the bigger stories of the day are."

The show is local for the 3 o'clock hour only and then they get a national audience for the next three hours.

Does Matt have a preference, local or national?

"Local for sure. Love it. The references are better. People really love that part of it. It's just more comfortable. It's where you live. Don't get me wrong, I enjoy the national show, it's great."

What is the main reason that 'Petros and Money' has taken off?

"I think because we're so different," Matt surmises. "I think when you listen to some sports shows and you hear them try to fit in non-sports content, you can feel it is being forced. I think that's something that just comes very naturally for us."

You never know what you'll hear on "Petros and Money." Matt guesses that 50 percent will be sports and the other 50 percent could be politics, pop culture, or current events.

The die-hard sports fans will let the pair know they aren't happy with the amount of non-sports they talk about. This is especially true when a new station comes aboard. It takes time to get a sense of the program.

"Especially when we first go on the air," Matt explains. "Whenever we pick up a new affiliate it does not go over well at the beginning. We both regularly get ripped in our e-mail. Every day."

Does it bother Matt?

"No. I mean, there are some things that will but for the most part it comes with the territory. You want people to have some sort of opinion. If they don't, they're apathetic and you're white noise."

ON PETROS

"He's a brilliant guy," Matt says of his gregarious co-host. "I think people may think he's just this bombastic, overwhelming, in-your-face, former football player meathead. And that's so not the case. He's a very complicated, complex person. His ability to recall lyrics or verses or passages is remarkable. He's a very smart guy."

Not too many 'former football player meatheads' drop English literature or bible references on a sports talk show as Petros does.

FAVORITE INTERVIEW

"Probably Didier Drogba," Matt says immediately. "Just cause I love soccer and he's such a giant superstar on the international stage. And we got him really at the peak of his career when Chelsea was at the top of the Premier League. Just to be able to talk to him about the Ivory Coast and his role in stopping the civil war in his country. It was very compelling. It was really cool."

OTHER INTERESTS

Besides the show, Matt puts his voice to work doing play-by-play of pro football, college basketball, as well as voiceover work for NFL Films.

He hopes to continue to do play-by-play, which started with him filling in for Spero Dedes on Lakers games. "Love it. Absolutely love it," Matt says. "Would love to do it forever." He also works for Compass Media announcing basketball and football.

Matt also loves music, politics, international relations, reading, and, of course, with a nickname like 'Money' he has a great interest in finance.

"I just consume. I like to consume a lot."

On his 35-mile commute to work he'll listen to educational CDs, NPR, and podcasts of other programs. One thing he doesn't consume is sports talk shows. Other than his own show, he doesn't listen to sport talk.

"I don't know why. I guess I'm just not interested. I mean I do from time to time. If I'm just kind of popping out to take the kids to school, on my way back home after I drop them off I've only got a five minute drive, then I'll pop it on."

Sid Rosenberg going for eight seconds

Sid Rosenberg with some friends

Sid Rosenberg with Brett Favre's friend, Jenn Sterger

Sid Rosenberg with former Miami Dolphin O.J. McDuffie

Tony Bruno with his dad, Orlando, and sister, Marie

Tony Bruno, right/middle, at high school dinner

Tony Bruno at WFIL in 1970

Tony Bruno at WCAU

Scott Ferrall throwing punches with Bernard Hopkins

Scott Ferrall picking a fight with Lennox Lewis

Scott Ferrall with former Globtrotters legend Meadowlark Lemon

Scott Ferrall hanging out with skateboarder Tony Hawk

Colin Cowherd in action

A very young Colin Cowherd

Colin Cowherd hosting his ESPN show

Arnie Spanier and son, Shea

Arnie Spanier at his high school prom

Arnie Spanier with Mavericks owner Mark Cuban and fellow talker Dave Smith

Arnie, the man!

Doug, left, and Ryan Stewart
a.k.a.—2 Live Stews

Ryan, left, and Doug when they were kids

Doug, left, working on some moves with Ryan

Brenda Stewart with her sons, Ryan, left, and Doug

Doug, having fun at a birthday party, behind a stunned Ryan

Ryan Stewart, left, isn't buying what Doug, was selling that day

Ralph Stewart with Doug, left, and Ryan

Greg "Greggo" Williams

Greg "Greggo" Williams

Petros Papadakis ready for vacation

Petros Papadakis at Palos Verdes Peninsula High School

Petros and his father, John Papadakis

Petros Papadakis playing Pop Warner football

Petros Papadakis, left, at USC with Traveler, the Trojan horse

Dan Sileo with NHL legend Bobby Orr

Dan Sileo heading to his next event

Dan Sileo while playing for U. of Miami

Dan Sileo with Red Wings great Steve Yzerman

Mitch Levy firing up the crowd

Mitch Levy as a ten-year-old little leaguer

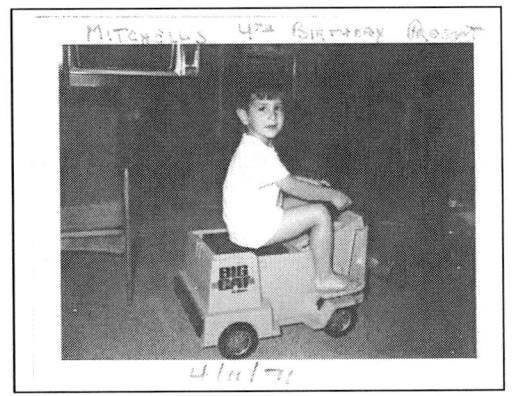

Mitch Levy taking a ride, on his present,
for his fourth birthday

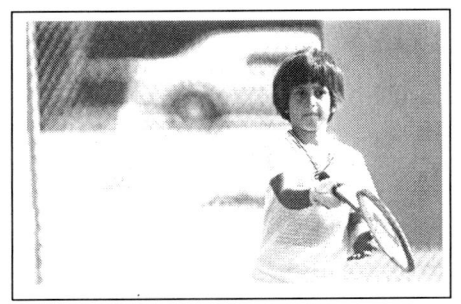

Mitch Levy hitting the courts as a kid

Howard Eskin, "The King of Bling"

Wayne Gretzky, left, with Howard Eskin and son

A beardless Howard Eskin, middle, age four

Allen Iverson posing with Howard Eskin

Kiefer Sutherland hanging out at a Flyers game with Howard Eskin

Kevin Wheeler, middle, at winter baseball caravan

Kevin Wheeler, left, relaxing with his family

The studious Kevin Wheeler on a high school road trip

Kevin Wheeler playing baseball while at the U. of Miami

Kevin Wheeler behind the plate while playing for the U. of Miami Hurricanes

Jason Smith with wife, Pam, and daughter, Zoe

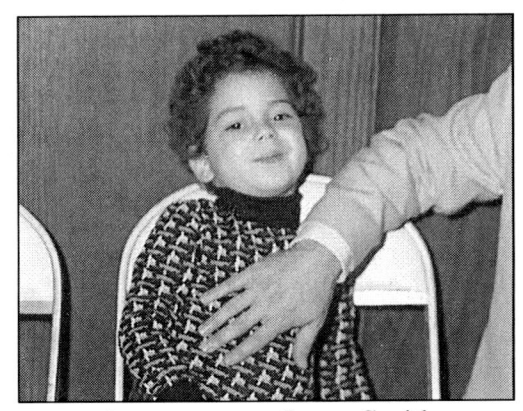

A very young Jason Smith

Jason Smith along with his dad, Walter, and Zoe

Jason and Pam Smith with Tom Cruise

Jason Smith with his parents, Gloria and Walter

Scott Van Pelt
"The Talking Terp"

Scott Van Pelt has hosted the aptly named 'Scott Van Pelt Show' on ESPN radio since July 2009. He anchors SportsCenter (which makes for some very long days and nights), and he's a regular host of ESPN's coverage of major golf tournaments.

Scott has put his degree in radio and television from the University of Maryland to good use thanks to some unique fortune on his journey.

FUNGO

We've all seen the kids who come home dirty after playing all day, no matter what the game or sport was. Scott was one of those active youngsters.

"Like a lot of kids, I grew up playing everything. As I grew older it was pretty obvious to me that I would get killed if I played football because I was 6'4" and weighed 170 in high school, so my nickname was 'Fungo.' Baseball and basketball were sports I was good at, but not great."

Growing up in the Washington, D.C., area, Scott's dad took him to Maryland football and basketball games as well as Redskins, Orioles, Capitals, and Bullets games.

"Sports were just a passion from an early age."

A FAMILY AFFAIR

It wasn't only his father who handed down a love of sports to Scott. It seems everybody had a hand in shaping his passion.

"My mom is a huge sports fan. My father was…he passed away when I was in college. My grandfather was a great sports fan. He was obsessed with the Yankees because he grew up in the city. He became a huge Syracuse fan (Syracuse being where he went to school) where my mom and my aunt went to school. He was also a Redskins fan. So really, my entire family [were] and [are] huge sports fans. It wasn't any one person in particular but certainly my father and I shared many, many days and nights together at Maryland games. If I'm honest with myself, that passion for Maryland that remains has a lot to do with that link to my dad that's been gone for far, far too long. It's a reminder of something we shared. The love for Maryland, he's 100 percent responsible for, but the love of sports is completely a family affair."

PLAYING

Despite anchoring SportsCenter and holding down his high profile radio show, Scott didn't envision that this is how his career would pan out. He didn't have those dreams when he was preoccupied with playing sports.

"I wasn't the kind of kid that sat around with a microphone, or a soda can pretending to be a microphone, doing play-by-play. That wasn't my thing. I was much more interested in playing them. I didn't necessarily think that I would spend my life talking about them (sports) but somewhere along the way it becomes pretty obvious that you're not going to make your profession doing this. The idea that I'm now talking about them will never stop being remarkable to me that this is what I do for a living. Never."

SCOTT TALKS TOO MUCH

Scott admits that there were times in school when he was a handful. Nothing too severe other than being a chatterbox.

"I think every teacher in seventh grade wanted to talk to my mom except for the gym teacher. I talked too much in class. That was just my thing. I enjoyed cutting up, I enjoyed making kids laugh, I was always pretty bright so the class maybe bored me a little bit, so I just did what I enjoyed which was being a clown. To this day I can quote my eighth grade math teacher, Mrs. Jackson. She used to say, 'Scott Van Pelt, why must you vex Ms. Jackson so?' She had to tolerate me. I was a pain in the ass is what it boils down to. I was just a class clown. I don't know if I was doing it for attention or if I was bored or what, but I was problematic definitely in school."

GRADES

They won't be erecting any monuments to Scott Van Pelt at Sherwood High School in Sandy Spring, Maryland, anytime soon. Not academic monuments anyway.

"I was a horrendous student all throughout. The ability to think and talk on my feet afforded me the ability to talk my way out of spots, I suppose. I was a lousy student. My average might have been around a B in high school, but my SATs were pretty good so I'm sure to any school that saw them, it was like, 'OK, here's a kid that's actually pretty bright but he's probably pretty lazy.' That's 100 percent accurate."

Some people might think that a B average isn't too bad at all. Some people reading this right now might be saying, "I wish I was that horrendous a student."

At the University of Maryland, Scott's grade point average was a little better than a 2.0. However, there were some extenuating circumstances. First of all, he liked to have fun. Sitting in a library on a Friday night and studying wasn't his idea of a good time. He also had two people close to him pass away.

"Early on I did alright. I'm not going to make excuses 'cause I enjoyed having fun and I was good at that. But my father passed away and my stepfather passed away within a three-month span, and you go from being 21 and having two dads to having none. I don't know, to this day, what toll that took and what kind of wreckage you have to navigate, and I took some time off in the middle there. But look, I was a lousy student when my dad was still alive."

HOOPS

A pretty decent basketball player in high school, Scott, who eventually grew to 6'6", had offers to some small colleges.

The Catholic University coach, the late Jack Bruen, tried to get Scott to play for him. Scott would be able to continue classes at Maryland.

They don't give out athletic scholarships at Catholic, so Scott told Bruen, " 'Coach, why would I pay 20 grand a year to go to Catholic and take classes at Maryland so I can play basketball for you, when I can just go to Maryland for about a tenth of the cost?' And he didn't have a compelling answer for that."

Bruen, who was teammates with Lew Alcindor in high school, eventually moved on to coach at Colgate University where he took the team to the NCAA Tournament. He was able to recruit Adonal Foyle to a small school in Hamilton, New York, but not Scott Van Pelt to Catholic.

BOARD MEMBER

There are some ironies that are just too juicy to pass up. For Scott, it's a story that he relishes.

"When I was in school at Maryland, I couldn't get into the journalism school and now I'm on the board. I enjoy telling that story. I tell kids it's proof that you literally are bound only by what you're willing to believe is possible. I always tell them that I learned more from the people I met than the classes that I went to. But then I would always be honest and say that I didn't spend a ton of time going to classes I was supposed to, because it wasn't nearly as interesting to me as these people that I met along the way. Finding out how much we all shared in common and that our lives were so much more similar than they were different."

Scott refers to two of his best friends. One is Puerto Rican from New Jersey, the other is a Chinese-Jamaican from Miami.

"THE POWERBALL TICKET OF ALL TIME"

Scott had no visions or goals of becoming a big-time radio and TV personality. He's amazed and appreciative of how he landed at ESPN.

"I don't know how much you know about how I got here, but it's the Powerball ticket of all time. I got an internship at Channel 5 in Washington, D.C., where I met a couple of guys who are still very close friends. The guy I met, who was the producer there, ultimately left to go to New York where he worked for HBO and MSG. Several years passed in between this internship and him going down to Florida to be one of the guys behind the scenes with the Golf Channel. I was not doing anything of grave consequence in Washington, D.C. I was working for a mortgage company. I was going to work for this company that sold life insurance and annuities and things of that nature for which I would have been woefully ill-equipped. He got in contact with me and said, 'look, this Golf Channel thing's starting up, you should come down here and give this a shot and work in production and who knows, you'll never know what will become of it.' So I went down there.

"I'd never been on television. And the story goes that there was going to be a show, 'Golf Talk Live.' And the host had never really been a host either so they needed to do some dry runs, and I sat in, in the role of Arnold Palmer who was to be the first interview. And in the control room the muckety-mucks from HBO are watching this host of theirs interview this idiot who's pretending to be Arnold Palmer and apparently at some point one of the honcho guys says, 'who is this guy?' And someone says, 'What do you mean, that's Peter Kessler, he's the host.' 'No, I mean this idiot who thinks he's fucking Arnold Palmer.' And I apparently did a decent enough job ad-libbing and being a bit of a ham that they thought maybe this guy has something. And they let me go out and do some reports because at the time the show was being seen in like 10,000 homes. So they could let me go out and try to figure out if I could be on TV or not. No one was watching."

They must have liked what they had seen because they expanded Scott's role. They also sent him to be a reporter at the 1995 NCAA Championship, the first event Scott ever covered.

TIGER

At the 1995 NCAA Championship, Scott met Tiger Woods. The two struck up a professional relationship that grew, even as Woods was moving up in the golf world.

"He gave me access that he didn't give other people and ultimately, after he won The Masters, he sat down and we did an interview that was a half-hour long special. He didn't grant anybody that kind of access but he did for me. And it got me noticed."

From never being on the air to interviewing Woods six months later was a major career boost for Scott.

"In the year 2000, Tiger Woods is having the greatest year in the history of golf. Jimmy Roberts, who covers golf for ESPN, leaves to go to NBC. ESPN's looking for a guy that has some kind of a working relationship with Tiger Woods and there I am. And I come to ESPN and it's been 11 years later. Now, none of what I just described is possible. I mean, none of that can happen. And all of it did."

If not for Tiger Woods, who knows what would have been of Scott Van Pelt, but he probably wouldn't be on ESPN right now.

"He would absolutely tell you that and I would agree. I mean, I'm 26, 27 years old and I'm working for a mortgage company. There's no way you could have given me an envelope and said, 'inside this is your future.' If I would have read it I would have just laughed."

REPORTING FROM ORLANDO

Scott was based out of Orlando, Florida, when ESPN hired him. He covered the Magic and the Tampa Bay Buccaneers. Whatever was going on in that region, Scott was there.

"When Dale Earnhardt died at Daytona, that was actually the first story I did that wasn't golf related. That was something of an epiphany for me because I was hired as this golf reporter and my phone rang and it was a news editor from ESPN. They said, 'Scott, we think that Dale Earnhardt may have died.' And I remember sitting there silently and saying, 'that's a bummer. How can I help you?' It didn't dawn on me that I'm the reporter that's an hour away from Daytona. This is my story. And literally that's a month into my hire at ESPN. And I'm driving up the road to file reports from there, so I hadn't done that. But that was what I had been hired to do, to be primarily a golf reporter but anything that was in the area."

That summer, ESPN called to see if Scott wanted to go to Bristol, Connecticut, to anchor a few SportsCenter shows. He had some anchoring experience with the Golf Channel.

"I said, 'sure, I'll do that.' But I didn't think it would ever turn into them asking me to be a host."

He actually did his first SportsCenter at the World Match Play Championship in Australia. Scott recalls watching the end of a basketball game knowing that as soon as it ended he was going on the air.

He had a producer speaking to him in his earpiece while he looked at the monitor in the desk scrolling the open to SportsCenter.

"You see this animation roll and it says 'this is a presentation of ESPN the worldwide leader in sports.' And in that moment, you have this realization that, 'holy shit, I'm about to be on ESPN.' That's the only way to describe it. If you know what I really thought, that's what I thought."

While Scott wasn't nervous, he knew his family was watching. He says, "It's an overwhelming moment because I didn't ever set out to climb Mount Everest, that was not my goal. Yet here I was at base camp so to speak. It was very, very powerful. And I don't think I've had a moment since then that felt quite like that. That one moment when you take a deep breath and you close your eyes and it's like, 'here we go.'" Scott adds, he had no reason to be nervous on his first SportsCenter, claiming, 'what's the worst thing that can happen? People will say you suck.'

While he thinks he would be mortified if he looked now at that first SportsCenter, he admits it was all a blur.

"The mechanics of doing television are essentially the same. There's a camera, there's something in your ear, you're doing highlights, you're talking to your analyst. It wasn't like I was suddenly speaking Portuguese and trying to make a bundt cake. There was nothing outside of my comfort zone. I honestly couldn't tell you how I did other than they let me do the next one."

RADIO

There is no doubt that Scott loves to anchor SportsCenter. He especially enjoys the immediacy of coming on the air after a big game or event.

"It's the show of American record on sports, period."

When he began working on the radio side at ESPN as well, the veteran TV broadcaster thought to himself, "how hard can it be?"

Although radio was foreign to Scott, he thought it would be easier than television.

He thought wrong.

"I realized, after doing radio for one day, that I was overmatched. Radio immediately struck me as something much more difficult to do than I thought it was. It's challenging."

One thing that has helped Scott's radio popularity is that he won't compromise his stance on an issue, even if it is an unpopular position.

"I think guys say stuff they don't believe just to piss people off. I'm never going to do that."

The best compliment Scott has received in radio came from a forwarded e-mail from a friend of a friend.

"He said, 'I really like listening to Van Pelt because I know that whatever he says, whether I agree or I don't, I know that he believes it.' I won't take a stance just because I think it will be a good radio topic. I can't be disingenuous. For what? So that I can rile up people over something I don't honestly think? If you're mad over something I really believe, fine. I recognize that people that are truly the most successful, I think, are the people that can get their devotees to listen and to get the people who hate them to listen just so they can get pissed off. I'm not trying to get everybody to love me, but I cannot do or say something that I completely disagree with just because it might make for a better topic."

ROUGH WEEK

In a span of one week on SportsCenter, Scott was phone pranked by a follower of the Howard Stern show claiming to be Eagles running back Brian Westbrook. Scott was also sick as a dog one evening and nearly passed out reading a story. He let an F-bomb slip when going to break. Hey, things happen, but Scott lets them roll off his back.

He uses a balance beam analogy. On the ground, people can easily navigate a balance beam. When it gets in the air, it gets a little dicey.

"Initially TV feels like this balance beam where you're like, 'oh God, I'm very nervous, I don't want to make a misstep here.' Once you realize that in TV, the balance beam is on the floor and if you fall off it and someone who's not Brian Westbrook says something about Howard Stern, you just laugh it off and say 'hi to YouTube.' And if you say 'fuck, going to break' and you think, 'that was bad,' what can you do? If you seize up and freeze up and think 'oh my word, this is the worst thing that's ever happened,' then you're done. And it's just television. Now, I would endeavor not to talk to Howard Stern crank callers and cuss on TV moving forward. I don't ever wish to do it again, I've done it. But the point is that in our medium if you take yourself seriously, then I'm not taking you seriously, I'm just not. I take what I do seriously but I don't take myself seriously. How could I?"

TAKE A SEAT, SCOTT

In 2009 ESPN Radio suspended Scott for a day for remarks he made about Baseball Commissioner Bud Selig, who happened to be listening that day to his show. Great timing on that one.

Scott said that he nearly choked on his own vomit when he learned of Selig's lofty $18.5 million per year salary.

He also compared Selig to a pimp.

"I don't know that anyone could ever grasp how surreal it is to be on the phone with Bud Selig trying to explain to him that a reference about a pimp cup is actually quite a compliment. What I was describing in using that particular word is, in urban language or street language or the way the kids speak, is actually if somebody's a pimp that means they're in charge. But how do you explain that to Bud Selig and expect him to understand it? By way of apologizing, I wanted him to understand that I was being strictly satirical. But as I look back at that, these are comments that are personal and there's a fine line to walk when you own your words. I have to try to be aware of it every day because you talk for three hours and you could slip up and say anything."

In his brief apology, Selig was very gracious to Scott. The rest of the half-hour conversation was spent talking baseball.

"The coolest thing that came out of that is I had a half-hour conversation with Bud Selig, and we spent literally 2 minutes with me apologizing and 25 minutes talking about how much I hated his Milwaukee Brewers for what they did to my Baltimore Orioles, and how I was at this doubleheader in 1983 with the American League East pennant hanging in the balance, and it was just great talk. But that was actually something really, really kind of sweet that came out of a situation that was far from my finest moment."

TIGER PART II

When Tiger Woods ran into marital trouble late in 2009, people were shocked and titillated. Scott saw it a bit differently.

"Well, I didn't know that he was doing what he was doing. And knowing Elin, which I do, and knowing him and having seen their interactions as people and having spent some time around them socially, it was just sad more than anything, that it dissolved. He'd be the first to tell you that he doesn't deserve sympathy because it was his mistakes that led to this. I will say this about Tiger, and I've known him a long time, I don't believe that he was very self-aware, even in the early days of his stardom, I don't think that he grasped the enormity of who he was. Because he lived the life of a prodigy growing up, like a lot of prodigies, I think he was fairly sheltered from the way other kids lived. And so, as he became self-aware and realized the scope of his star and what it would afford him, unfortunately it led to him making some really bad choices. All I can think of is the Chris Rock line that, 'a man is only as faithful as his options.' And I guess for Tiger the options became too many."

Scott added he's never shocked when a man makes such a mistake since so many have before.

Even though he reached out to Tiger unsuccessfully during this period in the golfer's life, he doesn't consider himself a close friend.

"I think we're professionally friendly people. To suggest that we're friends, I would never suggest that. I think that there's just a line I have to respect and so does he. But I would say that among people in our business, I know that I was as professionally as close as you could be, and I didn't hear from him and I didn't expect to."

Scott has been asked to write a book about Tiger Woods. He declined.

"My memories are not for sale."

FAMILY MAN

Scott isn't a family man at this time.

"Not yet but I'm hoping to be soon. It's going to be late in life for me. I know I'm going to be the old guy at little league games where people are going to say, 'hey, is that your grandpa?' My son's gonna have to put his head down and kick at the dirt and go, 'no, it's my dad.'"

NEXT SONG

Like many sports talk show hosts, Scott rarely listens to sports talk radio. He prefers to formulate his own opinions.

On the drive to work, Scott listens to music on his iPod.

"I put it on shuffle and whatever comes up comes up. Although, are you like me? Have you bought thousands of dollars' worth of songs, which when you spent that $1.29 you thought, 'I really like this song,' but when it comes up on iPod Shuffle you go next song? I spend most of my drive hitting 'next song.'"

He's a fan of rap music, which might surprise some people.

"I'm a middle-aged white guy. There are times you can get accused of trying to be this or trying to be that. I'm just me. Growing up in the D.C. area and playing a lot of basketball, I spent a lot of time being one of the only white dudes in the gym, and so my musical tastes I come by honestly. If I'm supposed to apologize for that I don't know why or to whom."

AWAY FROM THE JOB

When not working, what does Scott like to do? Read poetry? Art gallery excursions? Hike the Catskill mountains? Model train enthusiast? Raise cattle? What does he do?

"It's so sad. I watch sports, man. I'm just consumed by what they represent. The idea of who's going to win. I don't watch reality TV, I watch sports because every single day it's reality TV. It's unscripted. Something is going to happen that can't possibly happen."

He enjoys traveling, which he does frequently with ESPN.

"The world's a big, big place and I've been remarkably fortunate to see a lot of it."

THE FUTURE

Scott Van Pelt feels that he's been extremely fortunate and blessed to have ended up where he has. The man without a plan says he will trust his judgment on whatever possibilities are out there in the future.

"In the interim, I'm just aware of how fortunate I am and I'm thankful for what I get to do. And I trust myself and I know who I am. If there's something that presents itself then I'll know when I see it."

Dan Sileo
"Gridiron to Radio"

During the mid-1980s, Dan Sileo was an honorable mention All-American defensive lineman at the University of Miami. He played for the abrasive, despised, and showboating Hurricanes during Jimmy Johnson's reign of terror. That experience honed his skills for a career in broadcasting.

After a brief stint in the NFL with the Buccaneers in 1987, Dan eventually became a member of the media, the same media he didn't like so much as a player.

'The Dan Sileo Show' is broadcast each morning on WDAE Radio in Tampa, Florida, and no subject is off limits. Aptly the station's moniker is The Sports Animal.

SPORTS

Growing up in Stamford, Connecticut, Dan was raised by his Sicilian grandparents. His father left the family and Dan didn't get along with his mom. Dan was exposed to sports at an early age.

"I had the greatest childhood growing up with my grandparents. They were great to me. I enjoyed being around them. With their passing, the only thing that's gone is the tears. I miss them every day."

His uncle was the late pro-football Hall of Famer Andy Robustelli. Dan grew up playing with Jackie Robinson's kids. Dan's dad played golf with Jackie and Dan would go along for the ride in the golf cart.

"I also played Wiffle ball with Jackie. Jackie's numbers were pretty pedestrian if you put them next to a lot of people's numbers. As a kid you don't know the numbers, you don't know the history of the guy and the impact of the guy. I remember talking to him about what it was like to be a pro-baseball player and he said, 'hard work.'"

Former Giants assistant coaches Vince Lombardi and Tom Landry were also visitors to Stamford to see Robustelli.

"I've been in sports my whole life. Covering it, playing it, now being a sports talk radio guy for 17 years."

Dan played high school football at Stamford Catholic.

"Had to wear a tie every day. I went to Catholic schools almost all my life."

As a freshman, Dan was on a state championship team in 1978. It was his first year playing organized football. He was All-City and All-Conference three times.

"I had 28 sacks my junior year and by the time I left there I was the all-time state leader in sacks in Connecticut, of which Dwight Freeney's since broken."

Dan also lined up across the line of scrimmage from a guy who turned out to be pretty good quarterback

"I played high school football against Steve Young many times. He was at Greenwich. He was impossible to hit on the football field. I used to get flagged because I'd hit him late. I played baseball against him too. He was a tremendous, tremendous athlete. He struck me out. He was really a great baseball player."

Dan was a wrestler and played lacrosse, which he feels helped him along the line of scrimmage and taught him discipline. But he loved playing his favorite sport, baseball.

"I was a great baseball player. Bobby Valentine, when he was a third base coach with the Mets, used to come watch me play all the time. I was quite good at it. I was playing in the Cape Cod League. I should have stuck with it. I didn't really realize how good a baseball player I was, but I was a pretty good backstop."

STRONGMAN

Growing up, Dan was not only a big kid but the strongest one.

"I was always the strongest guy in the room. Every single place I was ever at. High school, junior high school."

Dan claims he was the strongest guy on the team at Maryland as a freshman and "the strongest player in the history of Miami."

We're not talking about a kicker or scrawny wide receiver here.

"I was a 550 (pound) bencher. I was a big dude. I was the strongest guy in the country when I played my junior year of college. I was on the All-America team for strength."

Always a robust kid, Dan got into his fair share of fisticuffs along the way.

"I didn't start them. But I was always the kind that believed in finishing what you started. So if that guy wants to start something I'm gonna help him finish it. I was more of a helper. I'd go, 'Hey, you got a problem? Well let's get this taken care of here.' So I really wasn't a guy that started fights but I didn't shy away from them." But according to Sileo, "That's retired Dan. Dan don't do that stuff anymore. The old Dan was a tough guy. I was always the toughest guy in the room."

ACADEMICS

Going to Catholic school in Connecticut, one can assume that grades were important to young Dan Sileo. That assumption would be incorrect. Dan's answer to the question, were academics important to you?

"Absolutely not. Couldn't give a shit about it. I cared about going and I cared about just having fun. Especially when I was in college I didn't give a shit about school. Who cares about that? If I wanted to be a lawyer I would have went to some other school. If I wanted to be a doctor I would have went to another school. I wanted to be a football player."

CORNBREAD AND KOOL-AID

When Dan was 15, he came home after a scrap and went upstairs to wash the blood off of his clothes. His opponent's blood.

"Some guy was giving me shit and I whipped his ass."

The next day, his grandfather, who was a fireman for more than 30 years, called his grandson to the living room.

"Were you in a fight last night?" he asked Dan.

"Yeah," was Dan's response.

"Well, the cops are coming to get you. You busted that guys jaw. You slammed it against the cement? They were watching."

"Gramps, help me!"

"Fuck no, I'm not helping you. You're gonna go sit in the can for a day."

Grandma was screaming and sure enough, the police arrived and Dan went to the slammer.

"They all fucked with me," Dan recalls. "It was kind of a lesson to learn. They were laughing at me. I had cornbread and Kool-Aid. They did a favor for my grandfather. I never did anything like that again. That stopped all that shit from me. I don't want to come off like some bully because I wasn't. I wasn't really like that. I had great friendships with everybody, but I wouldn't shy away from people getting in my face."

PUGISTIC DEBUT

Every scrapper has a first fight and Dan's debut came against a kid named Danny Lewis. Dan was in eighth grade and Lewis was a junior in high school. Dan claims that Danny's girlfriend liked him.

"I was always big for my age. I remember, he beat the piss out of me when he found out I was dating her. He went down to the junior high school. I used to hide all the time. During lunch breaks he would come to look for me."

The rematch went to Sileo.

"My freshman year I got all big and shit, and I'm lifting weights and I go back, all steroided up (more on that later) and all giant. And I found that guy and he's like, 'hey, Sileo!' And I went up to him and I beat the fuck out of him, man. And I crushed him and I go, 'justice!' That was the kind of guy I was."

Dan feels episodes like this shaped his radio career.

"I don't like people pushing people around. That's why on my radio show I'm more for the minorities and underdogs and all that kind of stuff now. I don't like the big bully pushing people around. I like people who can defend themselves. You may be the richest guy in the room but just because you got more money than me don't make you a better man than me."

CHANGE OF PLANS

The reason Dan played high school sports is because he loved them. He played for fun, not for an objective. His main goal at the time was completely outside of sports but was still physical and competitive.

"I was gonna go try to be a Navy Seal. I had already signed up and all that stuff. I was going to go to San Diego to try to become a Navy Seal. That's what I wanted to be. I wanted to do that."

The scholarship offers started coming in and eventually Dan decided to change course.

"I went on a different path," he says with a semblance of regret in his voice.

GET OUTTA HERE

Dan didn't begin his football career at Miami. It began at Maryland and would have probably ended with the Terps if Head Coach Bobby Ross didn't kick him off the team. Apparently Dan tossed a guy out of a dorm room window. Why? Over a girl, naturally.

"I get invited to this party by a chick, so I go up there and start talking to her. Dude taps me on the shoulder and he's got his five buddies with him. He goes, 'What do you think of the fact that that's my girlfriend?' I go, 'quite frankly junior, go back and drink some courage. I really don't care who she's with, she's gonna be talking to me now.' So, I hammered that guy, I knocked the other guy out. They threw punches at me, I got three of them down. Sure enough there was one dude left standing. I punch this guy in the chin and I grab him and I go, 'This is your girlfriend, huh?' And she's going, 'Don't do nothing!' So right by his heels I drop him out the window. He just like disappeared man. I was like, 'Oh my God, what just happened?'"

The guy landed in a snowbank and they had to dig him out.

Ross was fed up with numerous incidents involving Dan and felt he had to kick him off the team. While Dan claimed it was just a snowbank and the guy didn't get hurt, Ross said, "What if there was an air conditioning unit in that snowbank? I gotta toss you."

LETTERLESS

Dan was given a football scholarship to Maryland where he played in all 1983 ACC Championship games when the team was quarterbacked by Boomer Esiason. He didn't get a letter. Let's just say Dan wasn't pleased.

"I come to the banquet to get my letter. Denny Murphy the D-line coach doesn't give me my letter. I said, 'You fucking piece of shit.' I go to him and he goes, 'You should not be on this team, your attitude sucks.' And I go, 'Hey Denny, fuck you!' That was really beside the fact that me and him just never got along."

There was also an altercation between the two in the locker room in front of the entire team. Dan claims that Murphy pushed him.

"He pushed me and I said, 'If you push me again I'm gonna fucking break your jaw.' I go, 'test me. I want you to hit me,' right there in front of the whole team. I go, 'you put your fucking hands on me, Denny, I will knock you out.' Bobby (Ross) goes, 'Hey, you can't have that in front of the team.' I go, 'You can't put your hands on people either. I believe that is disrespectful to a man when you try to do shit like that. Those guys you have in your room are boys. I'm a man. I don't fucking play that game."

They sent Dan home.

"My grandmother and my aunt were crying. I'm sitting there and I go, 'you think the Seals will take me?' My grandfather goes, 'the only place you're going, man, is jail with that attitude.' I was so afraid I had thrown everything away."

He should have gotten a letter. It would have made things so much easier.

JIMMY JOHNSON

Options were few for Dan when he left Maryland. No team would touch him except for one. Although the helmets are white, they wore the black hat in college football in the 1980s. Jimmy Johnson, ringleader of the renegade outfit at the University of Miami, offered one final opportunity for the 6'2", 280-pound ball of fire.

"Jimmy Johnson calls me up and goes, 'I'll give you one more fucking chance in your career."

Johnson put Dan's locker next to the bathroom near the JV locker room. He had two weeks to prove himself to Johnson and earn a scholarship. He succeeded.

"Sure enough I went down there with no promises and Jimmy says, 'you won your scholarship.' I could never afford to pay 40 thousand a year to go to school at Miami."

Once Dan landed the scholarship, Johnson told him, "I'll back you forever. All you have to do is play like hell. Jimmy loved me, man."

Eventually, when Johnson was the head coach of the Dallas Cowboys, he cut Dan from the team.

CAMOUFLAGE

The last game that Dan played in his college career is one he remembers vividly, but it didn't have the result he desired. One of college football's classic games, Penn State defeated Miami 14-10 to capture the 1986 National Championship in the Fiesta Bowl. The game is memorable because the underdog, the Nittany Lions, shut up the trash-talking Hurricanes, a team loathed by much of America. It is also remembered because Miami wore battle fatigues to the game. The camouflage look was started by none other than Dan Sileo, but for reasons he says had nothing to do with the game.

"I used to wear the camouflage pants because they were comfortable. I didn't wear them to make a point but the media blew it up. They were big for my legs."

HURRICANE HIJINKS

The Miami Hurricanes were feeling pretty good about themselves during Sugar Bowl week in New Orleans following the 1985 season. Some of the guys, Dan included, headed down to Bourbon Street for a night on the town and met up with four lovely ladies. Or, what appeared at first glance to be lovely ladies. They were sitting on the players laps and a good time was had by all.

The bartender pulled Dan aside and said, "I'm gonna help you out. You're from Miami, right?"

"Yeah," replied Dan.

"Those are she-males. Chicks with dicks."

"I go, 'do me a favor, don't tell my friends.' I go back to the table and they're drinking and I go, 'no, I'm good, man.'"

At training table the next day, Dan was very eager to know how things went with the 'girls' last night. Maybe a bit too eager.

"They're like, 'hey motherfucker, you knew didn't you?' I go, 'hey man, I don't know. I just thought I was helping you guys out. So what happened? I saw you kiss a couple of them.' They were so fucking pissed off."

The angry Hurricanes promptly celebrated New Year's Night 1986 by getting their teeth kicked in by Tennessee, 35-7.

THE NFL

Dan was selected by the Tampa Bay Buccaneers in the third round of the 1987 NFL Supplemental Draft.

He played in just 10 games with the Bucs under head coach Ray Perkins. He also had training camp stints with the Dallas Cowboys and the Detroit Lions.

"There has really only been one coach to understand my background and what kind of guy I was, and that was Jimmy Johnson. Jimmy was the only guy to understand my kind of personality and I think that's one of the reasons my NFL career was cut short, because when I got to the NFL it was a let down. It really wasn't like my Miami times. It was nothing like it. I didn't enjoy it. I really hated it. It was more political than just who's the best guy and the coaches didn't get me right away."

He readily admits that he wasn't mentally ready to play in the professional ranks. Playing for Tampa wasn't easy either. He didn't get along with his position coach, Mike DuBose, and the losing weighed on him. In one year with the Bucs he lost 11 games.

"I didn't want to be around that environment. I

hated Ray Perkins and you know, when you get cut by the Bucs it's not usually a good thing. It just went around that I was a steroider and I was a head case, and it was my own fault in the fact that I was not mentally prepared to be a professional athlete and to understand. My stuff was mental not physical. You get aced out of the game when you're considered a problem kid."

At Miami, Dan says they were "rock stars."

"We would have parties at the Fontainebleau where they filmed *Scarface*. The University of Miami parties were in the ballroom. You gotta remember, the only thing whiter than me in that room were the napkins. It was an amazing time there. Outside of my daughter and my family, that was the greatest time of my life, being a University of Miami Hurricane."

The NFL doesn't give a rip about that.

STEROIDS

Steroids are and have been prevalent in sports the past 30 years or so. There is no denying that. Dan is forthcoming about his steroid use.

"My freshman year at Maryland I started taking anabolic steroids. Then is when it was legal. It all changed in 1990 when it became a controlled substance and it became a big time crime after 1990. So you gotta remember in '83 you could take steroids and they were legal. The federal government hadn't started that yet. That's funny now, everyone is all up in arms about steroids, I'm like, 'really?' Great. Me and [another Hurricane player] used to go to the Farmacia in South Florida when I was at Miami, and we would go up to the Cuban pharmacy and go, 'I'll take three Anadrol 50s and some Sustanon.' Sure. They gave it to you right over the counter back then. It was not illegal. People sold it to you. Then when people started getting an idea on how much this stuff was worth …ya gotta remember, the government, when they can see they can make a nickel on it, that's when they get involved. And that's what they started seeing with steroids. I was a massive steroid user. Loved it. It was one of the reasons I got to 630 in bench. I have no problems saying it on the air, I have no problems saying it to anybody, absolutely I was a steroid user."

He used steroids, like so many others, to gain an advantage physically and psychologically over his opponent. Was everybody using steroids?

"I would say so but not the brothers doing it. The brothers hated needles (laughs). They weren't real big on it."

Reflecting on his steroid past, Dan admits that he would do things differently.

"If I had to do it all over again I clearly would not have done that because I'm paying for it today. It was a weakness. It's like alcoholism or drugs. You think you need it when you really don't."

Back then, the side effects of using steroids for Dan were insomnia and acne. Today he has back, knee, and joint issues. He also feels steroid use will shorten his life.

"I probably took 15 years off my life but I always told people, somebody gives you a $600,000 signing bonus or a $700,000 signing bonus like I got from the Bucs, would you take five years off your life?"

When he was on the air at KNBR in San Francisco, Dan was in hot water with his program director Bob Agnew for calling out Barry Bonds and Jose Canseco as steroid users.

"Look at them, they're bigger than the Raider D-line. How do you not see that? I knew when I saw a steroider."

RADIO

One gets the feeling Dan has regrets how his professional football career went down. He wasn't about to let the next opportunity slip away. After floating around "doing nothing" for a couple of years, Dan made a vow to himself.

"If I ever got into a job, I would work my balls off and that's why I've been in sports talk radio for 17 years now. I said I would never get into a job I loved and had passion for again and never take advantage of it and I haven't."

Before making that commitment to himself, he dabbled in professional wrestling for three months in Austria where he was known as "Bonecrusher Sileo." When he returned to the states, there was a chance to play arena football. His cousin was a part owner of a team in Las Vegas and offered him an opportunity to play again.

"He goes, 'Hey, why don't you play for me,' and I go, 'fucking arena football? Come on man.' He goes, 'I'll give you 2,000 bucks a week and at the time that seemed like a lot to me.'"

Meanwhile, the radio guy for the team took an interest in Dan's colorful verbal skills.

"He goes, 'why don't you come down to the studio. You talk a lot of shit. Let's see what you can do on the radio.' I've been very versed in sports my whole life. I knew a lot about the history of sports, I loved it. All sports, not just football. Baseball was my passion. I got a chance to meet Mickey Mantle and (Joe) DiMaggio cause of my uncle at the old timer's games."

Like The Beatles on the rooftop in *Let It Be*, apparently Dan passed the audition. It was suggested that he get in touch with a new sports talk outfit based in Las Vegas called American Sports Radio Network. Eventually it became One-On-One.

"I started doing weekends out there," Dan remembers.

A few short weeks later he was doing mornings. He admits he didn't know what he was doing. But he was getting the radio bug.

"One night I'm driving home, I hear (Scott) Ferrall. He was fucking great, I loved him." Ferrall was working at KNBR.

Dan then got a call from KGO radio inviting him to San Francisco. After initially choosing not to go, Dan and his wife decided to head to the Bay Area.

"I walk into KGO with an old dak (a recording device), which we used to have back in the day. I put it on Ken Berry and Mickey Luckoff's desk and I said, 'if you like me, call me.' They listened and called me the next day. And before you know it, I'm on the mornings with Dunbar and Rosie. Out of the blue, Ken Berry goes, 'OK.' And I'm like, 'you're fucking kidding me.'"

Dan was doing sports updates for KGO in the mornings and they were finding shifts for him elsewhere during the day.

Eventually, he moved to KNBR.

"One day Ferrall does not come in. Ferrall started talking shit about Bob's (Agnew) daughters on the air and he was fucking going off as he always does. The thing with Scott is he's such a great talent, but he goes after management so viciously that they blow him out not because of talent. Bob ends up blowing him out. I'm doing updates. One day they had a fill-in guy doing 'SportsPhone 68' (KNBR) and sure enough the guy was stuck in traffic. So Bob goes, 'alright Sileo you're on.' He calls me up and goes, 'that's the best I've ever heard.' I said, 'ever?' He goes, 'ever. You don't know what you're doing but you're fucking fantastic.'"

Ferrall got whacked by the suits and Dan took over 'SportsPhone 68.'

"They partnered me with Rod Brooks in 'Ebony and Ivory,' which I thought was a fucking great show. Me and Rod hit issues on race and politics, it was great."

Then Randy Michaels called him up with a show

offer from Tampa, Florida.

"KNBR couldn't believe it when Randy Michaels called. Randy goes, 'I'm going to personally teach you radio' and to this day he still does. Randy Michaels made me what I am on the air today."

STYLINGS

The best way to describe Dan's on air approach is to let him explain it himself.

"Honest. Tell it like it is. Don't coat anything. I hit race, politics, religion. The three meters that move the world. The three meters that move my show. I think if you can implement those in any way, and I like making people uncomfortable, I say things that people won't and can't say or don't have the sack to say."

VIEWING AND LISTENING HABITS

In addition to watching sports on television, Dan also watches CNN. He doesn't listen to sports talk radio, preferring to take in Rush Limbaugh, Sean Hannity, or Glenn Beck.

"Sports talk radio guys, the majority of them, very flat. But you want to know what makes Rush Limbaugh $35 million a year, you watch a guy fucking run a show."

ClearChannel once sent Dan to West Palm Beach to watch Limbaugh do his show.

"I watched Rush Limbaugh do a week of shows and from that moment on changed my entire career. I learned not to take myself so serious. Rush Limbaugh laughs between every segment. It's delivery of content. That's what makes Rush Limbaugh the best radio guy. Not because he's smarter, it's his delivery."

HOME LIFE

It might be difficult for some to imagine that a Miami Hurricane during the Jimmy Johnson era could eventually settle down and actually have a normal family life. While on the radio, Dan is an opinionated and unyielding personality. Home is where the show ends and the bright lights of the studio dim. Away from the job, he simply likes to spend time with the family.

"I like to play with my daughter as much as I can. My wife, Kim, and I and Danielle have a nice little family deal. If you think about it, look at my job. People ask me all the time, what do I do for fun? Gee, I go to Bucs games, Rays games, Hurricanes games, I mean how much fun can I fucking possibly have? I go to sporting events, I go to Olympic games, I go to this and that, I go to the World Series. I've been to all these things because my job has afforded me the chance to do great things. For me, having the down time with my kid and watching my daughter grow up, that's really what I do. We go places, me and her and my wife, and we have a fun time. I'm not a partier, I don't go out. I'm home with them all the time. I refuse to play golf anymore, and I love playing golf, but I can't take four hours away from my kid as she's growing up."

LAST LICKS

"I want people to remember my show, that when you turned it on you were inspired and we told it like it was. Not like people wanted it to be, but how it was. That we were as truthful as we could possibly be. We've said some things obviously over our 17 years that we've regretted, but I really have no regrets in the approach that I had."

Joe Benigno
"From Fan to The Fan"

Joe Benigno parlayed his days as a frequent caller into a full-time deal with WFAN in 1995 and he hasn't looked back since.

Benigno, is in his 16th year with WFAN, holds down the midday slot with Evan Roberts.

MAZ, THE METS, AND JOE WILLIE
If you are going to have a first sports memory it might as well be a great one. That was the certainly the case with young Joe Benigno.

"I've been a huge sports fan my whole life. My first sports memory was Bill Mazeroski's home run, Game 7 of the 60 World Series. I was seven years old. That's the first thing I remember."

Benigno is well known among his listeners as a rabid Mets and Jets fan. While many media people like to downplay their fandom, Benigno makes no secret about the teams he pulls for.

"I became a Mets fan in 1962 because here was this new team I could see my whole life with. I became a Jets fan because Joe Namath signed with the Jets in 1965. I'd seen the Orange Bowl that year when he played for Alabama. I became a fan of his in that game even though he lost to Texas."

You can probably figure out that Benigno is also a Knicks and Rangers fan.

"I was always a Knicks fan. My father used to take me to the (old) Garden for the double-headers. You would see the Celtics play the Lakers in the first game and the Knicks against the Warriors in the second. I became a Rangers fan, not as big a hockey guy as I am the other sports but I guess it's a Garden thing. That's how it all started about me being a sports-crazed guy."

CREDIT DAD

Joe was a typical sports-loving kid growing up in Paramus, New Jersey, playing sports, watching sports, and talking sports.

"My dad was my biggest influence as far as being a big sports fan. He played basketball in high school. Unfortunately, he was drafted during World War II and was actually captured and spent nine months in a German prison camp. But he's the one that really got me into sports."

CALLING DR. BENIGNO

His life would change when his father, Joe, passed away when little Joe was just thirteen.

His mom and younger sister went to live with his grandparents, which didn't do much for Joe's love of sports.

"I always had a hard time with my grandfather. He would always give me a hard time about watching football on Sunday, and this is the heyday of Namath. I'm 13-years-old and totally engrossed in it. He was into boxing but nothing else. He was an old-school Italian and he looked at sports like, 'you're never going to make any money paying attention to that'. And of course he turned out to be wrong. I wish he was alive so I could tell him that today (laughs)."

Joe's mom and grandparents wanted him to become a doctor.

"I come from a family of doctors on my mother's side and that's what they wanted me to do. They were actually considering sending me to the Philippines to go to medical school. There was no shot I was going to go to the Philippines, I can tell you that. They pushed me to do that but I resisted. I had no desire to be a doctor. I went to college (Franklin College in Indiana) and ended up with a degree in political science. You can wipe my rear end with that."

THE FOOD BUSINESS

Joe's plan was to become a lawyer. One problem, and it was a big one, was he didn't have the grades. He didn't care about his grades, it was all about sports and having a good time at school.

After college and without any idea of what he wanted to do for a living, he got married in November of 1975.

"A mistake. Probably the biggest mistake I ever made. I was 22-years-old and didn't know my ass from my elbow. I really had no career."

He bounced around from job to job, including working at his stepfather's car dealership.

In 1978 he landed a career in the food business, an occupation he would keep until he transitioned into radio.

"I finally would up working for a food broker. A girl I knew from college actually turned me onto the job because she worked there in college and she knew I was looking for a job. That's how I ended up in the food business, which I was in from 1978 up until the time I became a talk show host."

JOE FROM SADDLE RIVER

Benigno would always listen to music in his car but when the 'Mike and The Mad Dog' show started on WFAN in 1989, he started listening to that. Mike Francesa and Chris Russo were the afternoon stars on The Fan, and Benigno became a regular caller to the show. Francesa still holds down the afternoon slot while Russo took his Mad Dog act to satellite radio in 2008.

With the moniker of Joe From Saddle River, Benigno called into the show a couple of times a week just for fun, still never thinking he would ever get a chance to do a show.

"I always knew I could do it, but I never thought about it because it was never realistic to me that I would get a chance."

IT WASN'T A CONTEST

It was December of 1994 and Benigno was working for Melba Foods, a gourmet food distributor in Brooklyn, New York. He was there for five years and the routine was the same. He'd get in early and read the sports sections of the *New York Post* and the *Daily News*. One day he was reading *Post* media critic Phil Mushnick's column and got fired up.

"I'm reading Mushnick and how The Fan is going to give a caller, this guy Eli in Westchester, a show. I'm a well-known caller at this point, but when I read this thing about Eli I said, 'are you kidding me?' They're going to give this guy a show and I'm probably 50 times better than this guy."

That was the first time the thought of becoming a sports talk show host entered the mind of Joe Benigno.

That afternoon Francesa and Russo were discussing the fact that Eli was getting a show and named some of their callers who deserved a show a lot more than Eli. One of the people they named was Joe From Saddle River.

When Joe got home that afternoon he called producer Bob Gelb, who put him on the air with Mike and Mad Dog to make his case for a show.

"I should be one of the guys who gets the chance to do a show," he said. "I know I can do it."

The Fan decided to give Eli and three other callers a chance to do a show and they called it Fan Appreciation Day. One of those guys was Benigno.

"I never thought it was a contest. They never ever said that whoever sounded best would get a show. That was never said, let me make that clear."

During the Christmas holidays, when the regular hosts were taking days off, is when Benigno and the others (Eli, Alan From White Plains, and Dick Corona) got their chance. Eli, though, got a two-hour show. The others just one hour, which ticked Joe off.

"For the first time it was in my head that this is an opportunity for me. I now have a door that is open and I've got to slam through this freaking door. Nothing was ever said that whoever sounded the best was going to get a show. Never said."

Is it misleading to say that Benigno was a contest winner?

"Yes. So instead of fighting it, because the story is very tedious as you can tell, I just go along with it."

THE SHOW

The mark of any successful talk host, sports or otherwise, is show prep. Joe was ready for his hour in afternoon drive.

"I went in with a game plan. I knew everything I was going to do. So I went in there and did the show. So after I got off the air that day, I'll never forget, the first time, the first signal if you will that things might happen, I got a call from Suzyn Waldman. So as I'm walking out one of the guys at the station says 'you got a phone call. Somebody wants to talk to you.' I said, 'hey, who wants to talk to me?' It's Suzyn Waldman. Really. She's complimenting me about what I had just done. So I said goodbye to the people there and I go and get in my car. I'm driving home and I'm listening to Eli do his show and he's totally crapping out. He really is. Whatever he said he would twist into a racial thing no matter what it was, it didn't matter. So now he has to deal with the callers and they just ate him up."

NO GUARANTEE

While Joe felt good about his one-hour show, he didn't know if it was a one-time thing or if something might come of it. He thought he did a good job but there was no guarantee he wouldn't just go back to being Joe From Saddle River with his talk show career consisting of simply being a caller.

The next day Joe took his two daughters to their mother in Massachusetts. On the way back he was listening to WFAN and Mike Francesa, who was flying solo without the Mad Dog.

Francesa was critiquing the shows of the four guys from the day before and said the only guy of the group who might have a chance to do this for a living was Benigno. Francesa was very complimentary and you can imagine what Joe was thinking in the car.

"I'm flipping out. This was the day before cell phones and I couldn't call the station right away and thank him."

No one from management ever got back to him although he remained a caller to the station.

Again, there were no promises and Benigno didn't do another show on The Fan until six months later. This after he went to broadcasting school and bought time at a radio station in New Jersey.

Bob Gelb told Joe that going to broadcasting school is all well and good but he needed to get on the air.

"I find this little station in Elizabeth, New Jersey, WJDM. I ended up paying $400 an hour to do a show. I was on Monday night from like, 6 to 7, whatever it was. I shelled out my own money to do this."

He of course kept The Fan in the loop about his progress.

"So I said to Bob (Gelb), I'm doing the show, maybe you can help me out. I said, 'Do you think I could get Mike and Chris on as guests on my show?' Absolutely.

It was a call-in show but I wasn't really getting any calls. I was just basically talking for an hour. Mike winds up doing the whole hour in this, maybe the fourth show I had."

It was during this program that Francesa alerted Benigno that there might be an opening on the overnight shift at WFAN. The overnight guy, Steve Somers, was moving to a day shift.

Joe called the station the next day and was told by Gelb that he might be getting a call from the program director, Mark Chernoff, about doing work at the station.

Eventually Chernoff offered some part-time overnight work for Benigno, which he readily accepted. He did two overnights over the Fourth of July weekend.

"I probably did five or six shows after that and they were paying me per show. So finally, it was coming up to the last week of August and they still hadn't made a decision on who was going to be the overnight guy. There were just a bunch of people filling in. So Mark says to me, 'can you possibly do a full week Monday through Friday?' I guess he wanted to see if I could handle a full week. So I did it."

After that Friday show, Benigno went home and went to sleep. He woke up at noon and one of his daughters told him to call Mark Chernoff at The Fan.

"Mark says to me, 'the job is yours if you want it.' If I accepted it, they were going to announce it on Mike and Chris' show. I went on with them that afternoon and that was it. I called the woman I worked for at Melba Foods and said I got the job and I appreciated everything she did for me. My first show was the day after Labor Day."

It didn't take long for Benigno to accept the offer.

"There was no question I was taking it if they offered it. I wasn't even thinking of money at that time. They were going to pay me $50,000 a year. They could have started me at 10 grand and I would have taken it. Bobby Gelb and Mike Francesa were the biggest help, giving me the vehicles to get into the business, and obviously Mark Chernoff was also very instrumental."

IMUS

As the overnight guy, it was up to Benigno to hand it off to the morning show at the conclusion of the program. In this case, he had to give the ball to the legendary Don Imus. It could have been very intimidating to have 'Imus In The Morning' following Benigno's show but that wasn't the case.

"I went up to him one morning to try to introduce myself and it was very funny. You don't approach Imus, but I did and I'm going to say hello, it's like a normal thing to do. I think it was a little weird and I think he did say hello to me. I think he always liked me. I'll tell you what, Imus has always been a supporter of mine. I've been on his show. He was always good to me, which is a good thing."

NO LOOKING BACK

The overnights became Joe's lifestyle. He didn't even consider himself a talk show host until years later. He loved doing the show and eventually made $100,000 a year.

"That was unheard of for overnight guys. I don't think anybody is making that now doing overnights so you know that became a big deal for me. It really told me how good I really was and just the way the whole show became."

The nine years he spent on overnights wasn't easy, but his wife made it easier.

"My wife had a normal 9-5 job, so I'd be coming home from work and she'd be getting ready to go to work. She put up with that for nine years and I have to give her tremendous credit that she was able to do that. She was always a great supporter of mine. All she had to do was turn on the radio to know where I was. And at that time I went to a lot of games. The only time I got to spend time with her was on the weekends."

THE LIGHT OF DAY

With Joe's contract coming up, there were whispers that he could be heading to the ESPN affiliate in New York. Not wanting to lose Joe, WFAN teamed him with Sid Rosenberg beginning in November of 2004.

Rosenberg unfortunately had issues with substance abuse and reliability. He didn't last much longer at WFAN.

"It's a shame that things turned the way that they did. It's too bad that he crapped out the two times that he did. But Evan (Roberts) and I have a great show and we really put some stability into the midday show. We have total respect for each other. But it's really a shame it never really worked out with Sid."

THE ATHLETE

Basketball was Joe's game to play. Although he didn't play in high school like his father did, he did play pickup games. A lot of pickup games.

"I was one of those guys that would sweep off the court when it was snowing so you can play. I'm a relatively short guy but I could play a little bit. I played basketball until about 10 years ago maybe. My legs are shot now. I did serious road running for about 20 years and it just destroyed my legs. So now all I do is play golf."

THE AUTHOR

Joe wrote a fun book called *Rules for New York Sports Fans*.

One of the rules is you can't be a fan of the Yankees and Mets.

"You cannot be a Met and Yankee fan. If you're a Met fan you're a Met fan. If you're a Yankee fan you're a

Yankee fan and you hate who the other one is."

Rule number two in the book is that you have to select a team by the age of 13.

"There is no changing after that. Women you can change and I have changed them, thank God for the better, much better, but your team is your team. There is an emotional attachment. I haven't seen my team, the Jets, go to the Super Bowl in 42 years, 42 freaking painful years with the Jets and no matter how this year ends (it ended with the Jets losing in the AFC title game, again) I can't explain that feeling of anticipation. There is no gray area."

We could tell you more. Better yet, go get the book.

MEMORABLE SPORTS MOMENTS

To Joe, the greatest sporting event that he attended was Game 6 of the 1986 World Series at Shea Stadium. Yes, that game. The Bill Buckner game. It was a hectic sports week for Benigno.

"It started out with the Monday night game at the Meadowlands between the Jets and the Broncos. The Jets started that year at 10-1 and they beat the crap out of Denver (Jets jumped out to a 22-0 lead and won 22-10). The Jets just beat them up that night. The next night I was in Fenway for Game 3 of the World Series, the game Lenny Dykstra led off with a home run. The following Saturday I was at the Buckner game and then maybe eight hours after that I was back at the Meadowlands to see the Jets beat the Saints. I'll never forget that."

MEETING HIS HERO

One of the nice things about being a sports broadcaster is you sometimes get a chance to meet people you otherwise wouldn't. Growing up, Benigno loved Joe Namath. He finally got the chance to meet him at Jets training camp in 2010.

"We are doing our show in Cortland and he was up there and I got to meet Namath. I got to interview him. It wasn't as long as I liked. I could do a whole show with him. I could sit down with him for three hours and talk about his whole career. I even got him to sign a couple of my old Sports Illustrateds, that I still have in mint condition with him on it."

THE IVERSON MOMENT

"I'm at a Nets game against the Sixers and I'm standing at the locker after the game and all the reporters are around Iverson. Allen Iverson is sitting there and in front of all the reporters he turns around and he whips out either his wallet or his money belt or whatever the freak he had and basically stands there and counts out in $100 bills in front of all the media. About $20,000 dollars like it was pocket change, to me, just to be an ass as far as I'm concerned. What are you doing that for? And what are you doing walking around with 20 grand in cash on you? That always kind of stuck out to me."

MUSICAL TASTES

"I'm into everything. I started out with the Beatles. Huge Beatles fan. I grew up with all of that. All the rock, all the Motown, I'm into Sinatra. I don't like rap and I'm not crazy about country music. Not really my thing."

THE MOVIES

"It's not even a question, *The Godfather*, the greatest movie of all time. Not even debatable. Gotta watch it at least once a year."

LASTING IMPRESSIONS

When it is all said and done, how would Joe Benigno like his media career to be remembered?

"Oh, just that I was a pretty damn good talk show

host. I think I already achieved this. This is one of the things that makes me proud. I want to be remembered as a factor in the New York sports world or New York sports media, and I think I have achieved that."

Mitch Levy
"Mitch in the Morning"

In an industry where self-promotion is rampant, Mitch Levy is not one to thrust his chest out and holler, "Look at me!"

While gaining information from Mitch for this book wasn't like pulling teeth, it did have some challenges. He approached this project with some trepidation at first. Once he grasped the concept and realized it wasn't a *60 Minutes* expose, he settled in and provided us with some great material.

Mitch is the host of the four-hour 'Mitch In The Morning' program on Sports Radio 950 KJR in Seattle.

Yes, Seattle; perhaps the last place Mitch Levy ever thought he would spend the past 17 years of his life.

PATH TO BROADCASTING

As a kid, Mitch didn't know exactly what he wanted to do when the time came to making a living, but he knew he wanted to be around sports and broadcasting.

"It became painfully obvious that I was never going to be able to make a living playing sports. I got into this broadcasting thing in terms of the interest. My first real memory of identifying that 'boy, that's a great gig!' was watching Howard Cosell, who became my passion, calling the boxing team the U.S. had in 1976 at the Montreal Olympics. Leon and Michael Spinks, Sugar Ray Leonard, Howard Davis was fabulous, he was the best on that team. I can remember Howard Cosell yelling at a nine-year-old Mitch Levy in my family room with my mom and dad, 'Look at Sugar Ray Leonard teaching the Cuban a boxing lesson!' (Mitch in his best Cosell impression.) And screaming. He was so excited about this. I remember becoming acutely aware of Howard Cosell in 1976."

That led to imitating Cosell and branching off and doing impressions of Marv Albert like so many kids of that time.

THE ARTICLE

In Florida, as a junior in high school, Mitch read an article in *Sports Illustrated* that changed his life. It was the March 12, 1984, issue with Royals third baseman George Brett on the cover.

The article talked about the great sports broadcasters that the Syracuse Newhouse School of Public Communications produced. The list is long and legendary. The announcers mentioned in the article included Marty Glickman, Marv Albert, Dick Stockton, Bob Costas, and Len Berman.

"Here I am in South Florida reading this article and I decided right then and there, I'm going to Syracuse."

His parents thought the broadcasting pursuit was a phase. His father was hoping that Mitch might follow in his footsteps as an attorney. But the kid's mind was made up, there was no turning back, and Robert and Ceil Levy threw all their support behind their youngest son.

INSECURITIES

Despite his Syracuse degree and his hunger to become a sportscaster, Mitch doubted that he could be successful in this business. Those early doubts can't possibly creep into Mitch's psyche these days, can they?

"Oh God, are you kidding? I still doubt it. I'm doubting it now! I'm waiting for this whole kind of fairy tale to end. I'm a glass half-empty guy. I'm wondering, how does it end? When does the journey end? Does my key card not work this morning? Is my office cleaned out? I'm perennially worried. I focus only on the bad shows that I do. The good ones are rare to me. I'm the harshest of self-critics. People say I don't enjoy when things go right, I'm really more preoccupied when things go wrong. So yeah, I have doubted it every step of the way. It gets to a point where you don't know how to do anything else. What in the hell would I do if I didn't do this?"

When did Mitch think he would make it in this business and that it would work out?

"This is the God's honest truth; I don't think I ever thought it."

While many people think that a sports broadcaster would be full of confidence and extroverted, many are not. Case in point, Mitch Levy.

"Terribly insecure. I'm awful in social settings, ask my wife. I try to avoid them like the plague."

In the studio, a controlled place behind a microphone is where he is comfortable. Outside of that environment, Mitch admits that he's "like a fish out of water."

He doesn't know why he gets the occasional request to make a speech or give a talk and he turns them all down.

"I can't do a speech. It would be humiliating. I would be terrible at it."

Plus he wouldn't want to hear himself give a speech anyway.

"Maybe it's the way I'm wired but I can't stand listening to myself. If I was forced to listen to myself, I would throw myself out of a building."

Mitch reads all his e-mail, every last one of them. He cops to feeling hurt when he gets negative correspondence. He wants people to accept him and wants to be well received.

"I think everybody wants to feel like professionally they're accepted. When I read all the negative e-mails and I get the calls and the notes, it's hurtful because I desperately want to feel like people enjoy what I do. They don't have to like me personally. If they enjoy what's coming out of those speakers every morning then I'm happy. I do the very, very best that I can do every day, and that people over the course of time enjoy what I do. That's important. If that's happening then I'm grateful and appreciative. If people don't accept what I do and feel like I'm loafing or this guy doesn't try hard enough, that's the worst indictment you could make of me."

MOM AND DAD

It's nice when a son has a good relationship with his parents. Mitch Levy has a great relationship with his mom and dad, Ceil and Robert. They both listen to Mitch's show every day and even had their new home set up so all they have to do is click a couple of buttons to get the internet feed over a speaker.

Mitch and his dad share a love of Syracuse basketball. They've made a pact to attend every Syracuse NCAA Tournament game each March. Mitch has it in his contract that he can go watch the Orange in the tourney. Ceil doesn't go on the trips and probably likes the peace and quiet while her husband and son enjoy themselves, especially when the 'Cuse win.

Mitch and his two older brothers were oriented towards sports growing up in Palm Beach County, Florida.

"We weren't the greatest athletes in the world but we played all the sports."

Mr. and Mrs. Levy encouraged their sons' love of sports and squired them around to sporting activities.

Robert was a basketball player in high school and went to the University of Pennsylvania, but when his son went to college, he adopted the Syracuse basketball team as his own.

The tradition of going to Syracuse NCAA Tournament games began back in 1989 when Mitch was a senior. Former Syracuse Athletic Director Jake Crouthamel gave tickets to Mitch for the Sweet 16 in Minneapolis where the Orangemen were playing Missouri.

Immediately, Mitch called his dad in Florida.

" 'Hey, I was just given tickets to the Sweet 16. Would you like to meet me in Minneapolis and go to the games?' I'll never forget his reaction which was, 'Why would I want to do that?' I said, 'maybe because you'll see basketball in person and you'll get to see your son!' He said, 'alright.' I kind of guilted him into it and he flew up from Florida and I went from Syracuse and we had the weekend together."

For the record, Syracuse defeated Missouri, but then lost to top-seeded Illinois with a trip to the Final Four on the line, ironically played in Seattle.

They had such a good time that when it came time to depart and go their separate ways in Minneapolis, Mr. Levy, the man who wondered why he would leave the comfort of his living room to go see basketball in Minnesota, said, "hey, let's do this again next year."

Mitch replied, "OK, we'll try."

They haven't missed a Syracuse NCAA Tournament game since.

They've also added the Big East Tournament to their Syracuse basketball itinerary. Sometimes a brother tags along as well.

BROWN AND KORNHEISER

In 1992 Mitch joined WTEM in Washington, D.C., with the task of producing 'The James Brown Show' and 'The Tony Kornheiser Show.' This wasn't producing 'The (throw in any local 'legend') Show' in Fayetteville, Arkansas, or some other outpost. This was producing the shows of two well-known personalities in a major market. The experience was invaluable and helped shape Mitch's career.

"A lot of the way I do my show, the way I approach the format, the way I approach myself really was kind of built from watching two guys at the tops of their crafts, like Kornheiser and Brown. But the neat thing about working with them for a few years as both a producer and on-air sidekick was how vastly different the two of those guys were and are."

Mitch found them both to be extremely talented, compelling, and entertaining, but completely different from each other on and off the air.

As mentioned, Mitch isn't a big self-promoter and he feels he got some of that from Kornheiser.

"I think that Tony's way of doing things kind of molded me the most. Tony was never a guy who would do commercials. I do commercials but only a bare minimum. He was never one to do promotional tours or remotes or anything that was outside the domain of the studio and doing his show. I think a lot of Tony has rubbed off on me. Hopefully whatever negative things people have about Tony have not rubbed off on me, but I've been told they have, too."

Since his show begins at 6 a.m., Mitch doesn't have the time to go to appearances or hawk products. For Mitch, it's all about the show. Just like Tony.

TONY AND JB PART 2

Mitch first met Tony Kornheiser a month before they went on the air in May of 1992. Tony entered the room first.

"He said, 'listen, I don't need this job, I don't want this job. I'm a writer. I'm not a broadcaster. I'm not a radio talk show host. I'm a columnist. I work for the *Washington Post*. I'm gonna do this for as long as it takes to earn money to send my kids to college then I'm gonna quit. I'm gonna do two hours. I need you to call me at 9:30 at night, each and every night before, not 9:28, not 9:32, you call me at 9:30 and tell me what we're gonna do on the show the next day. I don't want to talk to any athletes. Athletes have nothing to say. I want columnists. Get me Mike Wilbon. Get me Mitch Albom. Get me Bob Ryan. I want to talk to somebody who's intelligent, articulate, and has something to say. I don't want athletes. DON'T book me athletes.'"

Tony and Mitch went through a bunch of rules set forth by the host.

"If you can follow these rules, Mitch," Tony said, "we'll get along. If you can't, we won't."

They shook hands and Tony walked away.

"Look forward to working with you, Tony," Mitch said.

Five minutes later it was time to meet James Brown from CBS who was a local basketball legend at DeMatha High before going to play at Harvard.

James arrived wearing a three-piece suit complete with a pocket watch and perfect positioning of his handkerchief. He was displaying his usual friendly disposition.

He shook Mitch's hand, sat down in the same chair Tony was sitting in a few moments earlier, and said, "Mitch, I want athletes. I respect the job the columnists and the writers do, but I'm really somebody who wants the stars of the game. I want Magic Johnson. I want Michael Jordan. I want Larry Bird. I want Barry Sanders. I want the great athletes. Please don't load my show with columnists and broadcasters. I want you to call me at 9 o'clock every morning. I'll be on the treadmill and we'll talk about what's on the following show."

That was Mitch's welcoming into sports radio.

"They were as different as different can be and I loved them both," Mitch recounted. "I still love 'em both. They're idols of mine. They went about it in completely different manners. The sounds of those shows were completely different but boy, I cut my teeth with two of the really outstanding people. I know that might sound strange about Tony but trust me, as a guy who got to know Tony, if you get to know him and really get in on the inside, he is one special guy."

Mitch worked with T.K. and J.B. for two and a half years until the audition.

THE AUDITION

Mitch's agent in 1994 was Ellen Beckwith. One day, she gave Mitch news that she got him an audition. In Seattle. He was not doing cartwheels.

"I said, 'why in the world would I want to go to Seattle?' She said, 'Go to Seattle and audition. They want someone who does your type of show, the sports and the lifestyle and the cynicism and a little bit of pushing the envelope.'"

The station was looking for a midday show to replace 'The Fabulous Sports Babe.'

"I really resisted, but I went because she asked me to go. I did these two days in December in 1994, on the air, two midday shows. And I tell you, I was as bad as bad could be. It was dark outside and rainy and they put me up at this crazy hotel near the airport. I couldn't get out of here fast enough."

Mitch did the Thursday midday show and was committed to do a Friday show as well. He deemed the Thursday show "a colossal disaster." He changed his plans and was going to fly to Florida to meet with his parents a day earlier than scheduled.

He told to his parents, "I just gotta get out of here. This is awful. I'm not even going to do the second show. I'm getting out of Seattle as fast as I can. I'm never coming back."

Mitch was going to fly into Miami, an hour and a half away from where his parents lived.

Robert Levy asked his son, "Who's picking you up in Miami at the airport a day early?"

Mitch said, "You are."

"No I'm not. None of us are because you made a commitment. Did you make a commitment to do two shows? I'm not picking you up. No member of our family goes back on a commitment like that. You can walk from Miami to North Palm Beach as far as I'm concerned."

"Alright Dad. I'll do the next show."

Mitch did the next show and of course he rocked, right?

"It was equally as bad, I think. And I flew out and went home and I told my agent, 'You'll never hear from them again.' There's no way they could ever want me after those two performances. And if they did, I have no interest in living in that town."

The next morning he got a call from his agent.

"They like you and they want you."

Mitch's response was direct.

"They either don't know what a good radio show is or they gotta get their hearing checked."

Mitch also had offers from an outfit in Las Vegas and in Chicago.

After much prodding from Beckwith, he chose Seattle.

"I did it. I don't know why, but I did it."

Of course he didn't think he was very good for the first several months.

"The ratings went down the toilet as soon as I got here. Nobody could understand why any radio station would hire this goofball from the East Coast. He comes with this attitude."

Several months in, the radio station stuck by Mitch and insisted it would work.

Tom Lee, the program director, was very supportive.

Then they ask Mitch if he wanted to do mornings.

"No, I'll never do the mornings. I'm not a morning guy. I can't wake up at 4 in the morning."

Of course, he ended up doing mornings.

He went from 'Mitch in the Midday' to 'Mitch in the Morning.' And he's been the morning guy there ever since May 1996.

A THANKS TO PETER BROWN

Mitch Levy wasn't the only one auditioning for the midday host position at KJR. Peter Brown, a talented host, auditioned before Mitch did and Brown did exceedingly well.

Tom Lee was set to hire Brown until a miscue opened the door for Mitch.

The owner of the station, Barry Ackerley, also owned the Seattle Sonics. He was listening to Brown's second audition show when he heard the outspoken host rip the Sonics.

The Sonics were offering home games on a pay-per-view basis and Brown said, to the effect, "whose brilliant idea was it to make local sports fans pay for the regular season Sonic home games? That's the worst idea in the history of mankind. I can't even believe someone would do that. Who would do that?"

Ackerley, that's who. He was also listening.

A moment later, Lee got a phone call from the boss. "He's not our man."

Mitch reveals it was "because of that misstep by Peter Brown that Mitch Levy's career started in Seattle. The truth is, if Peter Brown did not do that schtick in that audition he would have been the midday host and I'd be on a street corner in Birmingham, Alabama, right now."

EAVESDROPPING

One would think that a successful radio host would be a killer public speaker. Instead of talking into a microphone in a studio, they just have to do the same thing in front of a larger audience. While true in some cases, that is not accurate for Mitch.

"Speaking into a microphone with one or two or three other people, while however many people are listening, eavesdropping on the conversation as I like to say it. Between that and getting up in front of a crowd with a microphone and being interesting and articulate and compelling, and that I think are two completely different arenas. I think most people would say, 'jeez, if the guy can talk on the air then he must be able to be a great public speaker.' I don't think that that's necessarily true because I think I'm a terrible public speaker."

One of the reasons Mitch may not be a good public speaker is that he devotes so much time and energy to his four-hour morning show. He does that by necessity.

"I do a four-hour morning show that takes a lot of work because I don't think that I'm as naturally gifted as some of the other people that are in your book and that are around the country doing morning shows."

MORE THAN JUST SPORTS

If you are looking for sports, sports, and more sports on your morning radio, then 'Mitch In The Morning' is the wrong place to go. While sports is naturally a big part of the show, it is much more than that. Taking a cue from Tony Kornheiser, Mitch sees his show as something that is transcendent.

"I always try to transcend the sports teams and the story lines around the sports teams. Yes, I use them and yes, I want to be popular when the Seahawks are in the news and when the Huskies are either winning or losing and when the Mariners lose 100 or win 116. I want to be interesting in those times. But I want to transcend that. I want people to say, 'hey, I gotta hear what Mitch and the crew say today' regardless of whether any of those particular storylines are present on that particular day. The people who can do that well, and I'm not suggesting to you that I do it well, that's for somebody else to decide. The people that can transcend the sports that they talk about are the ones that I think stay in it for a long time. Especially in the morning."

STORYTELLING

If Mitch finds something funny or ironic, he will certainly share it with his audience.

A recent example that he cited took place on an Alaska Airlines flight from Hawaii to Seattle.

Mitch thought about renting a digi-player for $12. The price didn't thrill him but he flipped through the programming guide to see if there was anything that would persuade him to cough up the $12. The table of contents included sports interviews, one of which was Mitch interviewing former Packers quarterback Don Majkowski.

"How it ended up being Don Majkowski and 'Mitch in the Morning' from KJR on the digi-player, that's for you to investigate. I found that to be funny. I'm actually the content on the digi-player so I have to pay $12 to listen to me. If I could somehow figure a way to listen to something else while I physically do the show I would. That should tell you how quick I was to pay $12 to listen to me. So I didn't take the credit card out. There's a story that's just perfect for radio, right?"

Indeed.

CROSSING THE LINE

Johnny Cash sung about walking the line. Mitch has not only walked the line, he's crossed it on many occasions.

"It happens more than regularly, more than I'd like to admit. My fear is you're going to ask me to cite examples."

Sure. Go ahead.

"I don't know that I can remember. It happens routinely and I'm on the air apologizing the next day. To

KJR and Clear Channel's credit, I can't remember the last time they said, 'Hey, come on. You went over the line. You gotta go do something about that.' In 16 years I don't think they've done that three times. Whenever I've gone over the line it's always self-recognized. It's always, 'Oooh, that didn't come out the way I wanted it. That wasn't as tongue and cheek as I would have liked. That was a little stronger than I would have liked it."

Which leads us to Sue Bird.

BIRD-LEVY WAGER

Sue Bird is one of the many great basketball players to come out of the University of Connecticut's women's program.

She was the first pick overall in the 2002 WNBA draft, selected by the Seattle Storm. Seattle is where Mitch Levy was and a storm was soon to follow.

Sue was a guest from time to time on 'Mitch in the Morning' and it served two purposes. It gave the Storm some much needed and desired publicity and it allowed Mitch to interview someone he admits he admired.

"Like most guys who watch women's basketball, I had a little thing for Sue."

Sue would go on the show a few times a year. Nothing earth-shattering about the interviews. They were basically fun, easygoing segments that delved into what was going on in her life. It was a little flirty in an innocent way, "which she got," says Mitch. "She understood it. She played along. She enjoyed it and looked forward to coming on."

The interviews were certainly not lengthy discussions on the Xs and Os of women's hoops.

A few years later, Bird was on the show again and started getting on Mitch for not going to the Storm's games.

"What do I gotta do to get you to go to the games

Mitch?" she asked him. "I want you to come watch Seattle Storm basketball."

Mitch had been to a few games but he wasn't a regular.

It was while looking at the first team All-WNBA point guard's stat sheet that Mitch got an idea.

"Too many turnovers," Mitch said tongue in cheek. "You gotta stop turning it over. I was kidding. She was laughing and I was laughing."

Mitch brought up the fact that her assist to turnover ratio was 1½ to 1 and he insisted it should be 3 or 4 to 1.

"It's gonna be better this year," Bird said.

"Are you guaranteeing me 3 to 1? 4 to 1?" Mitch asked.

"Yes," was the response.

They decided to make a friendly wager.

"What do you want," she asked.

"I don't know. What do you want if it is?"

"I want you to buy season tickets in the front row."

Mitch agreed.

Bird then wanted to know what Mitch wanted.

"I want to be able to spank you over the knee."

Uh oh.

"She starts laughing," Mitch recalls. "She says, 'You're kidding,' and I said, 'No.' And she kind of thought it was funny. 'And I'm not pushing this on you. It's up to you but this is what I wanted. But you don't have to worry about this of course because you're going to finish 3 or 4 to 1 anyway. So you're not going to have to worry about paying off the bet, right Sue?'"

Mitch says that Sue was not offended.

"She thought it was cute, she thought it was fun, she thought she had done nothing wrong. I thought I had done nothing wrong. Again, it's based on our previous experiences together."

The segment ended and the outrage began.

"How dare Mitch Levy make a wager to spank a female basketball player and how dare Sue Bird, a role model for young girls and for women who want to be empowered, how dare she subject herself to something like this," Mitch remembers. "It was all over the place."

It wasn't just a Seattle story, it was a national story, and Mitch turned down close to 50 interview requests, believing he wouldn't get a fair shake.

"It was done with only good intentions to promote the Seattle Storm."

Even though the Storm didn't have a problem with the wager and probably appreciated the publicity it generated, it was decided that the bet would be called off.

And who would have won the bet?

"ME!" Mitch says. "I'm still waiting for the opportunity to spank one of the best point guards who's ever played the women's game."

Bird has never been back on Mitch's show. Not because she doesn't want to, but Mitch says, "I've never known quite the comfortable way to do that interview."

SEAN McDONOUGH

Anyone who spends as much time on the air as Mitch Levy will have episodes that they regret. Normally, such things pass with time. Live radio leads to stuff happening.

There is one moment, though, in Mitch's broadcasting career that he can't let go and regrets to this day.

"I'll go to my grave upset that it happened. It involves one of the really neat guys, nice people and really talented people in our industry."

It also happened to involve a fellow Syracuse University alum who went to the upstate New York school a few years ahead of Mitch. We're talking about veteran broadcaster, Sean McDonough.

"I do nothing but respect the hell out of everything that he's done. He's just a pro's pro. There's nothing that he does that isn't good."

Alright, so far so good, Mitch.

The 1998 PGA Championship was at the Sahalee Country Club outside of Seattle, which was won by Vijay Singh.

"I'm a big golf nut," explains Mitch. "I was doing the show from the PGA Championship, which is very rare for me to get out of the studio. My producer was planning those shows and said, 'OK, what do you want to do about CBS announcers? Do you want to have any of them on?' This is a few days, a week or so before we went out there."

McDonough didn't do regular golf coverage except for when CBS would broadcast a major. He would then be added to the broadcast team.

"I said to the guys, 'Let's make sure when we have a golf announcer on from CBS it's one of their main golf announcers. Make sure it's a David Feherty, Gary McCord, Jim Nantz.' And that's the way we left it."

The day arrives when Mitch and company are at Sahalee doing the show and he gets word that they are driving over, from the CBS tent area, Sean McDonough.

Are you getting an uneasy feeling?

"And I said back on the IFB (direct line to the producer), during the commercial break to my producers in the studio, 'no no no no no. Remember, we want one of the golf guys that's week to week on the PGA Tour.' Obviously with no disrespect intended to Sean McDonough. I love Sean McDonough. And Sean came anyway. And he sat down at that table with me. We were about 15 seconds from going back on the air during a commercial break when he put his headsets on. And our producer at the time who will remain nameless, back in the studio, blurted into my headsets not knowing Sean had his headset on, 'Why in the world don't you want Sean

McDonough? What's wrong with McDonough?'"

Mitch was "in a state of shock."

Awkward is a word that comes to mind.

"Just another layer of why Sean McDonough is one of the great people in our industry. His reaction to that story is that he took his headsets off. He never mentioned it once. He took off his headsets as if to say, 'I'm hearing something that I'm not supposed to be hearing right now.' He did the interview. Did a great interview. Spent as much time as we needed. Shook my hand, said, 'Nice seeing you again, Mitch,' as if it never happened. Never once was there anything verbally or in his body language that suggested he was upset with me. He just let it go. I was humiliated. To this moment of my life I am humiliated over that. It haunts me what happened in 1998. I'll never get over it. Just another reason to be impressed with Sean. It was just one of those things that happened."

Mitch tried to explain things to Sean as he was leaving but McDonough stopped him and said, "Mitch, no offense taken."

McDonough showed how classy he is and it was a case of a couple of Syracuse guys sticking together. Live radio is great, isn't it?

INTERVIEWS

Around the industry, Mitch has a reputation as a solid interviewer. In true Levy fashion, he isn't about to beat his chest over those type of accolades.

"Trust me, I do as many bad interviews as I do good interviews. That you can write down in ink."

What makes a good interviewer?

"I think there are a few things. I think the art of listening is the most important thing in an interview. Not to go in there with question after question. You want to listen to what your interviewee is saying. Very often follow up questions, interesting and compelling questions come out of things that they say. Having a genuine interest in the person you are talking to. Some good research on maybe things that your audience doesn't know about the person. Even in interviews that come up because of controversial situations and I have to be serious, I like to try to find something interesting, fun about the person, bring it up and it kind of loosens the person up, if that makes sense."

He asks the questions that need to be asked.

"I believe in directly asking the important questions and maybe the uncomfortable questions. I can't think of many times over the years that I've shied away from asking question that might be uncomfortable to ask or for the interviewee uncomfortable to answer. I think there's a respectful, articulate way to ask any question. Even the hardest question. You have to find the right words and inflection and demeanor. I don't believe in being overly combative but I do believe in being direct."

Howard Cosell would be proud.

OPPORTUNITIES

While never having aspirations of becoming a national talk show host, Mitch did have a chance to work for Fox when his contract at KJR expired a decade ago. He explored resigning with KJR as well as other local Seattle opportunities.

Fox Sports Radio was looking for a morning show and Tom Lee, the programmer who hired Mitch at KJR, had moved on to Fox. He was looking for a new morning show host and had Mitch on his radar.

Mitch was offered the job and turned it down. He didn't want to live in Los Angeles where the show would be based. The counteroffer was Mitch could do the show in any city he and his wife chose. Mitch was thinking of moving closer to his family in Florida and his wife was from Washington, D.C., so the deal was verbally accepted. He said his goodbyes on and off the air at KJR and was set to move to Fox. His wife, Sharon, whom he met on a blind date before the WTEM days, quit her job. The movers started the process of gathering up the Levys' belongings for the trek to Florida.

The morning he was to sign the contract, he didn't.

"I got cold feet. I just felt like I was making a big mistake. I was on the treadmill at the gym. It was like 11 o'clock in the morning on the day before they were coming to sign me to a contract. I was just having terrible feelings that I was doing the wrong thing even though we had made our plans to leave. I had this terrible feeling in my soul that I was making a mistake and that I had something good here. When I left the gym that morning and came back to my home in Queen Anne there was a message on the machine from my agent."

The message said that KJR wanted one last chance to try to get Mitch to change his mind and stay.

Mitch called Sharon and his agent, and told them he wanted to stay in Seattle. They couldn't believe it. Tom Lee was very angry with Mitch.

Mitch's agent refused to make the call to Lee. He told Mitch to make the call.

"It was the hardest professional call I had to make because I owe so much to Tom. I was so friendly with Tom and I was putting him in such a terrible position, but at the same time, did Tom want me to go through with it knowing that my heart wasn't into it?"

Mitch doesn't remember the specifics of that conversation with Lee other than it was "horrible, terrifying, and nerve-wracking. He was very, very disappointed. It was very quiet. He couldn't believe it. He was shocked. I was embarrassed, ashamed, and I explained everything to him. That I was just getting this bad feeling. He was very upset. I told him I just can't do this, I can't sign this contract."

That led to a strained relationship between the pair

for several years but they have since ironed things out a bit.

Mitch resigned with KJR and didn't think much about a national show until ESPN started sniffing around a few years later when his old mentor, Tony Kornheiser, was giving up his show.

One of the concerns ESPN had with Mitch was that he was too much like Kornheiser. The deal would have been pretty complicated to complete.

The job eventually went to Colin Cowherd.

THE KIDS

Mitch loves doing his show, but there is one thing he doesn't like. He can't fix his two boys, 8-year-old Max and 5-year-old Brett, breakfast in the morning and take them to school.

It's safe to say the boys don't want to wake up at 4:30 just so Pops can fix them breakfast.

GOLF

"I'm a golf fanatic. I try to play as much golf during the summertime here in Seattle as I can. I love the game. It's my favorite thing in the world to do outside of being with my family. I've been playing since I was a little boy."

How good a golfer is he?

"Well, I guess it depends on who is asking. I'm like a 5-handicap."

ADVICE

While classroom experience is great, Mitch would suggest a hands-on approach for the aspiring broadcaster. While at Syracuse, Mitch did internships at NBC Radio and NBA Entertainment during the summers in New York City.

"Go get on the campus radio station, go be a DJ, go be a sportscaster, go do play-by-play. I used to sit in the corner at the top of the Carrier Dome with my microphone and tape recorder during football and basketball games and called the action. Get yourself internships. Get into TV stations, radio stations, get coffee and get breakfast and do whatever the grunt work is that needs to be done. But as you're doing that, learn to do things. Learn to produce, learn to book a show, go into a studio and do some fake sportscasts. Meet people and experience different aspects of our world. That's what I did."

REMEMBERING MITCH

How would Mitch Levy like to be remembered?

"Oh jeez, I don't want to answer that question. That's a horrible question. How do I want to be remembered? I want to be remembered as a guy who Sue Bird still owes a spanking! Who's thankful to Peter Brown for his rant against Sonics local TV and still wants to spank Sue Bird."

Tim Brando
"Iron Unkind"

Tim Brando has been in TV and radio longer than any other guy in this book. He was practically born into the business.

He's been an ESPN SportsCenter anchor, a play-by-play man, and he currently commands the microphone on his national show on Yahoo! Sports Radio (formally Sporting News Radio) and on CBS Television. He's done play-by-play for a multitude of sports and his smooth, easygoing demeanor and pleasant southern accent benefit his listeners on his daily sports talk show on Yahoo! There is no questioning his love of college sports and his ability to disseminate strong opinions.

LITTLE HUB

Tim was born in Shreveport, Louisiana, in 1956 as his father, Hub, was helping to establish television in that area.

Hub was a talented guy and eventually hosted three live shows, including 'The Hub Brando Variety Show.' The other shows were a local talent show and a kid's Saturday morning program.

Hub's musical band, Hub Brando and The Dreamers, put Tim to work at an early age as a drummer and singer. His older sister was part of the act as a dancer. They performed on television and took their show on the road to SAC Air Force bases.

"I was known around my hometown in the '60s as Little Hub," Tim remembers. "We even did 'Me and My Shadow' as a song and dance bit. I would also sing 'Too Old to Cut the Mustard Anymore' with him."

You can understand why performing or

broadcasting for Tim is second nature. He was a young boy hamming it up on television every week with his dad.

"Your dad's on TV and TV is brand new to the culture; it's a cool way of life. It's neat. I was around it. To me, the lights were as bright as being on Broadway."

Hub, who served in World War II, was an entertainer, a broadcaster, and sportswriter.

"He wore a lot of hats like a lot of guys in that generation did in their home markets," Tim says. "He was only legendary in Shreveport-Bossier, but that's all he had to be for me to be impressed."

Older people to this day go up to Tim and talk to him about his father.

"If you're over 60 and you live in the Shreveport-Bossier and surrounding area, you grew up on my father. So I'm constantly reminded at home about my father and it's actually a lot of fun. I enjoy that."

Tim's mother, Loretta, separated from Hub after 13 years of marriage. She was very concerned and cautious about her husband's career and eventually they parted.

"There was some bitterness as there would be in any relationship that ends that way in the '60s," Tim recalls. "But she always loved my dad until the day he died."

BEST FRIEND

When Tim began his stint at ESPN in 1985, Hub passed away from cancer at the age of 58.

"He got to see me realize a level of success and I think he was comfortable when he died that I was going to be successful, which makes me feel awful good."

Tim has been very successful and has had a varied and interesting career. It makes him think of his dad often.

"There are a lot of times when I would love for him to be around so I could say, 'Hey, can you believe I'm doing this? This is pretty cool!' We talked all the time. He was not just my dad, he was my best friend, too."

Tim says that his dad was a counselor and mentor and prepared him for the ups and downs and inevitable disappointments that go with broadcasting.

PLUNGING FORWARD

After his parents separated, Tim still worked with his dad. They called high school football games together beginning when Tim was 14. There was no way, despite a protective mom, that he was going to give up his broadcasting dreams.

Loretta was concerned that Tim might be wandering down the wrong career path, but things got better when her son was doing well away from Hub.

"When she started seeing me have success without him, both in school and speech and debate and that kind of thing, winning television announcing, oratory contests in high school and college, I think she knew that this was the direction I had to go in and she was very supportive. She was never, 'don't do this,' it was all about, 'just beware,' and I needed that. She offered balance to my upbringing."

Tim's mom is the only grandparent of his children that is still living.

"She's a huge basketball fan. She was a great athlete in school. She ran track and played basketball. She is exceedingly proud when she turns on a television set and sees her son."

SPORTS

When Tim was around 10 or 11, life changed. His parents separated and Hub's band broke up.

"I was no longer putting Brylcreem on my hair and combing it back and putting on tuxedos and shining my shoes to go on stage. I was actually a regular kid trying to fit in at school. Sports, obviously, was an avenue that I could redirect my life and feel good about myself and fit in with the other guys. When I was six, seven, eight, nine years old, I wasn't around to play pickup games in the front yard or the church lot. I didn't do any of those things."

That's unfortunate because it would have been fun to see a kid in shiny shoes with slicked back hair and a tuxedo playing pickup football in the neighborhood.

Hub eventually moved to California to pursue his entertainment dreams, which he could not do in Louisiana.

"I was the man of the house and had to make my own way, so to speak, and I ventured into sports that way."

What kind of athlete was young Tim Brando?

"I was a pretty good baseball and basketball player. In football, I played the Pop Warner stuff and all of that."

INFLUENCES

Some of the legendary broadcasters of the time became part of Tim's life through television.

"That's how I started developing, I think—my need and yearn for sports—through TV. I was watching Curt Gowdy and Jim Simpson and Jack Buck and Ray Scott and all of these great broadcasters call ballgames, and I was mesmerized because it was live TV and that's what I'd been around with my dad, live television. I thought to myself, 'That's the job to have.' Imagine you're Curt Gowdy and you're doing a World Series, a Final Four, a Super Bowl, and then when you got a little down time you're doing the American Sportsman out in a duck blind with Phil Harris pulling out a flask and having a toddy while you're waiting for the next groups of ducks to come in. To me, that looked like a good life. I was mesmerized by it and wanted to be like those guys."

To lead that life, he had to know his stuff so he began to prepare himself.

"I immediately started keeping up with all of the teams in all of the sports, football, basketball, baseball. When no one was around or no one wanted me to play in any of the pickup games, I'd go out with a Wiffle ball and bat or with a basketball in my front yard, and I would throw up my own fungos in baseball or throw up my own jumpshots in basketball, and also play a slow-motion video of John Facenda on NFL Films calling my own game as I played by myself."

Where he lived people would walk by, mostly women who were maids for families in the neighborhood. They would see Tim in the front yard playing and announcing his imaginary games.

"I'll never forget some looks on these ladies like, 'my God, that poor Brando boy is talking to himself again.' That went on all the time."

When he was 12, Tim knew exactly what he wanted to do.

"I knew I wanted to pursue it big time. I was really beginning to identify with all of the broadcasters and saying to myself, 'This is what I want to do.'"

A DIFFERENT GUY

In school, Tim played all the main sports. He also immersed himself in other extracurricular activities.

"In school I was sort of that nomad. I was the kid that was on the baseball team and the basketball team and the football team, but I was also the kid that was in the choir, sang solo, the kid that would be most likely to go into the speech club or the debate club, and be with the so-called kids that were seen as geeks because they talked a lot but didn't participate in sports. So the jocks would frown on me or not understand me for that, and I'd get the same from the kids that I was involved with in theatrical endeavors. I fit in with both actually. I found comfort in both social settings I was in."

ACADEMICS

Tim wasn't an exceptional student nor was he a numbskull.

"I was average," Tim says. "Not great, average. Just enough to get by. I was one of the ones that I think probably frustrated teachers that I didn't apply myself to the extent that maybe I should have. I was intimidated by math. I had the new math my generation had to deal with and I was scared to death of it."

Hub told Tim, "Don't worry about the things you're not good in, just find the one thing that you're great at and be the best you can be at it."

Tim says, with a laugh, "to a fault, I guess I followed my father's path."

OPPORTUNITIES

Being the son of Hub Brando made Tim a well-known figure in the Shreveport region. It certainly opened some doors.

"Opportunities did come my way. When I was a freshman in college, I was doing weekend sports on the NBC affiliate and I was doing an FM rock-jock shift on the major rock n' roll station on the weekends. The opportunities for me to work while I was in school were greater than anyone of my generation that I could think of in the South."

At times though, being so well known worked against Tim.

"I've got this thing down. I'm good. I think a lot of times you need a wake-up call, and I ventured to a point in my life where perhaps things came too easily, I needed that jolt. And I got it, like a lot of people do. At a certain point, you find out that you may have rubbed some people the wrong way."

The jolt came when a few programmers in radio and television laid down the law with Tim.

"They said, 'you know, Tim, you're talented. But you're not so talented that we can't tell you to get the hell out of here.'"

Point taken.

"I think we do want everyone to like us. I think that was probably my father's biggest downfall. He never could understand why everybody didn't like him. I was probably built the same way. I think my mother's influence really helped here because she said, 'Well, maybe you learned a lesson. You better be a little more humble and you better stick to what you need to do. Be on time. Don't think your talent will carry you.'"

It was at this time that he met his wife. Tim wanted to get married and when he did, he took a job in Baton Rouge.

"I needed to get away. I went to Baton Rouge right away in 1979 and I felt like this was a job I needed to keep. All of us in our business need to move if you're going to be successful. You have to take risks to be successful in our business."

He was 22 and in a new town where he had to prove himself. Being Little Hub wasn't going to cut the mustard anymore. It was time to get to work, which he did.

"I had to outwork people to get ahead and build my own name."

TERRI

Tim did pretty well with the girls growing up. Mostly because he was able to charm the parents. He was able to easily converse with them, which sometimes got the girl riled up.

"I'd win the moms and dads over big time, and then the girls would hate me because the moms and dads liked me."

When Tim was 21, he met Terri. They married a year later and they've been married since, more than 32 years. They have two daughters, Tiffany and Tara.

Much of Tim's evolution was due to Terri.

"Part of my wake-up call was finding a woman that not only loved me, but could slap me into shape when I was doing the wrong thing, when I was falling back on old habits. It helped that I ran into my wife, Terri."

In college, Tim worked at a radio station in a downtown building. He had to pass a business in the lobby in which the secretary could be seen through a glass window. They waved to each other every day as Tim went to the elevators to the 11th floor. The secretary inquired to someone at the radio station about Tim, which made him confident enough to ask her to lunch. The secretary was Terri.

So Tim, was it love at first sight?

"Yeah, pretty much."

BREAKS

In Baton Rouge, Tim was working an afternoon shift at his station and convinced the station owner to let him do a nightly one-hour sports talk show. There were no nightly sports talk shows there at the time in a city of more than 300,000 people. He told the owner that even though the show broke format, it would make money and fill a void.

Tim put his full effort into the show. There wasn't a press conference at Louisiana State University that he didn't attend. Golf, tennis, gymnastics, football, basketball, baseball, whatever. Tim was there.

"I would involve myself in the campus of LSU. I wanted to make everyone at the institution aware that they could use my airwaves to promote their product. I literally did everything in my power to be seen by everyone at that school."

In the early '80s Bob Brodhead became the new athletic director at Louisiana State. He had an idea to create

Tigervision, an outlet where people could watch cable telecasts of non-revenue producing sports of LSU teams. Back then even basketball was considered non-revenue. Tim was brought on to call the games.

"I started doing these basketball games and baseball games and whatever they threw my way on cable television, on Tigervision. Right about that time, Dale Brown's program was taking off. They went to their first Final Four in 1981. I was able to gather a lot of tapes of my calling several different sports, including college basketball, and I got some really good air check tapes to send out."

ESPN AND DICKIE V

Tim was prepared to call LSU basketball games when he got a call the last week of December 1984 from the talent coordinator at ESPN, where he sent his demo tape out a full year prior.

"I got this call from a woman who sounded like Fran Drescher from *The Nanny*. She said, 'This is Ellen Beckwith, I'm with ESPN.' OK, now my antennas are up a just a little bit. I had sent the tapes out so long ago that I forgot that I had not gotten a rejection letter from ESPN. I had not received any response from them."

Apparently, they held on to Tim's tape in a keeper file and Beckwith asked him if he was available to work an upcoming basketball game, on January 5th, in Charlottesville, Virginia.

"I never lost my cool. I learned this from my father; always make sure they know you're busy. So I said, 'Well, let me check my schedule.' I kind of put the phone down in my lap and tried to recompose myself because I was about to jump out of my shorts. And I said, 'It just so happens I'm available.' Which of course I was not, I was scheduled to work an LSU-Mississippi State game."

Tim worked the Duke-Virginia game that day and

made the going rate for freelance talent back then: $350.

Beckwith did pass this along to Tim.

"Just one thing, and we are concerned about it, you will have to work with Dick Vitale. Do you think you can handle that?"

Tim replied, "Listen to me, Ms. Beckwith. I really appreciate the phone call and I'm certainly happy that you've offered me this opportunity, but I want you to rest assured that I am a broadcaster first. I know I'm prepared to do this and I can handle any analyst you bring my way. I'm the play-by-play guy whether he's there or not."

After adding several more comments, Tim believed he got his point across.

"I think she liked my swagger. She kind of chuckled and said, 'Well Tim, we'll see. I wish you the best on that. Our people will be in touch with you.' I had no guarantee beyond that that they would call me back."

It was an on-air tryout for Tim with the six-year-old network.

"It went very well. Dick and I had a wonderful broadcast together. I'm pretty sure he went back and told all the producers this kid from Louisiana is pretty doggone good, and I think his reaction to working with me was very positive and it sort of blossomed into more calls from her for more jobs."

The next year, he got the job as a sideline reporter for college football on ESPN's Saturday night prime time game.

"CFA football on Saturday night on ESPN was the biggest show they had. That was the biggest show on the network. I had not been hired full-time at that point, but I knew when I got that opportunity the next step would probably be for me to move up to Connecticut and be a part of their staff."

He would make more than the $350 he made for his ESPN debut. It was a six-figure salary but not much more than that.

"It was a lot of money at the time, but the cost of living in Baton Rouge versus the Hartford, Springfield, and that area of Connecticut, my quality of life drifted downward big time even though I was making a lot more money than I ever made."

The moral of this story? If you send out tapes and don't get a rejection letter, maybe you'll get a call, eventually.

GARF

During Tim's first broadcast at ESPN with Dick Vitale, he noticed that his color analyst spent most of halftime on the phone. Tim was ready to go over the halftime stats and asked the producer, Bobby Feller, not the pitcher, if they needed Dick.

Feller said, "nah, not really. He'll just screw it up. You handle it. It'll be fine."

After the stats, Feller asked Tim if Dick was still on the phone.

"Yeah," Tim responded. "What's going on?"

"He's on the phone with Garf trying to find out how good he sounds," Feller said.

Garf being Howie Garfinkel, who ran the Five-Star basketball camps.

Tim says, "Dick was so insecure that at halftime of every game he would call Garfinkel to find out how good we were sounding and is there anything he needs to get in that he hadn't gotten in yet. And Dick had been doing this for six years! He had been doing this since the first year of ESPN in 1979. Now I'm insecure, but that's over the top. As soon as he got back to sit down next to me he turns to me and says, (Tim, in Vitale's voice) 'Hey kid, Garf says you sound great. We're good together.' Garf likes me. That's beautiful. I'll always remember that."

NAME THE GAME

Tim has called plenty of different sports. Make that more than plenty. At ESPN alone he called 25 different sports.

If someone at ESPN didn't want to call a sport, they would just ask Tim and he would always say yes.

"If they didn't want to do it they would just call me. I was like Mikey. Give Brando that. He'll do it. He'll do anything. He just wants to be on."

Here is where another one of his father's lessons came in handy.

"He said, 'If someone says, Tim, have you ever done this before, always tell them yes.' If you say no, that's a reason for them to say no to you."

They would ask Tim if he's done a particular sport and he would say, "absolutely." Meanwhile, he didn't know a damn thing about it. But that is why professional broadcasters do homework and put in the proper amount of prep work.

"I got to do every thing from Greco-Roman wrestling to Judo to Team Handball, you name it. Every imaginable off-the-wall sport, I would go out and do."

SOUTHERN MAN

While Tim was thriving at ESPN, there was a problem. He didn't particularly like living in Connecticut.

"I'm a Southern guy at heart," Tim says. "I probably didn't even realize it until I lived up there. I thought as long as I'm doing what I love, I can live anywhere."

He realized that other ESPN guys like Ron Franklin and Mike Patrick didn't live in Connecticut, but those were exclusive play-by-play guys. Tim did play-by-play but also studio work, including hosting SportsCenter.

"I loved the job but I didn't love living there. And I didn't want to do SportCenter at 2:30 in the morning anymore. Because I was getting all these plum assignments in football and basketball, it seemed every spring and summer I was doing the overnight shift and it was not real good with a young child and a wife that was a southern belle. And I would be leaving her in the frozen North when I went on the road to do basketball games."

In 1990 Tim renegotiated a new deal that allowed him to move back home, but management wasn't happy with him.

"I definitely fell in disfavor at that point with management, even though I got what I wanted."

He knew he was finished after the 1994 college football season. They were flying Tim to Bristol to do college football studio work, and they scaled back his play-by-play assignments. Once ESPN hired Mike Tirico to work in the studio, the writing was on the wall. Tim knew he was expendable and was told so. Time to look elsewhere.

Would Tim call it an ugly divorce from ESPN?

"No, no," Tim said emphatically adding that he had fond memories of working there. He didn't want to just be a studio star, he wanted to call games.

"I was old school. I wanted to be Curt Gowdy, not Chris Berman."

POST ESPN

After ESPN Tim moved on to Turner Sports, where he got the chance to call professional sports. He did Atlanta Hawks and Atlanta Braves games as well as the NBA playoffs in the mid-90s.

He then was hired by CBS Sports to do college football and other things.

When the NFL came back to CBS in 1998, Jim Nantz moved from the college football studio to the 'NFL Today'' desk.

"They still needed a host for college," Tim says,

"and that opportunity was afforded me in '98. I was hosting college football as well as doing the tournament (NCAA basketball) and those kinds of things. I went away from the booth and went back into the studio."

ESPN TODAY

Tim isn't a big fan of ESPN today.

"I think that the game should still be the main girl in town. Not the people that are projecting the game. We didn't even give credit to the producers and directors that were doing the games. Now it seems like you're getting beaten over the head with the credits. The whole idea of self-promotion, that impedes, I think, the event itself. I don't like that. I certainly have as much ego as anyone else. I certainly want everyone to know that it's me that's doing the game, but I don't think we should become bigger than the game. Again, that's an old school thing."

BUY A VOWEL

If Tim wasn't a sports broadcaster, what would he have done to make a living?

With his show biz upbringing he may have become a game show host. He loved game shows as a kid, such as *The Newlywed Game*, *The Match Game*, and *The Dating Game*. In 1988, Tim actually tried out and was a finalist to host *Wheel of Fortune* when Pat Sajak left to do a talk show. He did well in his tryout, but the gig went to former Chargers kicker Rolf Benirschke. Tim did get to meet Vanna White though, which was pretty cool.

"My destiny was to be with Beano Cook, not Vanna White."

Game show hosts were people that got Tim's attention.

"Some of these guys I really looked up to. I felt all along when I was coming up, if I couldn't be Curt Gowdy, I'd love to be Bob Barker or Wink Martindale."

CURT GOWDY

Curt Gowdy became a mentor to Tim in 1982. As you might expect, Tim was thrilled to meet Gowdy, the legendary broadcaster he grew up listening to and admiring from afar.

Bob Earle owned the radio station that Tim was doing his sports show from. Earle was an independent owner. He belonged to a group called Independent Owners Association and one of the people who was a member was Gowdy, who owned several stations.

The Independent Owners would get together a couple of times a year. Earle, who knew of Tim's love of sports and broadcasting asked Gowdy to listen to a few of Tim's tapes.

Gowdy liked the tapes and was impressed. He felt Tim was a talented kid.

A couple of years later, Gowdy was in New Orleans where Tim was working for WGSO radio. Tim had the chance to interview Gowdy, who was in town to work the Final Four at the Superdome, the one that Michael Jordan won for North Carolina over Georgetown with a dramatic jump shot in the waning moments. Tim was asked if he wanted Gowdy on his show to promote *The American Sportsman*.

"Are you kidding me?" Tim remembers. "He has no idea who the local guy is who is going to interview him, but I knew that he knew of me because those cassette tapes. He comes walking in and I said, 'Curt, I'm the guy that Bob Earle talked to you about a couple of years ago.'"

They did the hour-long show and Curt invited Tim to breakfast the next morning.

"I went to breakfast with him and Curt really took me under his wing. I told him I got to name my little brother Curt after him. I called my house and had my 11-year-old brother talk to him. Well, he got a little teary-eyed over that and I had a friend for life. It was a tremendous relationship and I miss him dearly. He was the best."

Gowdy passed away in 2006 at the age of 86.

SNR

Tim began his show at Sporting News Radio more than 10 years ago. It was a relationship that developed out of thin air. "I got a call, literally out of the blue," Tim recounts. "Out of the sky, asking me if I'd be interested in doing a daily sports radio show."

Tim had been doing a show that dealt intensively with the SEC called 'Conference Call,' which he did with Terry Bowden. While Tim wasn't the show host, he was one of the analysts, and he would go at it with the callers. They had their point of view and Tim had an honest, objective observer approach. He did it from his home and it was a fairly easy payday for him.

Somebody from Sporting News Radio must have heard 'Conference Call' and thought Tim would be a good fit.

They made an offer, which Tim says was so dynamic that he couldn't turn it down. He wouldn't have taken it otherwise, since he was concerned with his schedule.

"It was a decision that was not easy, even though it was one that was made easier by the financial package they offered."

Tim does his daily network show from a studio in his home.

"I think it brings a lot more of who and what I am on a daily basis to the show. It's like I wake up and have a cup of coffee and instead of talking to people at the 19th hole or at the water cooler, I'm talking to masses, people like me who love sports and it's a way of life for them. I think it's a lot more real because I'm doing it from home. And without question it's more convenient."

One of his goals is to beat out ESPN radio. Five

ownership changes and three relocation shifts has made that difficult, but it is still on Tim's mind.

"I don't think you should ever go on the air without wanting to be the best. Without beating the best. And ESPN has been the best at it for a long, long time. It's meant to be a compliment to them. I have a lot of friends still there. But when I go on the air I want to be better than them. And I want everyone to think we're better than them, meaning anybody associated with my show."

AL MCGUIRE

In a sports broadcasting sense, one of the highlights of Tim Brando's career was working the NCAA Tournament with legendary Marquette coach and colorful broadcaster Al McGuire.

"I think the three weeks that I worked with Al McGuire in '98 were probably the best three weeks of my life. In '98 I got a plum assignment to work with Al, to work a regional final with Al. I got to work with Al, which was a real thrill. I had worked with Vitale, I had worked with Billy Packer, and I had never worked with Al McGuire and I learned so much. We got through with the SEC championship in Atlanta and we're hurrying to the airport to try and make a flight. We're sweating it out just trying to make it to the airport and Al says, 'You need to stop and smell the roses. If you miss the flight we'll go back to the hotel, have a nice dinner and some wine and enjoy it. You're gonna die anyway, why not enjoy the fruits of your labors?' Life lessons were learned with Al that I had never thought about. In the world we live in we're always in a hurry, just slow down and enjoy it just a bit. That's what McGuire was all about. He was truly college sports first, flower child as a coach. He lived what he preached in a manner that no one else that I've ever been around ever has."

Leukemia took the irrepressible McGuire in 2001.

I'M BILL RAFTERY

One night, Bill Raftery was Tim's color man for a Vanderbilt basketball game. Barry Goheen, who made a habit out of making game-winning shots, did his thing with another buzzer beater. The ESPN producer was in Tim's ear telling him to throw it to SportsCenter right away. In his exuberance and haste, Tim wrapped it up by saying, "for Tim Brando, this is Bill Raftery, bye-bye everybody."

There was no time to correct it.

"Raftery is laughing at me like, 'You idiot!' They were on the air in Bristol right after I said it."

THE IRON UNKIND

Listen to a Tim Brando-called basketball game and you'll probably hear one of his trademark calls, "the iron unkind!" for a ball that doesn't get a friendly roll.

"When I was a kid we always referred to the rim as 'the iron.' Some say tin, some say rim, some coaches say 'take it to the hole.' I'm just in the middle of a game on ESPN one night, and the ball was halfway down the iron and hit the backboard and came back and circled it again a time or two and fell off, and I said, 'oh, the iron unkind!' It sort of just came out of my mouth. Vitale was working with me and I could see Dick was like, (in Dickie V's voice again) 'hey, that was pretty good! I like that! I never heard that!' It really did accidentally come out of my mouth. I thought I should keep it in my hip pocket and bring it out once a game."

Tim explains, "If the iron is unkind, it can also be kind."

The iron unkind, or kind, has become part of Tim's vernacular and fans and players alike identify with it.

"To this day, I'll see Doug Collins and he'll remember when his son Chris was at Duke and there was a game involving NC State and Duke in '96, and Chris hit a shot that literally hit the front of the rim, bounced off, hit the back board, hit the back of the iron and bounced in. It was a three-ball that gave them the lead with about eight seconds left. The game was in Raleigh at the old Reynolds Coliseum. So I said, 'the iron kind!' They in-bounded the ball and this kid, I can't remember his first name but his last name was Marshall, is playing for NC State at the time and he's hauling butt down the floor and he shoots a running bank shot that goes in the rim and round and round and round and out. I had honestly not used the term that day. I had waited. I had not seen a shot like that. And within 10 seconds with the game on the line we got an 'iron kind and oh, an iron unkind!' I'll see Doug at a Duke game when he comes to see Chris coach and every time I see him he says, 'Timmy B the iron is kind!' So it just sort of stuck."

FACTOID
Despite his celebrity, Tim does his own yard work.
"Absolutely. I'm a Southern boy. We do our own yards."

GOLF
While at ESPN, Tim played fast-pitch softball, but at 32, he was getting tired of the skinned knees, aches, and pains. It was John Saunders, though, that turned him onto golf. It became one of his passions. He lives on a golf course and breathes the game.

"It's not because I'm a great player, because I'm not. I work hard at getting better at it. It's such a hard game and it demands a lot of attention and patience and all the things that type A personalities like me are not."

He likes it to get away from the pressures of work and other things.

"For me it's cathartic. I really get into the golf is a way of life type of thing. I'm very much into the whole Bagger Vance thing. I'm really into golf, every aspect of it."

When Tim, a lefty and 12 handicap, isn't playing he's watching the Golf Channel.

THEATER

With his upbringing it comes as little surprise that Tim enjoys the theater as well as movies.

"I'm a big theater buff and movie buff. Whenever we go to New York during football season we take the girls to multiple musicals. We go to as many musicals as we can go to. I think we've seen *Jersey Boys* nine times. I just love musicals. I think it all goes back to my dad and being on stage as a kid. I'd say that golf and the theater are my two big passions."

CRITICAL AND ENTERTAINING

Part of Tim's job is to be critical and entertaining. While some guys can get personal in their criticisms, he tries to stay away from that.

"Can you be critical of a coach? Sure you can and I am all the time. It generally has to do with something that happened in the game. Personal attacks, and there are plenty of them in radio, I think, has given the business a really bad name. And I have tried my best to point out that you don't have to be that way. You can have some sanity and still be entertaining and critical. I'm doing radio and I think I'm doing entertaining radio, but make no doubt—this is Tim Brando from television that's doing a radio show. I will never stop being Tim Brando sportscaster on TV just because I'm doing a radio show. This idea that I'm going to make condescending comment after condescending comment, the Rome approach if you will, I despise that. And I hear so many watered down and diluted Jim Rome wannabees and I think that's awful. And by the way, Jim's done very well at being Jim. That's who he is. If you're an original then go get you some. I'm all for that.

But if you are just trying to do an imitation of what he's done in the past because you think that's the way to go, I think you're making a mistake."

ADVICE

"The first and foremost thing any broadcaster needs to do, whether he's on radio or he's on television, is understand one thing and one thing only. Know who you are. Be an original, be who you are. If you try being anything other than who you are, you're never going to get where you want to go."

FINAL SHOT

Through it all, the ups and downs, Tim remains grounded. A big part of that is his faith.

"I don't wear my faith on my shirtsleeves but I am a man of faith. I think I was blessed to have had a father that wasn't perfect but was very talented and was talented beyond people's recollections. I wish more people could have known him because I really did gain all my confidence from him telling me, 'You're not just good, you're great. You've got to believe that you're great to be believable to people. You can win people over and you've got to command respect by being as great as I know you can be. That little red light that's on the camera, people oftentimes say, 'What's it like to look into the camera and know that you're going to millions of people?' And I remember he taught me this very early, 'Don't think of that red tally light as being anything other than one person that you most want to convince that you're right.' Well, that one person that I always wanted to convince that I was right, that I loved the most, was my father. To me, for all these years that I've been doing what I've been doing, whether that light is an audio light for radio or a video light for television, it's the spirit of my father that lives through that camera that I broadcast to individually every time I go on

the air."
 The rim has been kind to Tim Brando.

Howard Eskin
"The King of Bling"

When you think of Philadelphia, you think of Howard Eskin. Well, maybe you think of other things first, like the Liberty Bell, cheesesteaks, pretzels with mustard, and Rocky. But when you discuss sports talk in the City of Brotherly Love, the conversation begins with Eskin, also known as the King of Bling. We'll explain that later.

Howard, after 25 years of hosting sports shows on WIP, entertaining, battling, and at times infuriating listeners, he is no longer doing the daily grind on afternoon drive on Philly's all-sports station. That came to an end in September 2011. His new contract at the station allows him more freedom to work on Eagles broadcasts and other shows on WIP.

One reason for Eskin's staying power? The guy pulls no punches. After all, he's in Philadelphia and in that sports-savvy town you can't pull punches. It can be a tough audience, but he's been at it for over 30 years with no signs of slowing down.

WIP

This past summer, word about Howard leaving his daily afternoon drive sports show made front-page news in the Philadelphia *Daily News*. Howard was looking for new challenges but the all-sports station wanted to keep him. A compromise was worked out, and he'll continue to remain an integral part of WIP.

"It will be nice to play some more golf, but I will probably work more soon," Eskin says.

ALWAYS ABOUT SPORTS

For as long as Howard can remember, he was always interested in sports.

His father, Donald, was very much into sports as was the entire Eskin family.

"It was all about sports. I was an average student and I'm the first to tell people that. I'm the luckiest person in the world to be where I am today, which I think is a success. Other people may debate that, who call me on the air."

Eskin describes himself as an average Joe who grew up in an average section of Philadelphia. While he thought about making a career out of sports that vision didn't truly come to him until later in life. There were too many games to play until then.

"As a child I just loved sports. We'd go out back and play stickball, handball, boxball, halfball, Wiffle ball, you name it I played it. Wireball, stepball, wallball, dodgeball, kickball, it was just something I grew up with."

DAD

As with many young boys, Howard's father was a huge influence on him, especially when it came to sports.

"There is absolutely no question about that. My father played in a softball league and was actually pretty good from what I remember as a kid. I just developed a love for sports. Back then everybody developed a love for sports. Kids today, the first thing they do is go to the computer. There's not as many kids going out and playing baseball 'cause kids don't like to stand in the outfield. I didn't care what I did as long as I played on a team. So I played little league, the whole deal, all the way through."

Howard's father passed away about two years ago in Clearwater, Florida, a place he used to take his family to for Phillies spring training.

"I guess I've been down to Phillies spring training

every year since I was 15 or 16 years old."

Donald Eskin bought a home right down the road from where the ballpark is today in Clearwater, and Howard says that's where his father wanted to pass.

THE ATHLETE

He wasn't a star player by any means and at times Howard found himself on the bench.

"We always think that we are better than we are. I thought I was good. I didn't think I was great. I probably wasn't good enough to play at the college level. It's kind of funny, I always concentrated on the things that are not in vogue today. When I played baseball, I always loved playing defense. I played third base, first base, and I pitched. Boy, I could throw hard until I hurt my shoulder. I could throw really hard. I was an average hitter but a very good defensive player. In basketball I'd rather pass the ball than shoot the ball. I was an average shooter but I thought I had really good court vision, and in football I was an offensive lineman, until I lost 60 pounds my senior year in high school and it kind of didn't work on the offensive line. But I had good hands."

Howard was a chubby kid who has fought his weight all his life. By his estimate he's lost and gained 400 pounds.

"I fight it now but I'm better disciplined with it. But when I went into television (1982) it was a matter of pride."

FAILURE NOT AN OPTION

Howard admits that he wasn't a big fan of school. He didn't go to college and went to vocational schools. It wasn't until after graduating from Northeast High School that he became truly motivated.

Part of the reason? His parents. His mother, Annette, was strict and his father just let Howard do his thing.

"I really got motivated after I got out of high school. I can't explain it. It was the fear of failure for my parents more than anything else. I had a fear of failing in the world. I just worked hard and all of a sudden the light went off and bang. My parents did so much for me, I was afraid to fail."

Again, sports was creeping into his mind as a way to make a living.

"Through it all there was always that vision of sports. I think somewhere around my sophomore or junior year in high school that I said, 'This is what I want to do for my career.' Now, I would have taken anything. I applied for the sports information director's job at Villanova before they won the National Championship in '85. I just wanted to be in sports."

DRIVE

The fear of failure produced a maniacal work ethic.

"I pushed and pushed and pushed and worked for peanuts," Howard recalls. "I worked for $1.60 an hour at a radio station in Atlantic City early in my career, and I was tickled pink, I had a job. And then I got $50 in trade at a delicatessen. That was living. I was living then. Those were all the things, those were all the steps. I just took all the steps and at the time I always had the vision I wanted to be in sports. I was a production engineer in Washington, D.C., I was spinning records for the guys at WFIL in Philadelphia. But I always wanted to make sure I had a vision. I just wanted to progress along the way and each radio station I went to, even when I was just on the other side of the glass back in the day, I just wanted to get better in every thing I did."

SHYNESS

If you listen to him on the radio or on TV you would not think that Howard Eskin was shy. But he was.

"I was insecure as a person because I was shy, and sports was my outlet. I was very shy as a child. But when I went out there and played basketball or baseball I was out of my shyness. I always played hard and I think it helped me in my career, because I played hard and now I work hard."

GEORGE MICHAEL

One of the biggest influences on Howard's career was George Michael, the sportscaster, not the singer. Michael, who had a long and memorable career, was probably best known for his highlight show 'The George Michael Sports Machine.'

Michael, who passed away in 2009, allowed Howard to spin records for him at a radio station in Philadelphia.

"I ended up doing a segment on his national show for 11 years. We always stayed in touch. He asked me to come down and work for him at Channel 4 in Washington, but I had so much going on in Philadelphia at that time it never happened. There were a couple of guys along the way, but I think I was self-motivated and it happened after I got out of high school."

Howard added that Michael was a perfectionist.

"He'd yell at me and I'd be fine."

ON HIS WAY

Jim O'Brien is another guy who was helpful in Howard's career. The late O'Brien was a radio disc jockey before becoming a television sports anchor, weatherman, and then news anchor in Philadelphia.

One day Jim became infuriated with Howard and it got ugly, at least by today's standards.

"O'Brien had me by the throat one day because I got a little sloppy spinning a record. But he got me to be better. Nowadays, can you imagine somebody yelling at somebody and grabbing them by the throat? I don't care, it made me better."

Eventually, when Howard was doing board op work, O'Brien said to him, "Man, I don't know what you're doing, doing this stuff. You should be doing what you should be doing, and that's sports."

Soon Howard got a job as a sports reporter at WCAU in Philadelphia, replacing Joe Banner, who eventually became the president of the Philadelphia Eagles.

That's where it started for Howard, in 1976, running around with a tape recorder and doing anything he could.

He did stats for visiting basketball announcers, with Marv Albert being his favorite.

"I loved Marv. He paid me $50 and everybody else paid me $25. It was great."

Certainly better than the $10 he got to keep stats for Ivy League football, although he didn't care. He was working in sports.

Those various assignments led to a sports talk show spot at WWDB in Philly, and soon after he began his foray into television at Channel 3.

TELEVISION

While Howard embraced the chance to work in TV, he wasn't about to leave radio, his roots. He's also not fond of the current state of television.

"It's a joke. The anchors are uncomfortable in ad-libbing, the sports guys don't really want to (ad-lib) with the anchors, and they at times are uncomfortable and people get locked into a teleprompter."

Howard's radio background gave him the ability to ad-lib. If something went wrong, he just looked into the camera and started talking.

He used to tell the anchors, "Don't tell me what you are going to say. Just ask it and whatever you ask I'll roll with it. That's what I did full-time for 11 years until I decided radio is where I really want to be."

According to Howard, they've destroyed television sports in America.

"They think everyone has to tune in for the weather. We can't get by without the weather. You know what, I'm looking at my phone and I can get the weather on my phone. In sports, if the guy's got a personality he can do something."

The first night Howard worked in television is one he'll always remember. He even recalls the date— September 20, 1982. It was to be the 6 o'clock newscast.

"The clock up on the wall says 5:09, the NFL players called a strike. Now I'm not just doing a sportscast, I'm the lead story of the news my first night in television. You've got to be kidding me! I'll never forget that. Never, never, never."

Howard worked at channels 3, 10, and 29 in Philadelphia. He even worked a night in Washington, D.C., when one of George Michael's guys had a heart attack.

Here's something that might be astounding.

"I never applied for a TV job in my life," Howard says. "And I've been working in television, like I said, since 1982."

Why has he has so much success on TV?

"Well, I think because I'm good on the air and I have a personality. I'm opinionated but people call me controversial. I have the energy that they like in broadcasting and I work hard, which is not a quality a lot of sports guys have in today's world."

CRITICISM

Howard, like any broadcaster, faces his share of criticism. Because he's not vanilla he probably gets more than his share.

When he started they didn't tell Eskin he sucked, but they told him in a different way.

"They would tell me they didn't like me because of what I said. I was so nice to people. I'm nice to people anyway, but on the air this one day I wanted to tell a guy off and I held it in. I walked out of that show and said, 'I should have told that guy he had no clue. None. An idiot.' I mean he had no idea and then I finally realized, you know what, tell people what you think. People could have told me I sucked and I wasn't good and I'm terrible, but they didn't tell me that way. They call me a hater because I criticize players, but they never really attacked my professionalism. It was love-hate, in either you loved me or you hate me and if you're somebody in the middle you better get off that fence because you got to decide with me in this town."

Once Howard was ticked off by a newspaper column that ripped him. He was angry and told former Phillies centerfielder Garry Maddox about a guy who was murdering him constantly in the papers. Maddox offered great advice.

"What are you all bent out of shape about? What are you pissed off about? Listen, if you're gonna be upset with what you read in the papers, you can't read them. If you read them, you gotta learn, don't get upset, let it roll."

Howard says he doesn't pay attention to the critics because, "I'm the first to know I'm not doing it well. Because I walk away from a show and I say, 'That wasn't good enough. I could have done this better and that better.'"

PREPARATION

Howard is a guy who admits he should take more days off, especially during football season.

"I push hard. If I don't go to Eagles practice I feel guilty. If I don't go to a game I should go to, and I go to most of them, I feel guilty. I expect more out of myself. You never know what you are going to pick up in terms of information. Not by watching the game but by talking to people after the game. Players and coaches will tell you things because they always see you there. I've gotten a lot from players and coaches because they trust me, because they always see me there."

Eskin calls Cal Ripken, Jr, baseball's Iron Man, a fraud—tongue in cheek, of course.

"I didn't have a sick day for 20 years, give me a break. Cal Ripken had three months off during the year and had days off during the season!"

MR. 5,000

They don't usually keep detailed stats in the radio broadcasting industry on how many shows a person has done. Certainly not like baseball stats. Some shows keep track, but most guys can only estimate how many programs they've done.

Howard apparently has kept stats on how many shows he's done. On September 20, 2007, he did his $5,000^{th}$ show and called Michael Harrison of *Talkers* magazine to see if he knew of anyone or could find anyone who has done as many shows. Harrison came up empty in his search.

ESKIN THE SKIPPER?

In 1983 the Phillies went to the World Series and lost to the Orioles under manager Paul Owens. Earlier in the season, the Phils fired manager Pat Corrales, and Howard decided he wanted the job.

"I said, 'I could do this'. So I called (Phillies President) Bill Giles, who I knew real well and said, 'I'd like to apply for the job of manager.' He kind of laughed and I said, 'Hey listen, a baseball manager, you don't have to wake up until the 6th or 7th inning. You just got to get players to understand you know what you're doing. That's all. If you've got a good pitcher, I'll take a nap, wake me up in the 6th inning and tell me where we are in the game.

That's what baseball is, and in the American League it's a complete joke because you don't even have to pinch hit, you just need to know when to take the pitcher out."

He told Giles that the job was easy but for some strange reason, Howard didn't get the Phillies managerial job.

Another time Howard applied for the Phillies' open general manager position.

"Hey listen, I know personnel. And I have the guts to make a move to get better. I thought I could do that job, too."

While he knew he wouldn't get the job, he felt he could do the job. Or as he says, "I knew I could do the job."

Was it a typical radio publicity stunt?

"No, I was serious. Dead serious."

He also applied for the 76ers GM spot. He didn't get that job, either.

THE KING OF BLING
We told you we would explain.

Howard went to a Philadelphia Eagles fashion show for charity. The players and their wives were modeling fur coats. Someone told Howard that he should be modeling coats, too.

"I'm a 5'10" white guy. I can't pull off a fur coat, gimme a break."

Several black guys then called his show and told him he could roll with the fur coat. So, one thing led to another and he talked to someone from a fur coat company. This all came during a bone-chilling winter in Philly.

"It was an Eagles-Dallas game, couldn't get any bigger. I come to the game in a full-length fur coat I got from the company. They just let me borrow it. A picture is in the paper, this is nonsense. It's BS, but sometimes BS works in newspapers and on the air. It became a thing people were talking about. So I said, 'OK,' and then I worked out a deal with the company. I was on a billboard with Jevon Kearse wearing a fur coat. It was nuts. The word I use is schtick. It was schtick, and then it was I'd come to a game with diamonds on the Rolex, I'd be blinged out with diamonds on the cufflinks. I only do it for the football games. You can't bling yourself out if it's not something that's big. It's gotta be big and football games are only once a week. So somebody called me the King of Bling. In the early '80s a guy on Channel 3 (before Eskin worked there) did a story on me and sports talk, and at the end of the story he called me the King of Sports Talkers in Philadelphia. OK, I didn't think much of it. I walk into the (Phillies) locker room the next day and Pete Rose says, 'Hey, there's the King.' Then the players started calling me the King and people started calling me the King. So then with the fur coats and the Rolex and all the other nonsense, it's really not nonsense, it's been a good kind of thing for me, it's fun. Then they rolled that into the King of Bling. So I'm still called King or the King of Bling. First of all it is absolutely wrong to give yourself a nickname. Can't do it. You're a fraud if you give yourself your own nickname. And people say 'Well you gave yourself a nickname.' No. It was a story on Channel 3 and then Pete Rose in the locker room, and then they all started calling me The King."

Even the players of today address Howard as the King. Which he of course finds quite humorous.

MEMORABLE GAMES

When the Phillies won the World Series in 1980, it was the first time Howard experienced a baseball championship in Philadelphia.

"It's hard to single out one game, but I'd have to take the 1980 World Series. I grew up going to spring training every year and I knew all the guys on that team. I guess it was that 6th game when they won the World

Series."

Another memorable game Howard attended was his first pro football game. It happened to be the Packers-Eagles NFL Championship game in 1960 in Philadelphia.

"It was the day after Christmas and I still have my tickets. If you want to dial it back to when I was a little kid, I was sitting on about the 20, 25-yard line on the south side of Franklin Field near the end zone where Tommy McDonald scored the touchdown. I remember the popcorn guy throwing the popcorn up in the air as Tommy went into the end zone. I still remember vividly everything that happened in that game."

The Eagles won that day, 17-13. It was their last NFL title.

WILD THING

Mitch Williams, the former hard-throwing lefty reliever for the Phillies, was about to sign a three-year contract in 1991. Howard's opinion was that guys who throw hard like Williams can lose it at any time and thought the Phillies shouldn't give him a deal of that length.

Williams caught wind of it and confronted Howard, calling him "hey you" in the Phils locker room.

Howard wanted to know what Williams heard.

"He said, 'I have a problem with what you said.' I said, 'Tell me what you heard I said and I'll tell you if I said it and why I said it.' Third hand is the way these guys get things most of the time. He just said, 'I don't want to ask you anything, I just want to punch you in the friggin' mouth.' I said, 'I tell you what, if you want to step outside I'll give you the first shot.' He looked at me and said 'You'll just get a lot of money.'" That's when it ended.

A few weeks later Howard and Williams talked things over.

"We get along great now."

Williams is now in the media as well as an analyst with MLB Network.

MIKE SCHMIDT

Being a former third baseman himself, albeit on a smaller level, Howard admired Phillies third baseman and future Hall of Famer Mike Schmidt.

"When I was coming through the business I kind of idolized him, and then I covered him and then I became friends with him. Just the steps along the way you look back on."

One of the perks of the sports broadcasting business.

THE FAMILY

Eskin doesn't like to talk much about his personal life but he does have a son, who went to Syracuse University, working on the air in Philadelphia on WISP. Another son went to USC's prestigious film school and is working in the entertainment field. A daughter works for an advertising agency and two other kids are going to school.

"That's the extent of it. I don't like to get into it, it's just another way for people to come after me. I got a lot of kids. I wanted to support the educational system in America."

LASTING IMPRESSIONS

While Eskin is not thinking about retirement, he'd like to be known as a guy who worked hard and wasn't afraid to express an opinion.

"I'm not a bad guy, I'm just a guy with a lot of opinions. I gave people everything I had and told them everything I thought. The people that know me know I'm a nice guy. People that don't know me, I can't worry what they think, but they have no real idea of what kind of person I am. The easiest thing to do is to be nice to people."

Kevin Wheeler
"From Behind the Dish to Behind the Mic"

If it were up to Kevin Wheeler, he would right about now be wrapping up a long and successful Major League career. While just about every kid has had those aspirations at one point, Kevin actually came closer than most, playing in the early '90s with the Miami Hurricanes. Unfortunately for Wheeler, a guy named Charles Johnson was the first string catcher for Miami, which relegated Kevin to the bullpen warming up pitchers.

But he had a backup plan and, fortunately for listeners of Sporting News Radio and now KMOX radio in St. Louis, that plan was broadcasting.

ERNIE, PAUL, GEORGE, AND AL

Growing up in suburban Detroit, Kevin was hooked on baseball. Listening to the Tigers broadcasters, Ernie Harwell and Paul Carey on the radio and George Kell and Al Kaline on television, enhanced Kevin's love of the game and gave him the idea that broadcasting could be a career path.

His interest in broadcasting then was in play-by-play, since there was no sports talk when he was a youngster. He hasn't done play-by-play professionally, but he says, "It's still on the list."

Kevin recalls his one in-person meeting with Harwell.

"It was at a Tigers game. I was probably in my mid- to late 20s. It was only briefly. A quick handshake and hello. But I had him on my radio show a couple of times, which was great to get a chance to talk baseball with him for an extended period. Especially when you have a record of it, not just the handshake, but the actual audio record of it, is pretty cool."

THE MOVE TO BROADCASTING

Some broadcasters had the bug early on and knew they wanted to be behind a microphone. Others are vague as to when they ventured towards an announcing career. Kevin knew the defining moment when he decided to become a broadcaster.

"Yeah, it was when I was told I was no longer good enough to play baseball," he said with some laughter.

"I kind of had it as part of the plan. I went to college to play baseball, obviously that was my first choice. I went to (University of) Miami because of their broadcast school. I knew if I wasn't going to play I was going to be a broadcaster. The time I decided that was what I was going to do was when I was no longer allowed to play baseball by anybody that mattered."

Another avenue Kevin explored was coaching. He met with Geoff Zahn, the former big league pitcher who was then the head coach at Michigan.

"He had just been hired recently and they were filling out their staff and I was just looking around to see if I was going to have that opportunity. But I found out right away that going into coaching, initially you don't make a lot of money. Actually, you don't make anything. You end up starting as a volunteer assistant and I was about to get married. So I figured I better get a paying job and that's where sports radio came in."

The cubicles that many people work in were not made for Kevin Wheeler. The thought of working a regular job in a cubicle for 40 hours a week made him shudder.

Since a big league career wasn't going to happen, the next best thing for Wheeler was to work in sports, in some capacity.

"There was absolutely no doubt that somehow, someway, that I was going to be working in sports, whether it was playing, coaching, or broadcasting, I had no doubt in my mind. I didn't think of anything else my entire life, that was going to be it."

YOUNG KEVIN

Wheeler grew up in a middle-class family and calls his upbringing "pretty typical," which included good Christmases and a lot of sports. His dad coached him in baseball and he played basketball. He didn't play organized football and although he wanted to play hockey he didn't. Kevin's father was a hockey referee and that might have been part of it.

He attended "Catholic schools from fourth grade all the way through the end of high school," Wheeler remembers. "Pretty disciplined household. My dad didn't put up with much BS."

Besides officiating, his dad worked his way into management at UPS, and when Kevin was in fourth grade his mom started working as a secretary, eventually moving into an administrative role. She still works at the same place where she started.

His two younger siblings were also good athletes. His brother, Sean, who lives in Atlanta and also went to Miami, dabbled in sports broadcasting and now works with the Nancy Grace show.

Since Sean is just three years younger than Kevin, did the Wheeler boys do any scrapping?

"Oh yeah, absolutely. A lot of good ones. Knock down, drag out ones. I think when I was 15 or 16 is when it all stopped, 'cause I was getting bigger and stronger and lifting weights for sports, and he was 12 or 13 and really hadn't gotten bigger yet. We had one fight where I absolutely destroyed him and I think that was probably the last fight we ever had."

His sister, Erin, 18 years younger than Kevin, goes to Central Michigan University.

"She's as good an athlete as my brother and I were. We both played multiple sports in high school. My little sister is every bit as good, if not better as a dancer. She's an unbelievable dancer."

THE CLASS CLOWN

Around his family, Kevin says he was kind of quiet and came across as shy. But away from his family he was anything but.

"From the time I was a little kid until basically the end of high school, I used to get straight A's on the report card except for personal conduct. I always got a D or a U for unsatisfactory. It was mostly for talking in class. I wasn't like a kid who started fights or anything like that. It was mostly just talking and trying to cut up and make jokes, that kind of stuff. Put it this way, looking back on it, people aren't surprised at what I do for a living."

He even got an award from his high school basketball team that was based on his personality. It was the Mr. Microphone award—a harbinger of things to come for sure.

"I guess you could say I was developing my skills as early as kindergarten. It's funny, my seventh and eighth grade teacher lives a couple of houses down from my parents now. So when I go back home, every once in a while they invite her over and she just looks at it now and she's like, 'All that time you were getting in trouble, you were just practicing.'"

Other than talking a lot in class, Kevin was a pretty good student. Not doing well in school was not an option for his parents.

"There was no such thing as a C on my report card, because if there was that would have been trouble."

In college it was a different story. He was enjoying the college lifestyle, playing baseball full-time, and he was only interested in having grades good enough to keep his scholarship.

"Nobody was going to ask me when I got out of college what my grade point average was. They just want to see the piece of paper that says I got my degree. I don't know if that was accurate by the way, but that's the way I viewed it."

THE BREAK

"I was waiting tables at a restaurant outside a mall in the Chicago area. There was a broadcast jobs fair at the broadcast museum in Chicago. My wife was just kicking me, 'Ya gotta go to this, ya gotta go to this.' I was like, 'I gotta work, I got a shift at the restaurant and they're not going to let me off.' So finally, I just called my manager at the last minute and said, 'Listen, I know you're gonna hate me, but I've got to go down to this thing. I've got a ton of resumes in my hand and I just gotta go start meeting people.' He said, 'Go do it. We'll cover for you, you don't have to worry about it.' So I went down there and passed out resumes, and I met a guy that worked at The Score, the first sports station in Chicago."

They set up a meeting that didn't come to fruition for a couple of months due to scheduling conflicts and such. CBS was in the process of buying The Score and a hiring freeze was put in place.

Kevin's contact, Henry Henderson, an executive producer, didn't want to lead him along any further. He graciously alerted Wheeler of another radio outlet called One on One Sports, out of Northbrook, Illinois, a Chicago suburb.

Henderson said, "Why don't you give them a call. They always seem to be looking for people."

Since Wheeler lived right down the road from Northbrook in Arlington Heights, he gave One on One Sports a call and a week later was hired as a 24-year-old intern.

He was ready to prove himself, even though they weren't going to pay him. He still had income from his restaurant job.

"My first assignment," Kevin recalls, "was to go get Ryne Sandberg on the phone to join the evening show from a live appearance where he was signing his books, and he blew me off. I even arranged this in advance. I called the publicist of the book. I set it all up, and she set it up with him that we were going to meet at this mall 15 or 20 minutes before the book signing and he would do the interview. I had one of those brick phones, that was our cell phone at the time, I was going to have him call into the station and just do it. It was all pre-arranged. He didn't show up until after the signing was supposed to start, so he was running late for whatever reason. The lady says, 'It's only an hour, would you mind waiting and doing it afterwards?' I can do that, I'm Mr. Intern. I called the radio station and told them what was going on and they said, 'That's no problem, we'll make room for him in an hour.' At the end of it all, he finishes and he's kind of like pretending that I'm not there and he starts to just walk away. And the publicity person comes up and says, 'I'm so sorry, but he and his wife decided they wanted to go shopping and the mall is going to close in 45 minutes so they are in a hurry.' I was like, 'OK, well I guess I'm going home now.'"

Wheeler has still never interviewed Sandberg. Not because of the mall rejection but because he's never had the opportunity to do so. But he said he'll bring up getting blown off if he does eventually interview the Cubs' Hall of Famer.

PAY ATTENTION YOUNG BROADCASTERS
Rich Bonn was the program director at One on One Sports and he was a straight shooter with Wheeler. Bonn told Kevin that he wasn't going to jump right on the air, but

if he worked hard Rich would find stuff for him to do.

That's all Wheeler needed to hear.

"I busted my butt. I did all sorts of extra research projects and passed them out to the hosts. Whenever an opportunity came up to do something more, he gave it to me."

SHEPHERDS

The gregarious Arnie Spanier, who is featured in this book, played a huge role in Kevin's development as a sports talk show host.

Wheeler was Spanier's associate producer for close to two years. "To be honest, I was his call screener."

But he didn't just sit there and answer phones. He was a sponge.

"Arnie was the guy I really learned from. He was the first guy I worked with. He was always great and always helpful. He knew I wanted to do shows so he was always saying, 'Hey listen, you gotta remember, this is what people are looking for' and all that. He is the greatest guy. There's no question that he had a major influence on how my career turned out. He would be number one along with Bob Kemp, the overnight guy at One on One Sports, and when it became Sporting News Radio he was still there. I ended up being his full-time producer. So I was around those guys all the time.

"The cool thing about it was they were so different. Arnie's loud and sometimes obnoxious. He's actually a total teddy bear off the air. On the air he likes to needle people, he likes to have fun, laugh, and make fun of himself. And Bob was more of the Joe Friday kind of guy. Very straightforward, likes to focus on facts and interviews and that kind of stuff. I feel like I'm kind of a mix of those guys, I learned from both of them what worked and how it fits into my own personality. Before I got there I didn't know how a talk show host worked. There were other guys but those were the main two."

THE WAGER

It was in 1996 when Kevin was working for Arnie Spanier that a classic radio bit took place.

East Carolina University was getting ready to play 12th ranked Miami at the Orange Bowl. Spanier had Pirates Head Coach Steve Logan on the air, since one of their popular affiliates was in Greenville, North Carolina, the home of ECU.

Arnie naturally teased the former Hurricane that his boys would lose. Wheeler said there was no way that East Carolina would beat Miami.

"I was laughing at him and telling him no chance. So we jokingly bet my car on the game. I said 'You can have my car if Miami loses the game.'"

They played up the bet leading up to the game, and obviously Arnie wasn't going to take Wheeler's car if Miami lost.

Arnie's Greenville listeners were naturally fired up over Wheeler's comments.

Sure enough, East Carolina throttled Miami 31-6, and the jubilant East Carolina fans brought Arnie into Greenville to celebrate. They were also eager to see Wheeler's car.

"The audience loved Arnie and they really bought into the bit. Arnie and the program director down there bought a $300 clunker and towed it to the appearance. They set it there and spray painted 'Wheeler's Car' on it, and let everyone come in and take a hack at it with a baseball bat. That's the kind of stuff Arnie did. He could turn something as goofy as a football game discussion into this great appearance that people were excited about. And that's something I learned from him. It's not just about knowing your stuff, although knowing your stuff is important, but you gotta be able to relax and have fun and not take everything too seriously."

INTERVIEW GONE BAD

One of the greatest moments in American sports history was the United States winning the gold medal in hockey at the 1980 Olympic Winter Games at Lake Placid, NY. Twenty years to the day, Kevin Wheeler was on the air and was interviewing players from that memorable team. A stringer in New York was getting players celebrating at the anniversary banquet and putting them on the phone with Wheeler.

"We had Mark Johnson, Mike Eruzione, and Kenny Morrow...it was a great show. It was a great night, I was having so much fun. I was just in heaven talking to all these players, everyone was in a great mood."

One can understand Wheeler's excitement. He was nine years old in 1980 and the Miracle on Ice was, he said, "the most memorable sports moment of my life."

His mood came down a few pegs though, when late in the show he had the coach of that team on the line, the late Herb Brooks. Brooks wasn't at the party in New York. He was coaching the Pittsburgh Penguins at the time and they had a game that night. And lost. Uh oh.

"They tell me Herb Brooks is on the line. I give him this great big introduction. I said, 'Herb thanks, appreciate your time,' and he's like, 'yeah, thanks.' Every question that I asked him, I said, 'I know you just lost tonight and I appreciate you coming on for a few minutes, but what does 1980 mean to you when you think back about it?' And at the time, he was in such a foul mood from having lost that game he goes, 'Ya know, that was 20 years ago. I really don't think about it that much.' I was just stunned. Honest to God, there must have been about five seconds of dead air. This is live on the radio and I didn't know what to say. I wanted to say, 'I can't believe you just said that.' I thought, wow, somebody's in a bad mood. I tried to squeeze in another question or two and I realized it was the same one or two word answers like, 'Yeah it was great but it's over, it's history.' At that point, it was two minutes in and I'm like, 'Well coach, we'll continue to enjoy the 20th anniversary, we wish you the best of luck with the Penguins, thanks for a couple of minutes.' It was the worst, most awkward, and most unexpectedly bad interview I've had. I was shocked about how little interest he showed in that event that night."

Wheeler came to have an understanding of Brooks, and coaches in general, after that interview.

"At first I thought, 'what a jerk.' But after time, it was kind of insight into what the life of a coach is. Every game is like a life and death thing. When they lose they're crushed. And that's what drives them, not wanting to lose. I understood that after the fact."

THE BEST INTERVIEW

Working as a national host with One on One Sports then Sporting News Radio, and now with KMOX, Wheeler has interviewed plenty of famous athletes and others. But one interview stands out from all the rest. It was with movie director and Knicks fan Spike Lee.

A couple of weeks after the 9/11 terrorist attacks, Kevin had a memorable chat with Lee, who has courtside seats at Madison Square Garden for Knickerbockers games.

"He was auctioning off his courtside seats to give the money to the families of rescue workers, firefighters, and policemen who died on 9/11. Obviously, it was for a great cause, it was really fresh in everybody's mind. He was unbelievable. He was just a great interview. Friendly, loved talking sports, we talked a little bit about movies, just an unbelievably good interview and he was totally into it, there was no boredom about it. As it turns out, somebody bid a ridiculous amount of money on those seats and gave those seats to a couple of kids who lost their dad on 9/11.

So it turned out to be this unbelievably cool story and I would say that was the best one. It wasn't the highest profile person or athlete I've had on, but to me that was the best one."

MR. HOCKEY

Growing up in the Detroit area, Wheeler was well aware of what Gordie Howe meant to hockey and to Red Wings fans. So when he got a chance to interview the legendary Mr. Hockey, he was, for one of the few times in his career, a bit on the nervous side.

"Gordie Howe was my dad's generation. He was the sports god in Detroit when I was growing up. If you thought of the biggest name in the history of sports in that town, it's Gordie Howe. So that was a pretty interesting moment, but he was so nice that initial 'Oh my God I'm talking to Gordie Howe' faded real fast, he was such a cool guy, once you start talking to him it's like talking to your friend."

THE DUMP BUTTON

Doing overnight shifts can make a radio guy do some strange things. One time while doing the overnight show at Sporting News Radio, Wheeler had to hit the dump button, also known as the seven-second delay. It wasn't because of what a caller said. Wheeler had to dump himself.

"I got so mad at a caller and I don't remember why, I don't even remember the conversation. But I dropped a bomb in the middle of my rant. And like a split second later, I remember making eye contact with my producer and we both had that look on our face like, "Uh oh!" So we both reached for the dump button and apparently we got it because nobody ever complained. That was a good thing."

Yes, the dump button can be a broadcaster's best friend at times.

DYSFUNCTION?

In the Colin Cowherd chapter in this book, Colin discusses and explains why he feels a good talk show host needs to be dysfunctional.

Wheeler, when asked if he agrees, immediately said, "No."

Kevin continued, "Maybe he thinks that because he views himself as being dysfunctional, I don't know, but there's nothing dysfunctional about me. I can't think of anything about me that would be odd or weird other than the fact I can be a doofus at times, but that's pretty normal. Absolutely you do not have to be dysfunctional. Even that idea, that someone would say that, is just stupid. I don't get that opinion at all. To me that's a very closed-minded viewpoint of things."

PERSISTENCE

Kevin Wheeler met his future wife, Susan, freshman year in college. They had mutual friends and the boring, but nice, story would be that they instantly fell for each other. That wasn't the case. She didn't like him at all. Not one bit.

"She hated me the first year that she knew me. If I walked in the room she would leave. No joke, she'll tell you the same thing. You have to understand, at that time, I was 19 years old, I was a college baseball player, I thought I was going to be a Major League baseball player. I thought I was a big shot, smart guy, academic scholarship, athlete, I was just a cocky 19-year-old kid and an incredible smart ass. We were always picking on each other, my group of friends and I, playing practical jokes on each other. It wasn't quite as extreme as you see in the Jackass movies but along those lines. She had no interest in any of that. So she was like, I'm out of here."

Kevin didn't have the same feelings towards Susan that she had for him.

"I was kind of in-between. I always thought she was cute but I figured she didn't like me, so I'm not going to be a jerk and bother her. I was friendly. I liked being around her. We had a lot of common friends, and she lived on a floor in one dorm with a bunch of people that hung out with guys that lived on my floor. We had this group of 10-12 people that were always milling around and hanging out together. That first year whenever I was around, she somehow mysteriously disappeared."

Things changed the following year.

"Sophomore year, she moved into another dorm with three of my other friends, obviously three girls. One of the girls was arguably my best friend in college. I was moving into the baseball apartments. But because she was there in the same suite as one of my best friends I was always there. It started off, I think I used to play jokes with her stuffed animals and put them in weird positions and goof around because I did anything that made people laugh. I don't care what it was, I don't care if it was making fun of me. I guess just being around enough, my awesomeness wore off on her (laughs). Really, the truth is all of our friends got jobs sophomore year so it ends up we were almost stuck together, just the two of us. That is where my growing on her began."

Susan runs everything in the Wheeler household, taking care of the kids and everything else that needs to be done.

Plus, she's a college football fanatic, making Kevin the envy of just about every guy who reads this book.

"She's a huge college football fan. On Saturday's during the fall that's all we do." Of course she's a Miami Hurricanes fan.

"She's middle of the road on baseball. She likes baseball when I'm playing but doesn't like it so much when I'm not." Wheeler still plays in an adult league and she watches him do that.

Kevin's daughter, Shannon, is heading into high school. She doesn't like sports.

"She could not care less about sports. She likes animals, music. She's a little brain. She scored 21 on the ACT as a seventh grader. She's a smart kid. She likes girly stuff. She's mildly interested in some sports. She'll sit and watch football games with us once in a while and ask a lot of questions. But mostly doesn't care. She likes going to games once in a while as kind of an entertainment event, but nope, sports are not on the list."

DOGS

Dogs are a passionate part of the Wheeler family. They do rescue work, are dog owners and foster for a rescue group, and do fund raisers and events. Former Cardinals Manager Tony LaRussa is also a huge animal lover, and with the Cards games back on KMOX radio, the animal rescue connection helped Kevin in his dealings with the sometimes salty skipper.

"That's one of the things we connect on. I've talked to Tony about that back when he was with the Oakland A's and I was at One on One Sports. Also when he was with the Cardinals as well to promote his annual event. I've talked to him about that off and on for 10-12 years. Tony says he doesn't go to the off season, he goes to the 'arf' season."

Jason Smith
"Up All Night"

Right before this book went to print, Jason Smith threw a curve and traded in his overnight radio program, 'Up All Night', for a TV position with the NFL Network. But because, like his loyal following, we like Jason, we felt his story was compelling and interesting enough to keep in the book. Plus, as you're about to read, Jason hasn't completely abandoned radio.

Another product of Syracuse University, from 2005 until his move to the NFL Network, Smith was a trusted friend of the people who go to sleep very late, the folks who get up very early, and those who can't sleep at all. Insomniacs need a place to go to on the radio dial to listen to sports and pop culture. Jason was their destination.

"I like going in at night and not only talking about sports but talking about my life as it pertains to sports."

So why the move to television and the NFL Network?

"It was a really hard decision. At the end of the day, I felt like there was more open to me for my future at NFL Network than there was at ESPN. ESPN is a crowded landscape, and being in Los Angeles and on late at night, it was difficult to cut through. I really like doing TV, as long as it's a forum where I can give my opinions and have fun — in short, an extension of what I do on the radio. I'm doing that now, also writing for nfl.com and still doing radio on our weekly show on Sirius XM. Radio is just too much fun for me, so I can't see myself not incorporating it into my life again. I'm excited about the different opportunities that will be afforded to me now coming off ESPN."

Here is Jason Smith's journey.

CHILD OF THE '70s

An only child, born in Syracuse, New York, Jason Smith's family moved shortly after to Staten Island, New York.

Jason's father, Walter, was looking to work in television and got a job as a production assistant in the sports department at CBS in New York City.

In the mid-70s, while just a young boy, Jason's parents divorced. His mother, Gloria, was very straightforward with her son, who had never really understood the arguments between his parents.

"I think because of the way she told me, my response was something along the lines of, 'OK. Will I still see Dad?' She said, 'Yeah, you'll still see him when he comes down to visit you and you can go see him.' She never told me about a divorce or getting separated. It was just like a matter of fact that he was going to live in Syracuse now."

He never felt his dad loved him any less and he didn't cry his eyes out.

"I just thought it was something that happened and I credit my mom for that a lot, for taking care of that. That could have been something that was really, really traumatic. Instead it was just kind of a little mysterious."

His dad moved back to Syracuse and Jason saw him just once from age seven until he went to college.

"He just wasn't around. I went through most of my teenaged years thinking, 'I'm just never going to see my dad again.' Because he never called and I never had the chance to talk to him. A couple of times he did call and my grandparents would intercept the phone. It was a very contentious relationship when they got the divorce."

Instead, he was reared by his mother and grandparents, Frederick and his wife, also named Gloria. His grandfather was the disciplinarian and instilled fear in the young boy.

"He had raised five children," Jason recalls, "and when I came around it was like, 'I'm going to take care of him like I took care of my five children.' So I was being raised in the mid-70s like he was raising a kid in the mid-50s. Where it was, I can't go past the corner on the street or if I don't take the garbage out I get in trouble, and I had to do all these different things around the house and I was like, 'this is kind of new for me. I didn't bargain for all this kind of stuff.' At the same time, I felt that was a discipline I got growing up."

His grandfather was a big sports fan, which Jason feels rubbed off on him.

"We watched the Mets and the Jets from when I was real little. We always watched TV at night, baseball especially during the week and then football on the weekends and he would always let me stay up late if it was a big game on. But at the same time, if I wasn't up and ready to go the next day to go to school then I got in a little bit of trouble."

Although short, his grandfather was an intimating figure. Jason recalls the time he got into some trouble for something minor and his grandfather told him to sit on the couch and not move.

"He went upstairs and I'm sitting on the couch in the basement by myself and I'm literally not moving. I think about that time and I go, 'why didn't I just lay down on the couch and then sit back up when he came back down?' But instead I sat on the couch and I did not move. I think I had to grow up a little bit in fear a lot of times of doing the wrong thing, and if that happened then the consequences were being in trouble."

QUESTIONS AND ANSWERS

After the divorce, Jason became used to his living situation. That didn't mean not having his father around became any easier. But it did bring up questions that didn't always have answers.

"I really wanted to talk with him because I remembered when I was younger, growing up, having such fun times with him. Then I'm starting to get stuff about divorce and why they're not together, and it was a question that I just never had answered. How do you go so long without talking to your son? It was a question I think that you're afraid to get the answer to."

Jason never got those questions answered.

"I never did. I always felt it was too hard for me to dive into. Honestly, I felt like I knew the answer. I felt like the answer was, well, for whatever reason that was the life he wanted at that time. He didn't want to have a life around his family. He could have moved somewhere else on Staten Island and got a job but he didn't. I think it was too scary to dive into. And to this day I still haven't asked him. Maybe the answer is a little bit simpler. Maybe the answer is, 'I tried thousands of times to call you and it didn't work out. I tried to come down and see you but your mom or grandparents wouldn't let me.' Maybe that's the answer and that would be a little bit easier, but other side I think is a little too hard to think about."

Jason describes his current relationship with his father as, "pretty good." But he doesn't know if this is the time for him to bring those questions up.

DEVELOPING PERSONALITY

While growing up with his dad out of the picture and his disciplinarian grandfather, Jason took time to enjoy himself away from home.

"When I was away from that situation, when I was out with my friends, I think I was much more outgoing as a result. I was much more willing to have fun and I liked to talk and be heard, and I think that made it part of who I am right now and I think a lot of that is by accident. If I grew up with an idyllic family or with my dad around all the time, would I have the same type of personality? I don't think I would."

MAKING THE GRADE

Deductive reasoning would indicate that if Jason went to Syracuse he must have been a pretty good student. That assumption would be correct.

"I was about a 90 average. I was in the top 10 percent of my class. There were kids that were smarter than me but I always did pretty well in school. I always did really well in English and history and I did horrendously in math and science."

Fear, it is said, can be a great motivator. The fear of bringing home poor grades helped make Jason an excellent student.

"If I came home with a bad report it would have been disaster. Luckily, I never came home with a bad report card, I always did pretty well. I think it was fear that made me a good student."

Despite the good grades, he did like to joke around and talk in class.

"I would get comments on the report card that would say, 'Jason got 93 but is a distractive influence in class.'"

Hey, just another future sports talk show host in training.

THE KEY

When Jason was 9 or 10, he was trusted to have a house key. Of course, he lost the house key one day and Grandpa wasn't happy. He told Jason, "It's going to be a long time until we're friends again."

For the next two and a half weeks, Jason frantically searched for the key. Meanwhile, his grandfather was distant. No kidding around, no talking about baseball or anything. He only spoke to the distraught youngster when he had to.

Finally, Jason found the key.

"It was under the couch in the basement. I found it totally by chance one day. I came up and I was so happy. I found the key! I remember telling him, 'Pop, I found the key, I found the key!' and he said, 'OK, we're friends again.'"

THE FIELD OF PLAY

Jason got good grades in school but he certainly wasn't a bookworm. He was a typical, active kid who played little league baseball and football in high school. Many kids would have their dads attend games but for Jason it was his grandfather who went to his games.

"He would come to every game and we'd analyze the game after. It's almost like after the game was over, he was a reporter that wanted to come in and ask me questions about the game. Why did this happen? Why did that happen? I had to have good answers for him. All I wanted to do was go get ice cream. It almost felt like I was getting interviewed after the game was over. He took a big level of interest in it."

One of his greatest memories of playing sports as a kid was when his grandpa was at one of his games, watching by himself, quiet with arms folded as usual.

Jason was 11 years old and was facing the best pitcher in the league, who was a flamethrower.

"The guy's name was Keith Reddick. I can't believe I remember his name. He would always hold the ball out and show it to you and then he would go into his windup and throw it. He would throw really hard. I came up with the bases loaded in the 4th inning of the game and he threw one, and I wouldn't say I closed my eyes and swung, but he was throwing really hard, but I swung a little late but I ripped a line drive into right field and it went for a double and the bases cleared. And I got to second base and I looked up and my grandfather was standing and clapping and yelling, and I couldn't hear what he was yelling, but I thought, 'Oh my God!' That memory stays with me to this day, that I got that hit and he stood up and cheered for me. That's probably one of the top one or two athletic highlights of my life because I don't have that many. You can be slow if you're tall, you can be fast if you're short. But I was slow and I was short. I think I peaked athletically when I was 12 or till kids started throwing curveballs."

Highlight number two for Jason Smith the athlete? An interception his freshman year in high school.

DAD AND BASEBALL

The only time Jason saw his father from the age of seven until he matriculated at Syracuse was when he was 11 and his dad visited him for a weekend. They stayed in a hotel on Staten Island and Jason was excited because his father would have the chance to see him play ball.

A third baseman and pretty good hitter, Jason normally played the entire game. But this particular Sunday morning the coach told him it was his turn to play just a half a game. Three innings. Jason was mortified.

"I said to my coach, 'Mr. Lilly, please, can I do it another day? My dad came down to visit and I really want to play a full game.'"

The coach looked at Jason and said, "Oh my God Jason, I'm so sorry. I already told these kids that they were playing a whole game and all their parents are coming. I'm sorry but you have to play a half game today."

Jason said, "Ok."

But he was stunned and after playing the first three innings rode the bench. He had one at bat and that was it.

Jason's team lost 5-3 and the kid who took his place came up with the bases loaded and two outs and, struck out.

"I remember after the game was over thinking, 'I would have got a hit. I would have drove in the runs and we would have won and my dad would have got to see it.' I still think about that to this day. Boy, if I could have played that whole game right there that would have been great. I would have got a hit and we would have won. Cause I know I would have got a hit. Instead my dad got to see me play and I played a half game and I batted once."

For the record, Jason can't remember what he did in that one at bat. But because he remembers being on base he thinks he got a hit. He also remembers his father being happy and smiling at the game. It was also a game his grandfather decided to skip since he didn't get along with Jason's father.

SYRACUSE
A career in sports was Jason's calling. He knew he couldn't play on a high level but he could certainly make a living by being involved in sports.

When looking for a college to attend, he saw such majors as finance and marketing and business. Those occupations didn't interest him.

"I came across communications where they would teach me how to work in radio and TV and so forth. I was like, well, I love movies. I love TV. I love radio. That's what I want to do. I applied to four schools that all had good communications. I applied to Syracuse, SUNY-Buffalo, Ithaca, and NYU. I got into all of them and I went to Syracuse because my parents went to Syracuse, and it was as simple as they offered me a big financial aid package. I really wanted to go. Syracuse was always the gold standard for communications and my parents didn't want me to go far away. And all the research I did, it was Syracuse. There were other great schools. I wanted to go to Miami but my mom told me, 'I'm not going to pay for you to go to college for a semester and drop off and live on the beach.' Syracuse became the school and it was the school and still kind of is. So she was okay with me applying there, and I think she was okay with me going up there and kind of finding my way and making my own decision now about my dad. I never thought that way until later in life."

When he made his visit to Syracuse, he met with his father for the first time in many years.

"I remember the first thing I did. I gave him a hug and picked up the hat off his head and I said, 'Wow, Dad, you're losing your hair.' We kind of reconnected over that weekend and we saw the campus and things were good and I felt like the years in between had kind of melted away. And my mom was always okay with it. She was always very good, always would ask about him, she would never badmouth him. She was always very nurturing in the relationship."

At Syracuse he got involved with the campus radio station where he did newscasts and hosted the morning program, 'The Crazy Morning Crew.'

"I did the morning show for a year and a half there. It was great. I was getting up at 5:30 every day, which stunk. But being on the air from 6 to 10 and doing the morning show was a lot of fun."

THE JOB HUNT

After Syracuse, Jason wanted to be a morning show host at a radio station. He felt he was ready and sent his tapes out. Not many other stations had the same belief that he had. One station told him in a rejection letter that he should start looking at markets 100 and lower, and not at the 25th market.

While looking for a radio job he was aware he had to get something. So he moved back to Staten Island and took a job working at a supermarket, the same place he worked at in high school.

"I would send out my resumes and wouldn't get anything back. I probably sent out over 100 (tapes and resumes) and I also had a head hunter agency helping me.

They would say they would present me 10 times for like $75 with potential jobs. And I went 0-10 there. And I think I tried it one more time and I went 0-10 again and I thought, 'I'm never going to get a job. I'm just never going to get a job.' I was ready to give radio up entirely."

While at Syracuse, Jason did a summer internship in the marketing department with ESPN in New York. It was there he made contacts. That led to an interview at ESPN in Bristol, Connecticut.

"It took them nine months to call me for a job."

It was an off-air job but he took it.

"To work at ESPN was so alluring. ESPN was it. How many hours did I spend watching it when I was a kid? And to be able to go up there and work in production and work on games, and with all the guys I would see on TV and Chris Berman and Dan Patrick and those guys, that was it. I was ready for that. I thought this was going to be the greatest thing in the world."

Good-bye supermarket, hello Constitution State.

HARD WORK

As a production assistant at ESPN Jason was stunned to find out the level of responsibility he had. He thought he would feel his way around for a while. But after a week of observing, he had important tasks to complete.

"They throw you right in. You're editing games, big games. And what you're writing down and keeping track of during the night is what Dan Patrick or Keith Olbermann or somebody else is going to be reading on SportsCenter. Everybody embraced it. Everybody worked hard. It was a competitive atmosphere where people want to move up and want to get noticed."

The duties given to relative novices shocked Jason.

"I think what people would be surprised to find out is that the backbone of ESPN, what you see on the air every night, are 22-, 23-, and 24-year-old kids who are doing jobs that you can't imagine they're doing to get ESPN on the air every night."

PRODUCTION STORIES

When Craig Kilborn was auditioning for ESPN's SportsCenter, Jason was his teleprompter guy.

"He was really personable, really nice guy. He was like, 'Hey, thanks a lot. I really appreciate it.' I remember him saying, 'Tell everybody I did a good job.' He's in his mid-20s at the time, too. I said, 'OK.' He's asking me to put in a good word for him, which I thought was pretty fun. But then he got the job. He started working and he and I always got along 'cause he knew me from prompting his audition. He said to me once, 'What are you doing here?' I said, 'What do you mean?' He said, 'What are you doing here? You should be on my side of the camera.' I said, 'Well, I always wanted to but it never worked out for me.'"

After revealing to the host that he did radio and some other things previously, Kilborn asked him if he still wanted to do radio.

"I told him I never thought I'd have the chance to do radio again. Two days later he comes up to me and says, 'Hey, a guy's going to call you from Monterey. I told him you're a real sharp guy and maybe you could do stuff for him. Maybe that would help you get back into radio.' I said, 'Wow, OK sure.' Sure enough the guy called me and we had a couple of conversations. I remember writing a couple of bits for him for the morning show, but it never really went anywhere more than that. I mean, I'm in Bristol and he's in Monterey. But I always thought that was really nice of him to do. Craig said, 'Look, in the end, did you make a contact? Great, I'm glad it worked out for you guys.' I never expected one of the talent when he got hired to look out for me."

Jason always had a very good relationship with Keith Olbermann at ESPN.

"He's incredibly smart. He could, in five minutes, write a piece that is award winning. It's really something to watch him work."

One thing Jason remembers vividly about Olbermann was his home in Connecticut.

"It was like a museum for baseball. You walk in and where most people have benches where you sit, like a sitting area where you take your shoes off, he had seats from Ebbets Field."

Another Olbermann memory is when they went to Hartford to take in a Whalers hockey game. The production crew and talent were friendly away from the job since they got to know each other so closely at work.

"I think it was a Whalers-Rangers game. I remember Keith saying one day, 'What's everybody doing tomorrow night?' I said, 'We're all going to a hockey game, you want to go to the game?' 'Yeah, sure.' 'Really?' 'Yeah, come pick me up.' So we pick him up and went to the hockey game and our seats are in the top row at the Hartford Civic Center. We sat in the top row and we were having fun the whole game, and we were making fun of people and I think Keith had a blast. And I thought, 'I'm sitting in the top row of a stadium with Keith, when normally he should be down right behind the bench or in some kind of luxury box.' Keith's just a good guy. He was a lot of fun."

ONLY IN LA

After three years of working at ESPN, Jason took off for the West coast, taking a job as a producer for KABC-TV in Los Angeles. Eventually he made the transition into sports talk radio.

"It was one of those only in LA type stories," Jason recalls. "I was producing at ABC and there was a show called *Monday Night Live*. It was on after every Monday Night Football game. It was a sports show, an hour long. It was a combination of sports highlights from the weekend. We concentrated on local schools, USC and UCLA. There were some comedy elements in it. It was a fun show to produce."

The host of the show was Bill Weir, who is now a co-anchor on *Nightline*. They hired Ellen K., who was Rick Dees' radio co-host. Jason produced comedy bits with Ellen during the week for *Monday Night Live*.

"I remember Ellen saying to me one day, and I'm 10 years out of college, 'Have you ever thought of doing radio?' 'I used to do it in college a lot, why do you ask?' She said, 'Well, I think a lot of the stuff you do, these bits, they're fun and you really have a good sense of humor and you know a lot about sports, and I know the sports station my husband runs is looking for talent.'"

That got Jason's attention.

"Really?"

"Yeah," Ellen said. "And since I know the boss I could definitely get you an introduction. So if that's something you would like to do, I could help make it happen for you."

When the excited 29-year-old Jason returned home that night, he said to his wife, "You'll never guess what happened ..."

While promoting *Monday Night Live*, Jason went with Bill Weir to the KIIS radio studio of Rick Dees and Ellen K. Upon entering the studio, Jason was taken back to his college radio days. He fell in love with radio again. It was overwhelming.

"The smell of the room. I can't describe it more than that. The wood smell, the machinery, it brought me back to college. Oh my God, it was like smelling the most delicious chocolate cake ever. And I thought, 'I have to do this now.' It was that moment. I still remember that smell."

Soon after, he met Ellen's husband and was hired to fill-in with evening talent Lee Klein, and that's where his dormant radio career was resurrected.

Only in Los Angeles.

TOTALLY SCREWED

Jason was anxious to do his first radio show with Lee Klein. He arrived at the stations two hours prior to air time, prepared and ready to go.

When the older Klein arrived he said, "Are you Jason Smith?"

"Yes."

"Alright, before we do anything tonight, I just want to let you know we are totally screwed."

How's that for your long awaited re-entry into radio?

"I'm looking at him like, 'OK, I can't believe you just told me that,'" Jason remembers. "Wow, this is my first show and we're totally screwed."

Apparently there were production and technical issues they had to deal with that night. They got through it and although understandably nervous, Jason made some nice contributions to the show. It was a fun show, Klein approved of Jason, and now the former TV producer was officially back in radio.

Jason and Klein became friends and would do things outside of the show.

"We'd go to lunch every once in a while and it was kind of like Jerry and Kramer. He's Kramer. He shows up and says, 'Hey come take a ride with me.' 'OK, where we going?' 'Don't worry about it.' Who knows what the adventure would be like that day. So that was kind of interesting."

FOX

In the fall of 2000, Fox Sports Radio was starting up. Jason eagerly sent in his demo tape and resume but heard nothing. Not a thing.

On a tip from Fox TV sportscaster Jeanne Zelasko, he sent his material to Tom Lee and an interview ensued.

"Four days later Tom Lee called me and said, 'Why don't you come in, I want to talk to you.'"

He was offered a chance to co-host a show on the weekend to do updates.

"Whatever you want me to do, I'll do it," Jason told Lee. "Only in Los Angeles can I go from a guy doing a couple of shows a week on a local affiliate and now I'm on the air on a network across the country. Without Ellen and without Jeanne, I don't know if any of that happens."

Yes, the ladies do love Jason Smith.

RETURN TO THE WORLDWIDE LEADER

After a few years at Fox, new management arrived. Jason, and his midday partner Jim Daniels were the only ones without contracts, and were going to return to their original overnight time slot.

Feeling he wasn't a priority, Jason couldn't agree to a contract and decided to leave Fox.

"It was a tough decision but at the same time I felt like I did what I did at Fox and now I'm looking to do something else."

Without a job, Jason's agent suggested he send stuff to ESPN, which he did.

Eventually he met with General Manager Bruce Gilbert in Bristol.

Gilbert told Jason that there were some things on his demo that he really liked, some stuff that was alright, and some things that he wasn't particularly fond of. It was at this point that Jason felt he was going to get the thanks but no thanks speech. He was just hoping they would keep him around to at least fill-in. Instead he was amazed at what Gilbert told him.

"I'll never forget him saying this, and I think I'll remember this for the rest of my life. He said, 'I've been a programmer for a long time and it kind of takes a lot to wow me. But because of what you've accomplished at your young age, we owe it to you to give you a chance with us.' I was like, 'Oh my God. Did you just say that to me, that you owe it to me?' I heard that and I thought there's no way I could ever let this guy down. He could have easily blown me off, he could have easily told me thanks, but he said, 'we owe it to you.' So from then on I wanted to make sure I did my best because he showed more confidence in me there than plenty of bosses showed in me."

LA BASED

Jason did his show from Los Angeles not Connecticut, which was good for his sleeping habits and quality of life.

"It's a heck of a lot easier for me to do a show that goes from 10 o'clock until one or two in the morning in Los Angeles than start a show at one in the morning and go to five or six in the morning on the East coast."

Some people would also say was an advantage not to live in Bristol, Connecticut. Jason however has a warm spot in his heart for Bristol. It's where he met his wife, Pamela.

"I always looked at Bristol as I'm two hours from Boston. I'm two hours from New York."

ATTITUDE

There are good things and bad things with every job. Instead of complaining and getting riled up at the things most people would get angry with, Jason takes a positive approach.

"I've always been somebody that's tried to say, okay, even if I absolutely hate something, I gotta find a way to make the best of it. How do I go positive? How do I try to have fun while I'm doing this? Because the alternative is to walk around in a fog. You walk around just unhappy and it really consumes your life. So even if it's something real tiny that you can hook into, you say, 'OK, well if I do this, at least this will be good.' Then suddenly things become always more bearable, things become always more fun."

Jason believes he would have enjoyed any occupation he would have done to earn a living, even if it were not in radio.

Surely the person you work next to every day also possesses the same positive and upbeat disposition of Jason Smith.

THE JETS

Jason is a big New York Jets fan, dating back to when he was a kid watching games with his grandfather.

When he was at Fox Sports Radio, Jason would be two different personalities according to how the New York Jets performed. If the Jets won, he was upbeat and at ease. When they lost, he wouldn't be as happy and would be more critical.

When this was pointed out to him he realized he needed to change.

"I realized that no matter what the Jets do, I have to put that to the side and still do my show that night."

SIMPLY E-MAIL JASON AT ...

One of the first shows that Jason ever did was also one that got him into a jam at home. His wife didn't even wait for him to get home to scold him. Pam called the station because Jason gave out their personal e-mail address on the air!

"She said, 'What are you doing? Get a hold of yourself. I can't believe you just did that.' She got really mad I did that."

He was talking with Lee Klein and the discussion revolved around Lee getting all the hate mail because they had his e-mail and not Jason's. So he let the listeners know where they could easily and conveniently reach him.

Pam immediately, and wisely, changed the home e-mail address and Jason hasn't made that boneheaded move since.

A TOUGH TIME

If you asked Jason what he talked about on his programs during December of 2008 he couldn't tell you.

His mother, who was diagnosed with leukemia in March of 2008, suffered a stroke in November of that year and passed away. At the time Jason's wife was pregnant with their child, Zoe.

Jason's first show after the death of his mom was not an easy time for him.

"I don't even know what I said. I don't even know what my personality was like for those two weeks on the air. I didn't talk about my mom dying because it wasn't the time. I didn't feel comfortable with doing it. I couldn't tell you one thing I said on the air for two weeks. I do remember leaving the studio at night and thinking, 'what did I just do for three hours?' It was really, really hard."

A year later his mother-in-law passed away, resurrecting some difficult memories.

"I was sad because I knew exactly what Pam was going to go through the next year. With time going on, things do get better."

Jason admits that he thinks of death more than he used to. With a wife and young child he has responsibilities he didn't think about in his younger days.

"I know that I have amped up my fear of flying that I had a few years ago. I'm scared for me when I fly, I'm scared for Pam when she flies, I'm scared for Pam and Zoe. I'm scared for all of us when we fly."

BAD INTERVIEWS

All talk show hosts would love for every interview to be dazzling. It doesn't always work out that way. Every host has had an interview or two or many go bad. Jason Smith is no exception.

"I remember once I talked to Carmelo Anthony. It was right after Syracuse had won the National Championship. I had gone to Syracuse and I was excited to do the interview. He was getting ready for the NBA draft. And he was obviously driving in his car and he was doing something else, and I'm sure he didn't want to do the interview. I interviewed him for six minutes. We actually went back and looked at this after it was done. I talked for five minutes and 24 seconds of the interview. He talked for 36 seconds in a six-minute interview, just because he wasn't into it. I feel like, 'It's Carmelo Anthony and eventually I'm going to get something out of him.' But after five or six minutes you realize, 'OK, this is not going to work.'"

He also had an unforgettable interview with William "Refrigerator" Perry.

"I'm pretty sure he was playing poker while we were doing the interview with him."

He kept saying "check" during the interview, which led Jason to surmise he was either playing poker or working at a hat check room.

"But that turned out to be hilarious because he's playing poker during the interview."

JOE WILLIE

Ask any Jets fan over the age of 40 who his guy was and they would say, without hesitation, Joe Namath.

One of the guys Jason was able to cross off his want-to-interview checklist was Broadway Joe.

It occurred on the red carpet at the ESPY's award show where Jason did his radio program.

A producer asked him if he wanted to interview Namath. Of course the answer was a resounding "Yes."

"Right after the interview, it was like a minute and a half long, I couldn't remember one thing I said to him. It was fun. I told him, 'Hey Joe, growing up me and my family were buying soap-on-a-rope, we were buying the Hamilton Beach Popcorn Popper, and he says, 'Let me see your legs, are you wearing panty hose? Then I know I did my job.' I listened to it after and I was saying, 'I can't believe I just interviewed Joe Namath and the main thing I talked to him about was the products he endorsed in the '70s and that he wore panty hose.' That was really a surreal moment and it took me like five minutes to come down from that."

JASON, PAM, AND TOM?

Jason and Pam moved to California in September of 1996. A mere three days after moving into their Marina del Rey apartment, across the street from the house being used to shoot the film *Jerry Maguire*, they met a fellow named Tom. Tom Cruise that is.

"He came by us before he went into his trailer. He saw that there were four of us standing around and he said, 'You guys want a picture?' We said, 'Yeah.' I can't believe it, I got my arm around Tom Cruise and we're taking a picture. And I'm taller than he is. I thought that was pretty cool. And we used that as our Christmas card for about three years. Hey, Merry Christmas from Jason, Pam, and Tom. He was cool, he was very cool."

ADVICE

Young broadcasters, and not so young ones, are always asking the Jason Smith's of the world for pointers, for tips to reach their goals. Jason's top advice was given to him by sports talker J.T. The Brick.

"The best radio advice is that you will succeed more

because people in front of you implode than you will on your own merits. I found that to be 100 percent true."

The worst advice?

"Sitting back and letting things come to you. There's no way that that works."

LASTING IMPRESSIONS

Jason Smith isn't sure how long he will remain in radio. But he does know how he would like to be remembered.

"I'd like people to say, 'You know what, he was fun to listen to. I enjoyed listening to him.' I think that's about all you can ask. 'I enjoyed the time I spent with the radio on listening to him.' To be able to do that, I think, is the ultimate for me to accomplish."

The Authors

David Brody

David Brody has more than 25 years of on-air and talent coaching experience.

He has worked as a play-by-play announcer, sports talk show host, and update anchor in Philadelphia; Hartford, CT; Youngstown, OH; and Princeton, NJ. From 1993 to 2003, David was a familiar voice on America's first national sports talk show network, Sportsbyline USA. He has also freelanced as a pre- and post-game studio host for the Oakland Raiders, Oakland A's, Philadelphia 76ers, and University of Alabama football.

David currently owns and operates Broadcaster Marketing Services (www.sportsbroadcastingcoach.com), co-owns the website www.ussportspages.com, produces the Sports Prep for Westwood One/Dial Global, and teaches sports broadcasting at Kennesaw State University in Kennesaw, GA.

Bill Rogan

Bill Rogan has been a radio and TV sports broadcaster for 27 years. He has hosted sports talk shows and called play-by-play for various sports including Army hockey and basketball for 11 years as well as five seasons of minor league baseball.

He currently is the sports director at KNUS radio in Denver where he is part of the popular "Kelley & Company" morning program. He also calls high school football and basketball for Channel 8 in Broomfield, Colorado.

Bill lives in the beautiful state of Colorado with his wife, Gwyn, and cat, Jeets. He has authored three other books: *A Renegade Summer*, *Turf Tales*, and *More Turf Tales ...Taking the Serious Out of Sports*.

His website is www.turfsports.net.

Dustin Rhoades

Dustin Rhoades has spent 15 years producing local talk shows in Chicago and on national networks.

He began his radio career in 1996 at One-On-One Sports/Sporting News Radio and worked for 10 years as a Senior Producer on shows featuring Tim Brando, James Brown, Tony Bruno, Troy Aikman, Papa Joe Chevalier, and Peter Brown.

After 10 years with the network, Dustin moved on to the nationally syndicated Mancow Show, where he worked as Executive Producer.

Dustin currently serves as Executive Producer for the Mully and Hanley morning show on 670 The Score in Chicago, and he is also the co-owner of USSportspage.com and produces the Sports Prep for Westwood One/Dial Global.